Law,
Soldiers,
and
Combat

Contributions in Legal Studies
Series Editor, *Paul L. Murphy*

Stability, Security, and Continuity
Mr. Justice Burton and Decision-Making
in the Supreme Court, 1945-1958
Mary Frances Berry

Philosophical Law
Authority, Equality, Adjudication, Privacy
Richard Bronaugh, editor

PETER
KARSTEN

Law,
Soldiers,
and
Combat

CONTRIBUTIONS IN
LEGAL STUDIES,
NUMBER 3

GREENWOOD PRESS
WESTPORT, CT • LONDON, ENGLAND

Library of Congress Cataloging in Publication Data

Karsten, Peter.
  Law, soldiers, and combat.

  (Contributions in legal studies ; no. 3 ISSN 0147-1074)
  Includes bibliographical references and index.
  1. War crimes. I. Title. II. Series.
JX5419.5.K37   341.6'9   77-87976
ISBN 0-313-20042-4

Library of Congress Catalog Card Number: 77-87976
ISBN: 0-313-20042-4
ISSN: 0147-1074

First published in 1978

Greenwood Press, Inc.
51 Riverside Avenue, Westport, Connecticut 06880

Printed in the United States of America

10 9 8 7 6 5 4 3

Dedicated To
Warrant Officer Hugh Thompson
and those of his calibre
throughout the world

Men who take up arms against one another in public war do not cease on this account to be moral human beings, responsible to one another and to God.

> Francis Lieber, "General Order No. 100, Instructions for the Government of Armies of the U.S. in the Field," April 24, 1863

The Japanese have no justification for making war on China. If they think they have, then do it as a civilized people is expected. Crush the Chinese army and incidentally lay waste a part of China if they must and can. Why should they carry on indiscriminate bombing, sink fishing junks, kill ex-soldiers in cold blood, burn cities after capture, and indulge in large-scale looting, rape and murder wherever they go? They have so behaved themselves with no corresponding barbarities on the part of the Chinese. They have committed atrocities not even under the pretext of reprisals. They are at war not only with China, but also with law, humanity and civilization.

> Shuhsi Hsü, *The War Conduct of the Japanese* (Shanghai, 1938), Preface.

Contents

Acknowledgments

Military personnel, academic colleagues, and other friends have been helpful or encouraging in one or more ways. I am especially grateful to Benjamin Franklin Cooling, of the Military History Research Collection, and Colonels James B. Agnew and Roy Barnard, of the Oral History Program, at the Army War College; Captain Bill Goodman, USAR; Colonel John Roehm; Dr. Ronald Spector and his colleagues at the office of the Chief of Military History; Beatte Schempp, research assistant for the German dimension of this study; Professors Michel Roublev, Hal Sims, and James Clarke, of the University of Pittsburgh; James Kemper and Mazie Coleman, of the Army Judge Advocate General's Office of the Clerk of Court; the staff of the Federal Records Center, Suitland, Maryland; Ingrid Glasco and Lee Krieger, of the University of Pittsburgh's Hillman Library; Major Robert G. Totten and the members of the "Officer Responsibilities" seminar at the Army's Command and General Staff College; Colonel Mel Wakin of the Philosophy Department at the Air Force Academy; Professors J. Glenn Gray and Fred Sondermann, of Colorado College; Margot Mazeau, of the Arms Control and Disarmament Agency; M. J.-L. Cayla and M. Yves Desceudres, of the International Committee of the Red Cross in Geneva; Professor Edward Sherman, of the Indiana University School of Law; Professor Morris Janowitz, of the Sociology Department, University of Chicago; Professor Klaus Knorr, of Princeton's Center of International Studies; members of the Fifth National Security Education

xii   ACKNOWLEDGMENTS

Seminar; Bart Lami, Dean Zarganis, Eileen Finnegan, and other members of my History 159 seminar; Greg Mattson of the U.S. Foreign Service; Frank Simonie of the U.S. Coast Guard Academy; Czeslaw Raczkowski; members of the 1973 West Point Senior Conference; D. G. Brennan of the Hudson Institute; and the American Council of Learned Societies, the Inter-University Seminar on Armed Forces and Society, and the Center for Arms Control and International Security Studies of the University of Pittsburgh, which organizations provided financial aid, facilitating the research and writing of this book. None of these persons or organizations, however, is responsible for any errors or omissions herein.

Introduction

In the days of the Roman Republic (190 B.C.) a Roman commander, Aemilius Regillus, accepted the surrender of the Greek city of Phocaea in exchange for the guarantee of its safety. But, ignoring his orders and those of his officers, his soldiers attacked the Phocaeans and pillaged for some time before finally being restrained. Another commander, Scipio Aemilianus, accepted the surrender of the Spanish city of Locha in 203 B.C. as his men approached its fortifications with ram and scaling ladders. He ordered the soldiers to halt their attack and give quarter, but they ignored him and sacked the city. When Aemilius Regillus and Scipio Aemilianus eventually regained control of their men, they punished those chiefly at fault, restored the freedom, lands, and goods of those victims whose lives they had been able to preserve, and offered public atonement for the deeds.[1] These incidents do not constitute the earliest instances of the violation and enforcement of rules comparable to our modern laws of war, but they are among the earliest clear recorded examples of such violations and observances, and as such their mention may serve to introduce this essay.

For thousands of years, in every corner of the globe warriors have clashed, and for many of these years those warriors have been formally ordered to conform to a number of rules — among them, rules governing the treatment of noncombatants and their property, the types of weapons and warfare allowed, and the taking of, and treatment of, enemy personnel *hors de combat*.

Wherever such rules were, in fact, treated seriously, we may say that the army in question observed the laws of war. The rules may never have been recorded in any formal way by the state's officials, but when they constituted widely held norms and actually regulated behavior, they amounted to customary law, and their observance or lack of it is the proper subject of our attention, for we are concerned here with violations and observances of the laws of war.

For as long as states have resolved to restrict their modes of warfare and to treat with compassion noncombatants and prisoners, there have been some who have declined to go by the rules and others who have scrupulously observed them. Here we shall attempt to identify the reasons for this divergence in the behavior of combatants, and to recommend steps that may be taken to reduce the likelihood that violations of the laws of war will occur in the future. Why have the laws been broken? And what may be done to increase the chance that they will be observed more often in the future?

Obviously, the task is an enormous—indeed, a presumptuous—one. In exploring the literature, however, I find very few writers who have systematically addressed the questions we have just raised. As William V. O'Brien, one prominent student of the laws of war, puts it, few concerned with the subject have approached it from the perspective of "what might be called the 'sociology of war.' " And many display "a singular disregard for military history and modern military science. To the extent that these failures are present and relevant to a war crimes controversy, they should be recognized as limiting the usefulness and fairness of seemingly authoritative subsidiary sources [such as legal treatises]. . . ."[2]

How can I, then, add something of value to this discussion? To begin with, let me explain what I mean by the laws of war and clarify when states may be said to have adopted one or more of them (Chapter 1). We shall not concern ourselves too long with the behavior of warriors in the past whose norms did not include any of the modern laws of war. Instead, we shall focus our attention on the behavior of those who have been obliged to observe one or more such laws, for we want to know why norms are ignored. We wish to detect the means by which such norms might be strengthened, and where there are no norms, there can be no deviations, from which we might learn. *Mens rea* (the culpable state of mind) is a necessary condition for the commission of a war crime. A war criminal is one who knew, "or should have known,"[3] that an act he committed violated the law. Hence we shall restrict ourselves to the consideration of such acts and persons.

Once we understand what we are talking about, we can begin to analyze a substantial number of clear violations and, in contrast, scrupulous observances of the rules of behavior that presently constitute the laws of war.[4] We shall examine the My Lai massacre and place it in the context of the several reasons for these violations, and we shall seek to isolate and identify these reasons (Chapter 2). Given these reasons, we may then be able to offer some specific prescriptions designed to reduce the likelihood of future violations (Chapter 3). Detecting "causes" may be much easier than discovering workable "solutions." Psychiatrists are often able to determine why a patient is mentally ill, but find it quite another thing to cure him. Moreover, if one *were* able somehow to determine that a "solution" offered would *work*, one would still want to know how to persuade the powers that be to adopt it. Anyone who has had experience as a "policy studies consultant to one or another federal agency has observed that policy recommendations are rarely given much attention (to say nothing of adoption) even when they have been specifically commissioned. But if someone is truly troubled by violations of the laws of war, then he will try to help reduce their occurrence in some way.

Let me begin with three statements: first, I do believe that combatants should observe the laws of war; I accept these laws[5] and believe that if nations go to war, they would do well to "play by the rules." War crimes are reprehensible on moral, ethical, or religious grounds, on the grounds that they constitute violations of legal norms, result in injury to the innocent and defenseless, degrade a belligerent's purposes and principles, weaken discipline in one's military forces, leave the violators with guilt or (worse) a sense of social sanction, injure one's relations with other nations, and may provoke reprisals by one's opponents. The laws governing the conduct of armies in the field have both practical and ethical roots. They are both reasonable and humane. This may strike some readers as an unremarkable position and an unnecessary defense, but it is offered because of the frequency with which it is said that "all's fair in . . . war," that "in war, anything goes."[6] In effect, I reject that view wholeheartedly. All is *not* "fair" in war, nor should it be. War is grim enough as it is. We have learned over the years to try to limit the contest to a fraction of the population and to restrain the behavior of that fraction. We would be foolish, indeed, were we to allow ourselves to slide back to the conditions existing before such norms were internalized by civilized states.

Second, although the "laws of war" include the decision to go to war in the first place (the *ius fetiale* of Rome, for example), I am arbitrarily excluding that subject from consideration.[7] We are concerned instead with but one facet of the *ius gentium* — namely, the law governing the conduct of combatants. This does not mean that we shall completely ignore the civilian leadership or its decision to order the armed forces into combat, for such decisions may well contribute greatly to the formation of what has been called the "atrocity-producing situation."[8] But we shall restrict our consideration of civilian decision makers to those moments when their decisions (regarding matters such as military recruitment, training, deployment, command and control, etc.) affect the ability of combatants to conduct themselves according to the laws of war. This should not be taken as an absolution of policy makers for their initial decisions to go to war. That issue will simply not be addressed in this book.

Third, I admit that a disproportionate amount of the evidence is drawn from the record of U.S. military engagements, and I find this evidence especially troubling. In fact, my research activities began shortly after I had heard of the massacre at My Lai, albeit my interest in the subject as a whole predated that event.[9] As an American citizen, I quite naturally take a considerable interest in the conduct of the American military. But this interest is balanced by attention given to the behavior of the armed forces of other nations. If American examples appear disproportionately in the book, this is largely due to the relative ease with which I have often been able to detect them. We shall also deal with examples from the military experience of ancient Greece and Rome, England, Russia, Poland, Germany, Switzerland, Italy, Spain, Portugal, France, modern Greece, Cuba, Korea, Japan, India, and Vietnam. We shall be concerned with the behavior of heavily armed forces of an imperial power, but I shall also have something to say about the behavior of guerrillas. I have tried to be as comprehensive as possible, for it is only by analyzing all types of war crimes that one may offer useful generalizations on the subject. And, as I shall argue in Chapter 3, a war crime committed by a "committed freedom fighter" is no less reprehensible than one committed by a "sadistic imperialist lackey."

NOTES

1. Mars M. Westington, "Atrocities in Roman Warfare to 133 B.C.," University of Chicago Ph.D. disseration, 1938, pp. 78, 101; Alberico Gentili, *De Iuire Belli Libre Tres* (1612 ed. [first published 1588], trans. John Rolfe, Oxford, 1933), II, 217.

2. O'Brien, "The Law of War, Command Responsibility, and Vietnam," *Georgetown Law Journal* 60 (February 1972): 612. Compare Robert W. Tucker, *Just War and Vatican Council II* (New York, 1966), 9n; Daniel Frei, "The Regulation of Warfare," *Journal of Conflict Resolution* 18 (December 1974): 628, 630; and Jacques Van Doorn, *The Soldier and Social Change* (Beverly Hills, 1975), 133: "Even smaller is the number of studies on war atrocities. . . . Serious and systematic analysis from the side of the social sciences is lacking."

I do not mean to fault the superb work of scholars like Jordan Paust, William O'Brien, Morris Greenspan, Joseph Kunz, Telford Taylor, Richard Falk, and others; I am simply pointing out that such scholarship relies almost exclusively on international protocols, published manuals, and formal trials and courts-martial. Legal scholars generally do not treat certain types of data (recollections of and letters describing events that did not end in a trial, reports of psychological experiments, unsworn testimony, etc.) that form part of the evidence in this book.

3. See Morris Greenspan, *The Modern Law of Land Warfare* (Berkeley, Calif., 1959), 477, 486.

4. In searching for our violators and observers I have examined historical accounts, autobiographies, legal treatises, court-martial records, recorded testimony, and other relevant works, and interviewed a substantial number of combat veterans, legal officers, chaplains, and

other military personnel. Some sources were necessarily suspect and are not considered herein. Thus although I sought confirmation of every violation of the laws of war described to me by a combat veteran, I was understandably unable to verify many. The shortcomings of this technique were evident, both from my own experience and from reading reviews of Mark Lane's *Conversations with Americans*, and therefore less weight has been given to such evidence than to, for example, the records of courts-martial.

In all I have evidence of over 200 clear violations or observances of the laws of war. Obviously, this is but a small sample of the total universe of such cases, and I have surely missed some well-reported ones, but the number is sufficient for our purposes; clear patterns can be discerned that allow us to form credible generalization. And, in any event, it is not evident that any larger number, subjected to more sophisticated forms of quantification than I have employed here would add measurably to our understanding of the subject. In short, I stopped searching when the new data began to become repetitive.

5. See the final section of Chapter 3 for a qualification of this statement, dealing with the need for the *extension* of the laws of war to new conditions and technologies.

6. This view is not just a popular one, but has, on occasion at least, been approached by prominent legal scholars. See, for example, William O'Brien in *World Polity*, II (George Washington University, 1960), 81-84; and Joseph Kunz's critique of such scholars, "The Chaotic Status of the Laws of War. . . ," *American Journal of International Law* 45 (1951): 37-61.

7. For the author's views on the question, see Peter Karsten, "Response to Threat Perception . . .," in Klaus Knorr, ed., *Historical Dimensions of National Security Questions* (Lawrence, Kansas, 1976); and A. F. Allen, P. Howell, and P. Karsten, *Military Threats* (Center for Arms Control and International Security Studies, Univ. of Pittsburgh, 1978).

8. Robert Jay Lifton, *Home from the War* (New York, 1973), 42.

9. In the navy I once served as a legal officer on a heavy cruiser, and later, in graduate school, I gave some attention to the subject while taking courses at the University of Wisconsin's law school. For the "first thoughts" I and a number of coauthors offered, see E. Berger, et al., "ROTC, Mylai, and the Volunteer Army," *Foreign Policy* 1 (Spring 1971): 135-60, reprinted in slightly altered version as "Professional and Citizen Officers" in J. Rokke and R. Head, eds., *American Defense Policy* (Baltimore, 1973), and in Charles Moskos, ed., *Public Opinion and the Military Establishment* (Beverly Hills, 1971).

Law,
Soldiers,
and
Combat

CHAPTER 1

The Laws

Nullum Crimen sine lege.

What are the laws of warfare, and what are their origins? How did they come into being? Let us answer these questions by briefly surveying the ancient, the medieval, and the modern worlds in order to describe and explain the evolution of what we now refer to as the laws of warfare.

THE ANCIENT WORLD

Human societies engaged in warfare have not always possessed a set of rules or laws designed to restrain one another in the treatment of prisoners or noncombatants. Early man and primitive societies may well have limited themselves to nominal casualties, and their combat was (and, where such societies remain, still is) generally governed by certain rules and ritualistic behavior, but their norms governing the treatment of "enemies"—be they warriors or noncombatant women and children—were often unlike those of modern societies. To such intensely "local" premodern societies, all nonmembers of the tribe, or "outsiders'," were largely fair game.[1]

As ancient societies became more developed and sophisticated—that is, as their economies and commerce became more complex, their governments more centralized and efficient, and their social and occupational structures more stratified and specialized—they slowly developed greater regard for prisoners and noncombatants. This was in part due to the fact that such societies began to generate excess wealth, freedoms, self-respect, and codes of honor that were by some generalized into a morality due all mankind. But it was in larger measure due to the fact that such ancient societies sought to create empires wherein the conquered peoples might prove useful and valuable as slaves, vassals, and feudatories. Unlike their more primitive predecessors, sophisticated ancient civilizations (the Athenians, the Romans, the Vedic Indians, the Incas, etc.) were able to mount and sustain complex, expensive, and long-term military operations and to maintain elaborate colonial administrations. With such capabilities, these ancient empires had less to fear from "barbarians" than had less powerful, simpler societies who were without the ability to garrison frontiers with well-armed, well-trained, professional warriors. The appearance of outsiders to the more primitive, militia-defended societies was extremely frightening. It might evoke memories of the devastation that hordes of mounted Scythians, Huns, Turks, or Mongols may have wrought in the past. In short, the more vulnerable the society, the more threatening its neighbors might appear to be and the more ruthless its behavior might be toward outsiders.

More developed ancient empires, then, were not as bent on slaying outsiders in combat as were many more primitive societies. But they were still far from modern in their treatment of such prisoners and noncombatants. Indeed, the earliest Middle Eastern powers (the Assyrians, the Hebrews, the Chaldeans, the Egyptians) were probably *more* brutal than their more primitive predecessors. The Hebrew prophet Nahum claimed that when the Assyrian capital, Nineveh, was to fall, the victors would righteously "dash to pieces" the young Assyrian children "at the top of all the streets," and this serves us both as a credible description of what actually *did* happen when Nineveh eventually fell in 612 B.C. and as a useful and revealing measure of one prominent Hebrew's sense of what a victor could legitimately do to the vanquished in 650 B.C. in the Near East. The Assyrians had been ruthless; they suffered a like fate.

Nahum's norms were understandable. After all, in 1280 B.C. Moses had instructed the Hebrews to "let nothing that breathes live" in the lands of the Hittites, Amorites, and Canaanites, as this was considered land that God meant the Hebrews to have. And Joshua, the Hebrew commander, appears to have done just that. He killed all in Jericho, Ai, and several other cities, and he enslaved the supine Gibeonites. Moses, however, *did* indicate that God intended that there should be some limits: Cities beyond the lands set aside for the Jews could be put to the sword, if necessary, but the women and children, although fair prey as spoils, need not be put to death. Captive women who were physically attractive were to be wed before they could be raped. During a siege, the besiegers might not cut down certain of the enemy's trees, for fruit trees were "meaty" and vital to "man's life." Nonetheless, in 849 B.C. Elisha reported that God wanted Israel and Judah to "fell every good tree and stop all wells of water, and mar every good piece of land" belonging to the rebellious Moabites.[2]

Why was there such brutality? Part of the answer lies in the fact that the Jewish nations had equally brutal neighbors, the Egyptians, the Chaldeans, and the Assyrians. Their annalists reported being raided by Midianites and Amalkites about 1100 B.C. The crops of the Hebrews were destroyed, and they were forced to retreat to the mountains. Later, in about 400 B.C., the prophet Joel, addressing the Phonecian leaders of Tyre and Sidon to the north and the Egyptian and Edomite lands to the south, complained of their destruction of the trees and vines of the Hebrew people and of the enslavement of Hebrew children: "I will sell *your* sons and *your* daughters into the land of the children of Judah, and they shall sell them to the Sabeans, to a people far off [in Arabia]: for the Lord hath said it." In the future, Joel maintained, "no strangers" would be allowed to approach Jerusalem.

When in 587 B.C. Judah was defeated and the people of Jerusalem were carried off as slaves by the Chaldeans, their conquerors "had no compassion on young man or maiden, old man, or he that stooped for age."[3] Warfare in the ancient Middle East was "total," and retribution, slaughter, and enslavement were the common plight of the vanquished.

There is another reason for the "total" character of this warfare—religious fervor. If an intensely religious people believe that they have divine sanction for the seizure of lands inhabited by others, if they feel that God wants them to "punish" or annihilate nonbelievers, they may well enter into the business with considerable elan. The Hebrews were hardly unique in this regard. Their contemporaries, the Vedic rulers of ancient India, had noble rules of conduct for wars with other Vedic peoples, but they were free to slaughter and plunder nonbelievers with abandon. And the same may be said of Islamic armies and Christian Crusaders.[4]

The ancient Greek states were sometimes ruthless, but then, like the Israelites, they were rarely free from the fear of attack. Pausanias, the Spartan commander at Plataea (479 B.C.) gave "no quarter" orders to the Greek forces, and thousands of defeated Persians were slaughtered. As they had invaded Greece, no one regarded their fate as particularly unwarranted. The rapine and slaughter attending the close of the Peloponnesian Wars can be understood in terms of the uncertainties all had endured. And one thinks of the brutal treatment meted out to prisoners taken after the failure of the Athenian assault on Syracuse. The leaders of the expedition were slain "with ignominy," and the rest, some 7,000 men, were sent to the stonequarries, where they remained for ten weeks, each subsisting on a pint of barley meal per day. Exposure, exhaustion, and disease killed many before the survivors were branded and sold. The Athenian response to this behavior was predictable—retaliation. Four Syracusian triremes were captured and the crews dispatched to the quarries near Piraeus. The revolt of subject cities and colonies, or even the posture of neutral neighbors, could produce the same fears and provoke the same behavior. Thus Apollonides packed 500 captured rebels into a wooden building and burned them alive in 315 B.C. And Athens sacked the southern isle of Melos during the Peloponnesian Wars simply because Melos refused to join with the Athenians, who regarded the isle as strategically vital and wanted to frighten other neutral states into supporting their cause.[5]

To be sure, the Greeks devised and engaged in some self-restraints, but these were often unclear and unstable. In 400 B.C.

the Athenian general Xenophon told his men to behave with moderation and honor during their retreat through Asia Minor and not to plunder any people who were not contesting their passage. But although Xenophon was a gentleman, his motives were certainly as much inspired by pragmatism as by propriety or humanity. Pausanias slaughtered the defeated Persians at Plataea, but he did reject as barbarous a proposal that the head of the Persian commander be placed on the end of a spit in retaliation for comparable acts. In 315 B.C. some leaders of rebellion were dragged by Cassander and his men from refuge in the sanctuary of Artemis and turned over to angry citizens who killed them. Diodorus objected to this "violation of Greek international usage," but the deed was done, and the rebels had been guilty of similar acts.[6]

When Antigonus, one of Alexander's more able commanders, was lectured on law and justice by a Sophist, he is said by Plutarch to have reproached the lecturer with: "Justice! What is justice to me? My business is the seizure of cities belonging to others." Polybius had kinder words for a descendant of Antigonus, Antigonus Doson, the conduct of whose soldiers was to him unexceptionable (given the norms of the age), but he was angered by the "blind passion and insanity" of the forces of Philip V, who "deface[d] temples and like edifices in pure wantonness, and without any prospect of weakening the enemy or strengthening themselves," and he was outraged by the behavior of the people of Mantinea, who massacred the 500 troops of the Achean League garrisoned by invitation in their city. This conduct was "in violation of the law recognized by all mankind." It was "a crime of the most impious description." And when Antigonus Doson sacked and razed Mantinea in retaliation and carried its women and children off as slaves, Polybius regarded the act as just:

This [razing] is only what, by the laws of warfare, awaits even those who have been guilty of no special act of impiety. They deserved, therefore, to meet with a punishment even more complete and heavy than [it was] ... nothing worse befell the Mantineans than the plunder of their property and the selling of their free population into slavery.... [The historian Phylarchus was unfair in being] unwilling to compare with this alleged cruelty of the Achaeans the conduct of the same people in the case of the city of Tegea, which they took by force in the same period and yet did no injury to its inhabitants.[7]

In short, if it was the case that Greek warfare *need* not have ended with the slaughter of the army of the defeated state and the enslavement of its people, it appears that it was still considered *legal* for it to end in such a fashion. In criticizing Philip V's improper defacement of religious edifices, Polybius readily granted that Philip *was* free to destroy "the enemy's forts, cities, harbours, men and crops, and other such things by which an enemy is weakened, and our own interests and tactics supported," as these were "necessary acts according to the laws and rights of war."[8] Cities generally contained women, children, and the elderly, who were not warriors. And if it was not deemed proper to *kill* such persons, one of the more important reasons for this deficiency was that they often were desirable as booty—as slaves. Ancient civilizations consisted, in large measure, of wealth and comforts acquired by the right of conquest.[9] And the enslavement of conquered peoples was a major component of these civilizations.

What of the Roman Republic's rules of war and combat behavior? They were not unlike those of other ancient civilizations, but they do move us a few short steps closer to today's laws of war. Romans saw in captives the same market value as did other powers.[10] And they too were fearful of powerful neighbors and competitors, such as the Samnites and the Carthaginians.[11] This fear certainly informed the treatment meted out to some prisoners and noncombatants. And there is no denying that the Romans could be very brutal.[12] But they could also exercise self-restraint.

Alberico Gentili (1552-1608) was so struck by the ambivalent nature of Roman combat behavior that he published two essays on the subject, one entitled *De institia bellica Romanorum* [*On the just warfare of the Romans*], the other, *De iniustitia bellica Romanorum* [*On the unjust warfare of the Romans*]. What Gentili noted was on the surface an inconsistency between the laws and disobedience. But a degree of consistency emerges once one takes a closer look. The *ius belli,* or customary law of warfare, did exist. It constituted protection for heralds, ambassadors, religious sites, persons with safe-conduct passes, persons in sanctuaries (such as temples), and persons who had been guaranteed quarter; it protected captive women from rape and dead foes from mutilation; it prohibited poisoning and most forms of treachery; and it provided for the exchange of prisoners of war.[13] Most consuls and commanders expected their men to show "good faith" *(fides)* and to observe the rules, such as they were. Thus those who assume that Marcus Tullius Cicero's famous remark — *inter arma silent legis* — refers to the absence of the rule of law in warfare[14] are mistaken. Cicero was no less anxious to have Roman soldiers behave properly than other Roman leaders. (His words refer to the private right of Titus Annius Milo to defend himself against assailants.[15]) Roman statesmen and commanders were often relatively "civilized," humane people. And they were well aware of the practical role of *fides* and generosity in the success of campaigns.[16] But, as we noted in the opening pages of this book, these leaders were not always able to restrain their men. And the soldiers of Aemilius Regillus and Scipio Aemilianus were not unlike those of Marcellus (unable to check his men at Syracuse in 200 B.C.) or those of an earlier age who ignored the orders of the consuls and slaughtered prisoners of war during the Second Samnite War.[17]

Other early civilizations developed codes of conduct for their warriors, but we know less about them. The ancient Vedic Indians possessed noble rules and high ideals, though we know little of the actual behavior of their soldiers. Early Muslim *jihad* (holy war) armies were instructed to avoid unnecessary harm to fruit trees, bee hives, wells, camels, noncombatants, and religious persons and places; and they were prohibited from using poison arrows or from impaling the heads of their victims on their spears. Inca warriors were ordered to treat conquered peoples fairly; they were not to abuse them or steal from them. Again, we cannot say how widely any of these rules and orders were observed, but they did exist, and their purpose was clear — unnecessary harm done to property and prisoners was not practical. It led to retaliation, and it destroyed the very fruits of conquest.[18]

We know more of the development of the laws of war in the West, and these are more relevant to us, for, ultimately, they lead directly to what today constitute the international laws of war. The collapse of the Roman Empire and the migrations of Germanic and Asiatic war bands surely weakened the various restraints developed by the ancients, but throughout the Middle Ages scholastics, international lawyers, and classicists, the Church, and feudalism revived them and added restraints of their own.

THE MEDIEVAL WORLD

With the passing of Roman hegemony, Europe and the Mediterranean basin again witnessed brutal warfare. Various confederates of the Empire—Visigoths, Lombards, Alans, Franks, Saxons—struggled with one another and with outsiders—Vandals, Thuringians, Huns, Vikings, Magyars. Like many of their "civilized" predecessors they pillaged towns, murdered prisoners and noncombatants, destroyed fields, vines, fruit trees, and sacred buildings. The potentates of the surviving Eastern Empire did not measurably display more admirable scruples. Basil II, for example, blinded thousands of captured Bulgar soldiers in 1014. Moreover, though the ceremony of knighthood may have provided dignity to the process by which one was admitted to the higher circles of the war band, it was (at least initially) no guarantee that the recipient would conduct himself with restraint and compassion on the battlefield. Knights in King Stephen's England, for example, did not appear to be governed by any principles comparable, let us say, to the ancient Vedic Code of Manu. "In their savage outbursts of anger or their cold ferocity, nothing restrained them; neither regard for weakness nor religious fear had any influence over them; they killed unarmed men without mercy; they burned nuns in their convents."[19] Not exactly what one might deem worthy of those heir to the mythic mantle of Sir Galahad.

The Church, reflecting substantial social pressures felt universally throughout Europe, sought to moderate the violence within

The pillage of a Gallo-Roman villa by Huns, as imagined by a nineteenth-century French artist.

its domain. On one level, it announced the Peace (A.D. 988) and the Truce (A.D. 1095) of God, which (among other things) protected churchmen, the helpless, and peasants (by prohibiting warfare during planting and harvesttimes). On another level, its scholastics and theologians pronounced the characteristics of "the just war" (St. Augustine and Francisco Suarez), which characteristics included an emphasis on the inviolability of noncombatants, and the "Principle of Proportionality" (St. Thomas Aquinas), which proclaimed that the damage done by the force offered should not exceed the military advantage thus to be gained.[20] On yet another level, at the Second Lateran Council (A.D. 1139), it tried to prevent the use of the crossbow—except against "infidels." (And, on yet another level, it declared war on the "infidels"[21] in the Holy Land in order to help siphon off warriors from the European continent.)

The feudal world produced other restraints, reflections of feudal culture and social structure. As a gentleman of heroic and virtuous proportions, the chivalrous knight was expected to be gentle to the weak and infirm, generous to the vanquished, and fair to foes. Inasmuch as the practice of subinfeudation sometimes caused countrymen, friends, and relatives to be pitted against one another on the field, it was logical for knights to agree to treat their captive caste fellows with some respect. After all, a prince, a lord, or a knight was worth ransom monies to the captor; he might be related to the family of one's wife, and abusing him might provoke the injured man's relatives or vassals to retailiate or to cause the guilty party to be brought before virtually international courts-martial composed of fellow knights, where his feudal bonds often provided him with little or no protection.[22] Moreover, since his protected military status was his chief badge of social distinction and his chief claim to economic support, he did not look kindly on those using unsanctioned (and often dangerous) new weapons or on uncommissioned irregulars or *banditti*. Such men were, as Balthazar Ayala and Alberico Gentili put it, "the common enemies of all" and were fair game to any who seized them.[23] In this regard their laws were not unlike those of the ancients, who also regarded pirates and brigands to be the common enemies of peaceful men.[24] These *banditti* threatened the security of peaceful citizens, but they also threatened the sovereignty and legitimacy of the power elite and the status of knight-warriors. If they would not subject themselves to the orders of a sovereign, such men were not to be offered the privileges of the customs of war. Room would not be made for "legitimate" irregulars or guerrillas in the laws and usages of nations until more modern times.[25]

Finally, classicists and international lawyers revived and embellished the ancient laws and usages of warfare. Baldus de Ubaldis (1327-1400) concluded that the victor was not lawfully impowered "to take the lives of those surrendering if they were merely enemies, and not traitors." Pierino Belli (1502-1575) agreed, and added that cities capitulating before the battering ram was actually applied to their gates should properly be given quarter. Gentili concurred, and noted that, whereas in the past warriors captured by the enemy were thus disgraced, with the advent of the *ius gentium* and the professional army (of which more in a moment) no disgrace attached to honorable surrender and there was no cause for captives to be abused. Gentili also observed that treachery and poisons were illegal and that women, children, and fruit-bearing vines and trees ought by right to be spared. Francisco a Vitoria (b. 1400) maintained that, in the event of an enemy's breach of faith, only *military* hostages should suffer. Honore Bonet (1341-1406?), echoing John of Legnano (fl. 1360), maintained that captives and peasants ought not be mistreated, as, too often, they were: "I do not call [such acts] war; it seems to me to be but pillage and robbery." Hugo de Groot (Grotius (1583-1645]) called for the "moderation of warfare" (*temperamenta belli*) and the exchange of prisoners of war. Emmerich de Vattel (1714-1767) and Immanuel Kant (1724-1804) insisted that the degree of "justness" attaching to a given war was at least as much a function of "the legality of the means" employed in fighting the war as it was of "the justice of the cause" of the war itself. In Vattel's words:

All damage done to the enemy unnecessarily . . . is a licentiousness condemned by the law of nature . . . [for] if you once open a door for continual accusation of outrageous excess in hostilities, you will only

augment the number of complaints, and influence the minds of the contending parties with increasing animosity; fresh injuries will be perpetually
springing up, and the sword will never be sheathed till one of the parties
be utterly destroyed.

Kant made a similar statement:

A state ought not during war countenance such hostilities as would
make mutual confidence in a subsequent peace impossible: such as,
employing assassins (percussores), poisoners (venefici), breeches of
capitulations, secret instigations to treachery and rebellion (perduello) in
the hostile state . . . [for] some kind of confidence in the disposition of
the enemy must exist even in the midst of war, or otherwise . . . the hostilities will pass into a war of extermination (bellum internecium). . . . Such
a war . . . , and also the use of all means which lead to it, must be absolutely forbidden.[26]

What provoked these jurists and seers to take such positions?
We can recognize four impulses: First, they possessed a basic humanity, derived from their religious and ethical training and from
reasonably comfortable surroundings and leisure. Second, they
were erudite, having devoted years of thoughtful study to past
human behavior and legal codes. (Surely their study led them to
note the relation in classical times between brutality and the desire to retaliate.) Third, they gained experience through their own
professional activities and daily associations, which led
international jurists like Gentili (a professor of international law
at Oxford and an adviser to the Earl of Essex) and Grotius (counsel to the Dutch East India Company in their challenge to the
papal degree of 1493) to sympathize with those whose lives and
property had often been subjected to the whims of an ill-disciplined
or vengeful soldiery. And, finally, they disapproved of the brutality often associated with the religious wars of their day (Grotius
suffered imprisonment for his defense of the Arminian province
of Holland before its more Calvinistic Netherland fellows, and
spent his last years trying to bring together the warring factions
of Christianity). But, whatever their reasons, and whatever the
reasons of churchmen and feudal functionaries, three forces—
the Church, chivalry, and jurisprudence—produced a climate
that allowed the ius belli to grow.

The climate was not without its changes. The introduction of the English longbow, the Genovese crossbow, the Swiss pike, the cannon, the musket, the grenade, and other new weapons accelerated the displacement of knights by *routiers, conditerri, ministerialis, landsknecht,* Swiss pikemen, English "crackers," and other mercenaries. And these *nouveaux arrivés* to the profession of arms were often initially unaware of, or unwilling to defer to, these laws and usages of war. Moreover, when a war had ended and the mercenaries had been dismissed, they often continued to pillage and forage at will. The Swiss and the South German *landsknecht* were particularly brutal—even toward one another. Consider a French saying (ca. 1500) of the *landsknecht:* *"Un lansquenet repousse du paradis ne peut avoir acces en enfer parce qu'il ferait peur au diable"* (A *landsknecht* thrown out of heaven couldn't get into hell because he frightened the devil.)

The fourteenth-century Florentine *conditerri* Pippo Spano was understandably hated by his opponents because of his practice of cutting off the right hands of prisoners before releasing them. Simultaneously, in France, noncombatants often suffered grievously, unless field-grade officers were on hand. Honore Bonet noted that "the man who does know how to set places on fire, to rob churches . . . and imprison priests, is not fit to carry on war."[27] But the new, mercenary professionals of the late Middle Ages soon decided that this sort of behavior constituted "bad war"— that is, warfare that was *too* cruel, *too* ruthless. Hans Delbrueck and, more recently, Fritz Redlich and Michael Mallett have demonstrated that conventions ensuring a "good war" were slowly developing among such mercenaries by the sixteenth and seventeenth centuries: Common soldiers and noncombatants were to be treated generously; affluent captives were subject to ransom but not abuse; looting, burning, and other such attacks upon inhabitants and their property were restricted to acts vital to the success of the military objective; and in consideration for their subsequent loss of loot and booty, mercenaries were given provisions and regular pay.

This last practice, the provision of adequate supplies and of decent and regular pay, went a long way toward ending some of the vilest of habits. But the men were not always paid on time, or as much as they had been led to believe they would be, and in

Three artists' versions of "good war" and "bad war" in the sixteenth century:

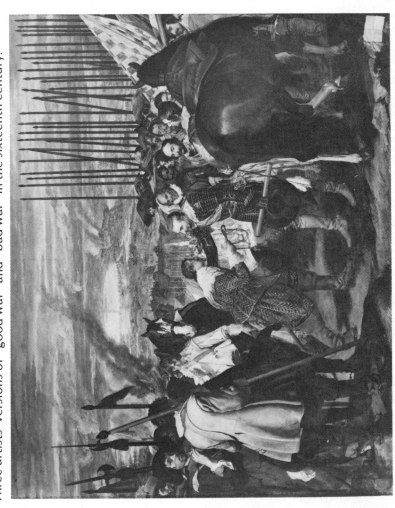

Velasquez celebrates the generous treatment offered the Dutch by the Spanish commander at the "Capitulation of Breda" (1581). The Prado, Madrid

Francois Dubois depicts the French massacre of Huguenots on St. Bartholomew's Eve (1572).

An unknown engraver offers a view of the killing of Antwerp burghers by French troops (1583).

such instances they reverted to plundering for revenues. William Worcestre advised the English monarch in 1475 of the need to prevent his "officers roialle" from withholding the wages of the king's "souldeours," who thereupon simply stole from the king's subjects. The result was that the "oppressed" subjects had "turned their [hearts] frome us, breking theire allegeannce by manere of cohercion for such rapyn, oppressions and extortions." Count Ernest von Mansfeld, the military commander of the Bohemian forces in 1620, complained to his employers that "it was impossible" for him to "restraine so many malcontents . . . and hold [the soldiers] under Discipline if their wages be not paid them. Neither they nor their horses can live by the ayre; all that they have whether it be arms or apparell, weareth, wasteth, breaketh. If they must buy more, they must have money. And if men have it not to give them, they will take it, where they find it, not as a part of that which is due unto them, but without weighing and telling it." [28]

Many professionals of the standing armies of the early modern European monarchies, be they aristocrats or "common" mercenaries, came to agree with the jurists that (as Sir Philip Sydney put it) "cruelty in war buyeth conquest at the dearest price." Gustavus Adolphus was said to have kept a copy of Grotius' *De Jure Belli ac Pacis* by his side throughout the Thirty Years' War; it is known that his articles of war included one (no. 97) that warned his soldiers not to abuse religious persons, scholars, the poor, women, and children "upon pain of death." The Stuarts in England included the same rule in their own articles of war (no. 5, sec. 5). Sir James Turner cited Grotius frequently as an authority on "the modern laws of war" in 1671. In 1692 the French and the Holy Roman Emperor agreed to regularize the size of foraging parties (to be no fewer than fifteen men per party) in order to eliminate the freebooting, undisciplined foraging habits that prevailed when small groups of men foraged without the supervision of an officer. General Wellington clearly observed this practice in the wars of the early nineteenth century. [29]

THE MODERN AGE

In short, a sense of moderation and restraint was advancing. Brutality seemed both unethical and uneconomical. When Louvois ordered the devastation of the Palatinate in 1689, he may well have restricted himself (as Albert Sorel put it) to *"les usages etablis"* and may have applied them more systematically than his contemporaries, but his orders still provoked cries of outrage from those same contemporaries.[30] The fact of the matter was that the rest of Europe was simply leaving Louvois and his "strict interpretation" of the laws behind in its search for a more humane mode of warfare. Guglielmo Ferrero's insightful (if unnecessarily pessimistic) view is worth quoting: "Restricted warfare was one of the loftiest achievements of the eighteenth century. It belongs to a class of hot-house plants which can only thrive in an aristocratic and qualitative civilisation. We are no longer capable of it. It is one of the fine things we have lost as a result of the French Revolution."[31]

In the next chapter I shall argue that Ferrero is only partly correct—that one needs only a qualitative civilization, not an aristocratic one, in order to limit war's horrors with humane rules. But for now we shall pass over these remarks to a consideration of his last sentence. Why did he regard the French Revolution as damaging to the *ius belli*? The reason is that he felt it was often ignored by the Revolutionary French proponents of "total war."

Actually, the French were not generally as brutal as Ferrero implies, but on occasion they could be atrocious in their treatment of prisoners and noncombatants. The repression of the revolt in *La Vendée* may be an unfair example of this to offer, for the counterrevolutionaries were not, strictly speaking, protected by existing features of the *ius belli* (nor might such forces hope to be until the Geneva Conventions of 1949). But the initial efforts to repress the revolt by Deputy Carrier and Generals Turreau, Boucret, and Westermann were so ruthless as to offend some of their fellow republicans-in-arms, to say nothing of nonrepublicans. The peasant rebels had themselves committed numerous atrocities, but consider Westermann's report of retaliations taken: "I have crushed the children under the hoofs of the horses, executed the women . . . who will thus breed no more of these brigands. I have not a single prisoner with which to reproach myself. I have wiped out all. . . . The roads are strewn with corpses.

. . . [I]t would be necessary to feed [prisoners] with the bread belonging to Liberty."[32]

The Jacobins, of course, correctly believed themselves to be
locked in a life-and-death struggle with these Royalist foes. And
full of such fears, they were capable of acts of "total war." The
lack of professionalism in Westermann's army certainly counted
for something too in this regard. But we leave for the next
chapter such causal considerations. The point we want to make
here is that the warfare waged by some French revolutionaries
was ruthless and "total," and in this regard the French were not
unique. American revolutionaries and their British opponents
had been guilty of similar atrocities. Wellington's Penninsular
army was apparently also capable (in his words) of a number of
"outrages . . . committed on [an Iberian] people who have
received us as friends." German recruits were later guilty of
some similar acts, which acts, I think, the disciples of Baron Carl
von Clausewitz could be said to have provoked.[33] The mass,
ideological character of unprofessional Revolution and post-
Revolution armies surely lent itself to some violations of the laws
of war, or so we (like J. F. C. Fuller) shall argue. In any event, many
nineteenth-century jurists and statesmen feared a "backsliding"[34]
(such, it might be added, as that actually experienced in the days
of the Social Wars of ancient Greece, and in a fourteenth-century
Europe of new weapons and professional mercenaries).

Consequently, these jurists and statesmen organized a number
of conferences throughout the nineteenth and early twentieth
centuries to revive, clarify, strengthen, and codify the law of war.
In 1856 the delegates of several major nations met and signed
the Declaration of Paris, designed to abolish irregular naval warfare (privateering). The republican United States, still a minor
naval power, refused to accept the declaration, claiming that
such guerrilla fleets were necessary for weak, nonimperial powers.
But later, when the Union blockaded the Confederacy with strong
squadrons, the Union's diplomats accepted the Declaration of
Paris and sought to prohibit Confederate privateering. In 1859 a
Swiss gentleman, Jean Henri Dunant, visited the battlefield of
Solferino, where he witnessed the suffering of tens of thousands
of the abandoned wounded. In 1862 he wrote *Un Souvenir de*

Solferino, which prompted the 1864 Geneva Convention for the Amelioration of the Condition of the Wounded and Sick in the Armies in the Field and the creation of the International Committee of the Red Cross. Geneva Conventions in the 1920s and 1940s fixed a minimum set of obligations that armies owed to irregulars, noncombatants, and combatants who were *hors de combat* due to sickness, wounds, or capture.

Another group, distressed by the treatment of prisoners of war, called for an international conference in 1874. The Russian government had recently championed the outlawing of bullets that caused unnecessary suffering (the 1868 Declaration of St. Petersburg by an "International Military Commission"), and it now proposed that such a conference consider the general question of the usages of warfare. The conference met in Brussels, chaired by Baron Henri Antoine de Jomini, but was unable to produce a protocol acceptable to all. In 1880 the Institute of International Law drafted such a protocol, and, armed with these antecedents, at the turn of the century delegates met at the Hague (in 1899 and again in 1907) to define and codify the rights and duties of belligerents in the field, particularly with regard to the employment of weapons, the conduct of field forces, and the disposition of noncombatants' property.[35] Towns were not to be pillaged "even when taken by assault." Prisoners of war were not to be regarded as personal prizes but were to be regarded as passing immediately into the hands of "the hostile government" itself. Hague Regulation 23 (g) of 1907 specified that it was not lawful to destroy property belonging to citizens of enemy nations unless such acts were "imperatively demanded by the necessities of war"—strong (if still not prohibitive) language—stronger language regarding property than had ever been used before. Hague Regulation 25 (1907) also prohibited "attacks of bombardment, by whatever means, of towns, villages, dwellings, or buildings which are undefended," the phrase "by whatever means" being inserted in order to include a new potential weapon, the aircraft.

Much of this codification sprang from the concern men had with the fruit of technology—the new weapons of devastation—bombs, planes, mines, cannon, gas, submarines. An 1899 clause outlawed the dropping of bombs from balloons, and the ban was renewed in 1907, but a number of states indicated reservations, and in 1908 the British jurist T. E. Holland declared it "defective." Nonetheless, in 1916 the British treated Zeppelin crews as war criminals.[36] Explosive bullets below 400 grams (first attacked in the 1868 Declaration of St. Petersburg) were outlawed, as these were deemed to possess the potential for unnecessary cruelty. Efforts to outlaw uncontrolled submarine mines[37] and to oblige all naval combatants (including submarines) to care for the survivors of sunken vessels were ratified but often ignored in World War I and thereafter—albeit in the 1920s the Allies sought to punish some German U-boat commanders for attacks upon hospitals ships and victims of torpedo attacks. The United States refused to agree to outlaw asphyxiating gases in 1907, but later began to observe such a restriction when gases were outlawed by others at Geneva in 1925.[38]

The 1907 Hague Conference also sought to allow for the survival of as many of past, customary usages as possible with Convention IV (The "Martens Clause"):

Until a more complete code of the laws of war has been issued, . . . in cases not included in the Regulations [herein adopted], the inhabitants and the belligerents remain under the protection of and the rule of the principles of the law of nations, as they result from the usages established among civilized peoples, from the laws of humanity, and from the dictates of the public conscience.

This and other portions of the Hague and Geneva Conventions were utilized by the International Military Tribunal in 1946 and 1947 during the trials of German and Japanese war criminals at Nuremberg and Tokyo, Specifically, the charter of the tribunal defined war crimes to be:

Violations of the laws or customs of war which include, but are not limited to, murder, ill-treatment or deportation for slave labour or for any other purpose of the civilian population in occupied territory, murder or ill-treatment of prisoners of war or persons on the seas, killing of hostages, plunder of public or private property, wanton destruction of cities, town or villages, or devastation not justified by military necessity.

Central to many of the trials were two issues: (1) whether obedience to orders should be considered a sufficient defense and (2) to what extent a commander should be held responsible for the behavior of subordinates. The International Military Tribunal answered the first as follows: One ought not to obey an order one knows, or ought to know, to be illegal,[39] but the final test of culpability was not the order itself "but whether moral choice was in fact possible." In the event that one's commander threatened imminent and deadly peril, one could not be expected to disobey, but "threats of future injury" or other discipline were insufficient. The second question, that of command responsibility, was addressed by the International Military Tribunal and by the United States in several opinions—among them, those of the *List, Von Leeb, Kimura,* and *Yamashita* cases.[40] Briefly, the courts held that the commander was obliged: to instruct his men to observe the laws; to investigate their behavior in order to ascertain whether his orders were being obeyed; and, in the event that he discovered noncompliance, to take those steps that were necessary "to prevent thereafter the commission of war crimes and to satisfy himself that such orders are being carried out."[41] Commanders who fulfilled these duties were not to be held responsible if, despite their efforts, subordinates were still guilty of committing atrocities.[42]

The taking and the eventual executing of hostages by German troops were not punished in the *List case,* but disapproval of this usage had been building for some time, and in 1949 delegates at Geneva agreed (art. 34) to prohibit the practice altogether.[43] In 1874 delegates had met at Brussels in an attempt (among other things) to delineate the laws relating to irregular or guerrilla forces. But its members found agreement difficult, and the resulting declaration was never ratified.[44] Various nations dealt with guerrillas within their own law codes, to be sure. The Union army's Lieber Code (General Order No. 100, drafted in 1863 by Major General Ethan Allen Hitchcock and Francis Lieber, an international lawyer) had specified (arts. 82 and 84) that irregular

forces without commission and regulation from their government were not entitled to be granted the protections offered
prisoners of war, as they were no better than the brigands of
old.[45] The U.S. Attorney General, approving the code's application, observed:

> The horrors of war would indeed be aggravated if every individual of
> the belligerent states were allowed to plunder and slay indiscriminately
> the enemy's subjects without being in any manner accountable for his con-
> duct [to the sovereign, its commissioned officers, and its courts-martial].
> Hence it is that, in land wars, irregular bands of marauders are liable to be
> treated as lawless *banditti,* not entitled to the protection of the mitigated
> usages of war as practiced by civilized nations.[46]

Formal language, sanctioning organized guerrilla bands that
observed the laws of war and distinguished themselves from
noncombatants when engaging the enemy, was agreed upon at
Geneva in 1949.

   The laws of war are, theoretically, at least, enforceable by
international tribunal, but that means of enforcement is rare, as
are the instances (most of them medieval) in which an accused
citizen of one state is released to the custody of courts of
another state for trial. Most enforcement is accomplished by the
courts-martial of the state exercising jurisdiction over the
accused person, for most conduct constituting war crimes is also
domestic crime. Hence, for the most part, the relevant and
operative law is to be found in the articles of war, the field
manuals, rules of engagement, and general orders of each armed
force. In the United States today, for example, the Department
of the Army's Field Manual 27-10, *The Law of Land Warfare* (most
recently revised in 1956), constitutes the U.S. Army's primary
guidebook, and the articles contained in the *Uniform Code of
Military Justice* (act of May 5, 1950), together with general orders
in the field, constitute its basic substantive law. To date, all U.S.
servicemen charged with violations of the laws of war have been
tried by military or naval courts-martial for specified breeches of
one or another of these articles or their antecedents.

Recently, the International Committee of the Red Cross (ICRC) and elements of the diplomatic and legal community have sought to reaffirm and to add to the body of international agreements or laws regulating the conduct of warfare. Delegates met at Geneva in 1956, at Vienna in 1965, at Istanbul in 1969, and again at Geneva in 1971, 1972, 1974, 1975, 1976, and 1977. New protocols (discussed in Chapter 3) were accepted and forwarded to the participant states for ratification in December 1977. (See Appendix 3 for some of the more important articles of these protocols.)

In summary, the laws of war are the products of humanitarians, of legists, of military professionals, and, most significantly, of *practical* statesmen. They emerged as societies sensed that certain restraints in wartime were both appropriate and possible ends. Nonmilitary property, civilians, truce parties, prisoners, and those *hors de combat* slowly acquired protected status as policy makers and the informed public alike came to agree that such protection as was to be afforded made sense. Captured and taxable property would not be lost by the conquering state; troop discipline could more readily be preserved; outnumbered forces should be more willing to surrender; professional soldiers could conduct themselves with honor; defenseless noncombatants could have less fear in time of war. War was no less horrible, and there were always violations of the laws, to be sure, but each society that condemned "inhumane practices" or "superfluous injury," for whatever reasons, preserved *some* defenseless souls from "unnecessary suffering."

This account of the development of the laws of war is, of course, but an abbreviated sketch. But it should serve to introduce the reader to the laws and norms relevant to our inquiry. We are concerned with the reasons behind a number of identifiable violations of these laws of war. It is to these that we must now turn.

NOTES

1. See, for example, John G. Kennedy, "Ritual and Intergroup Murder . . . ," in Maurice Walsh, ed., *War and Human Race* (1971), 40-61; Quincy Wright, *A Study of War* (Chicago, 1942), I, 163; Rafael Karsten,

"Blood Revenge Among the Jivaro Indians . . . ," in Paul Bohannan, ed., *Law and Warfare* (1967); N. Chagnon, "Yanamomo Social Organization and Warfare," in M. Fried, M. Harris, and R. Murphy, eds., *The Anthropology of Armed Conflict and Aggression* (1967), 109-60; H. H. Turney-High, *Primitive War* (Columbia, S.C., 1949); William Divale, ed., *Warfare in Primitive Societies* (Santa Barbara, Calif., 1973). Compare Robert S. Bigelow, *The Dawn Warriors* (Boston, 1969).

2. Coleman Phillipson, *The International Law and Custom of Ancient Greece and Rome* (London, 1911), II, 203; Nahum, III: 10; Deuteronomy, XX: 10-19; XXI: 10-14; Joshua, VI: 22; VII: 18-29; IX: 1-27; X: 25-38; II Kings, III: 19-24.

3. Judges, VI; Joel, III: 5-21; II Chronicles, XXXVI: 17. For a modern example of such *bellum internecium* see J. B. Glubb, *War in the Desert* (London, 1960), 307: "Every Ikhwan engagement was a war of extermination."

4. Sarva D. Singh, *Ancient Indian Warfare with Special Reference to the Vedic Period* (Leiden, 1965), 153 ff; Zoe Oldensbourg, *Massacre at Montsegur* (translated by Peter Green, New York, 1962). Compare Philip Hitti, *Islam* (Chicago, 1970), 86-88, on the destruction of the Umayyads by the 'Abbasids and Shi'ites in A.D. 750.

5. W. Kendrick Pritchett, *Ancient Greek Military Practices,* Part I (Berkeley, 1971), 70 ff; Thucydides, *Peloponnesian War,* III, 82; Peter Green, *The Year of Salamis* (London, 1970), 270; Green, *Armada from Athens* (New York, 1970), 345 ff, 347n. Compare A. H. Jackson, "Plundering in War and Other Depredations in Greek History from 800 B.C. to 146 B.C.," unpublished Ph.D. dissertation, Cambridge University, 1970; Walker, *A History of the Law of Nations* (2 vols., Cambridge, 1899), I, 42.

6. Green, *Salamis,* 270; Michael Rostovtzeff, *The Social and Economic History of the Hellenistic World* (3 vols., Oxford, 1941), I, 142.

7. Phillipson, *op. cit.,* II, 203-6; Polybius, *History* . . . (trans. Evelyn Suckburgh, 1889), I, 58; V, 11. Walker, *op. cit.,* I, 131-33.

8. Phillipson, *op. cit.,* II, 249.

9. Rostovtzeff, *op. cit.,* II, 606.

10. *Ibid.,* 1258 ff.

11. See, for example, J.P.V.D. Baldson, *Rome* (London, 1970), 24.

12. Rostovtzeff, *op. cit.,* II, 606.

13. Phillipson, *op. cit.,* II, 221-23; Mars Westington, "Atrocities in Roman Warfare . . . ," University of Chicago Ph.D. diss., 1938, 10-21, 25-26, 38, 48, 51, 60, 95, 104, 121; Piganiol, "*Venire in fidem,*" *Revue Internationale des Droits de l'Antique* (1951).

14. See, for example, William T. Hutchinson's introduction to *War and Law,* ed. Ernst Puttkammer (Chicago, 1944); R. D. Heinl, *Dictionary of*

Military and Naval Quotations (Annapolis, 1966), 166; Captain S. P. Adye, British Army Deputy Judge Advocate, cited in F. B. Wiener, *Civilians Under Military Justice* (Chicago, 1967), 120; Representatives Rhett (S.C.) and James Seddon (Va.), *Congressional Globe* (1846), 23-24; and Ralph Gabriel, "Military Occupation of Conquered Territory," in J. C. Kerwin, ed., *Civil-Military Relation in the U.S.* (Chicago, 1948), 632.

15. Cicero, *Pro Milone*, IV, 11; *Pro Balbus*, VI, 15 C. D. Yonge, in *Select Orations of M. T. Cicero* [New York 1859], III, 178).

However, Plutarch *does* claim that Pompey took a position quite comparable to that of Antigonus, when he allegedly remarked: "When I am in arms, am I to think of laws?" (Cited by Grotius in his *Prolegomena, De Jure Belli ac Pacis* [Paris, 1625], 3.)

16. Westington, *op. cit.*, 25-26, 104 ff.

17. Westington, 10, 78, 95, 101; Alberico Gentili, *De Iurie Belli Libri Tres* (1588 ed., translated by John Rolfe, Oxford, 1933), II, 217.

18. We can, however, note that such customary laws of warfare exist and are observed among many sub-Saharan West African tribes. See ICRC *Bulletin*, no. 4, May 5, 1976, 5. See also Singh, *op. cit.*, 138, 153 ff; Majid Khadduri, *War and Peace in the Law of Islam* (Baltimore, 1955), 102-5; Joseph Bram, *An Analysis of Inca Militarism* (Monographs of the American Ethnological Society, IV, New York, 1941), 47. We should note that Arab civilization developed a class of chivalric warriors, the *rabitos*, comparable to the Western knights (Walker, *A History of the Laws of Nations* [Cambridge, 1899], I, 88).

19. R. S. Hartigan, "Noncombatant Immunity: Reflections on Its Origins and Present Status," *Review of Politics* 29 (1967); Sister Dolorosa Kennelly, "The Peace and Truce of God," unpublished Ph.D. dissertation, Berkeley, 1963; J. Flack, *Les Origines de l'Ancienne France*, II, 567-68, cited in Edgar Prestage, ed., *Chivalry* (New York, 1928), 5-6. Compare Walker *op. cit.*, I, 64-66, 123-124; J. R. Strayer and D. C. Munro, *Middle Ages* (New York, 1942).

20. See, for example, R. S. Hartigan, "Saint Augustine on War and Killing: The Problem of the Innocent," *Journal of the History of Ideas* 27 (1966); Y. de la Briere, *Le Droit de Juste Guerre* (1933); and Joan Tooke, *The Just War* . . . (London, 1965).

Suarez distinguished between the just killing of a Saracen infidel and the unjust killing of the Saracen's young children.

21. Walter Wakefield, *Heresey, Crusade and Inquisition in Southern France, 1100-1250* (Berkeley, 1974), 99-100.

22. Maurice Keen, *The Law of War in the Late Middle Ages* (London, 1965), passim; Charles Oman, *History of the Art of War* (London, 1898), 384 (quoting Oderic on the fate of 140 French knights captured at Bremule in 1119): "...because of the fear of God and the fact that they were known to each other as old comrades, there was no slaughter."

23. Balthazar Ayala, *De Jure et Officiis Bellicis* (1582), bk. 1, chap. 2, par. 15.

24. Rostovtzeff, *op. cit.,* I, 196.

25. See p. 104 and p. 165 for more on this subject.

26. Ubaldis, *On Code* (1389), VII, vi; Belli, *A Treatise in Military Matters and Warfare* (1588 ed., trans. Herbert Nutting, Oxford, 1936), 86, 232-33; Gentili, *De Iuire Belli Libri Tres* (1588 ed., trans. John Rolfe, Oxford, 1933), 145 ff., 210 ff., 213, 251, 275; Grotius, *De Jure Belli ac Pacis* (Paris, 1625), passim; Vattel, *The Law of Nations* (originally published 1758, trans. Joseph Chitty, 1834), 369, 381-82, cited in J. F. C. Fuller, *The Conduct of War* (London, 1961), 17-18; Kant, *Perpetual Peace,* I (1795, trans. M. C. Smith, New York, 1948), 6-7; Walker, *op. cit.,* I, 228; Honore Bonet, *The Tree of Battles,* ed. G. M. Coopland (Liverpool, 1949), 152-89.

27. John Barnie, *War in Medieval English Society* (Ithaca, 1974), 34; John Schlight, *Monarchs and Mercenaries* (Bridgeport, 1968), 16; Sir Charles Oman, *The Art of War in the Middle Ages* (Ithaca, 1966), 76; Oman, *A History of the Art of War in the Sixteenth Century* (New York, 1937), 66, 328; Keen, *op. cit.,* 190; Anthony Mockler, *The Mercenaries* (New York, 1969), 42, 83, 86, 93, 100; Hans Delbrueck, *Geschichte der Kriegskunst im Rahmen der politischen Geschichte* (Berlin, 1920), IV, 73-79; Michael Mallett, *Mercenaries and Their Masters* (New York, 1973), 35-43, 200-201; *The Sand Creek Massacre,* ed. John Carroll (1973), 159. Compare George Tamarin, *The Israeli Dilemma* (Rotterdam, 1973), 185-190.

28. J. R. Hale, "International Relations in the West," in *The New Cambridge Modern History,* Vol. I: *The Renaissance* (Cambridge, 1957), 291; Worcestre, in *The Boke of Noblesse* [1475] . . . , ed. J. G. Nichols (London, 1860), 72; Fritz Redlich, *The German Military Enterpriser and His Work Force,* I (Wiesbaden, 1964), 512. Compare Richard Hellie, *Enserfment and Military Change in Muscovy* (Chicago, 1971), 210.

29. James Anson Farrer, *Military Manners and Customs* (New York, 1885); Sir James Turner, *Pallas Armata* (London, 1671), 335-36, passim. W. W. Winthrop, *Military Law of the U.S.* (Washington, 1886), 6n; *The Letters of Private Wheeler,* ed. B. H. Liddell Hart (Boston, 1952), 115. In 1743 a similar agreement was concluded between the French and

Austro-Hanoverian armies, "by which each undertook to respect the hospitals of the other" (T. E. Holland, *A Lecture on the Brussels Conference of 1874* [Oxford, 1876], 7).

30. Sorel, cited in Sir George Clark, *War and Society in the 17th Century* (Cambridge, 1958), 78-79, 85. (Fritz Redlich, however, maintained that the rape of the Palatinate was *not* in accord with existing practices. See *De Praeda Militari* . . . [Wiesbaden, 1956], 24*n.*)

31. G. Ferrero, *Peace and War* (London, 1933), 63-64; first cited in J. F. C. Fuller, *The Conduct of War* (London, 1961), 25. Compare John W. Wright, "Sieges and Customs of War at the Opening of the Eighteenth Century," *American Historical Review* 39 (July, 1934), 629-44.

32. Fuller, *op. cit.*, 31, quoting from Hoffman Nickerson, *The Armed Horde,* 91; Charles Tilly, *La Vendée* (Cambridge, Mass., 1964), 330-39; Peter Paret, *The Vendee, 1789-1796* (Research Monograph No. 12, Princeton Internal War Project, 1961), passim. Compare Redlich, *De Praeda Militari . . . ,* 76.

33. Clausewitz, *On War* (London, 1908 ed. and trans. F. N. Mande), I, 3: ". . . to introduce into the philosophy of War . . . a principle of moderation would be an absurdity." Compare J. H. Morgan, ed., *The German War Book* (Toronto, 1915), and T. E. Holland, *The Laws of War on Land (Written and Unwritten)* (Oxford, 1908), 12, quoting General von Molke: ". . . all means of waging war [are legitimate] save those which are absolutely objectionable." But see the argument of Michael Howard and Peter Paret, eds., *Carl von Clausewitz on War* (Princeton, 1976).

Here, and in several of the preceding paragraphs, I find myself in agreement with, and in the debt of, Fuller, *The Conduct of War,* 37, 61.

34. For example, Francis Lieber, the German-American codifier of the laws and usages of warfare, explained that he had been motivated by "history, reason and conscientiousness, a sincere love of truth, justice and civilization." He was also a veteran of early nineteenth-century European warfare (Holland, *op. cit.,* 72).

35. See F. F. Piggott, *The Declaration of Paris* (New York, London, 1919), passim. Compare Kenneth Andrew, *Elizabethan Privateering* (Cambridge, 1964).

36. Holland, *op. cit.,* 41-42; Stone, *op. cit.,* 611*n.*

37. Hague Convention VIII (1907) prohibited mines active for more than one hour that were sowed "with the sole object of intercepting commercial navigation (art. 2). It has been circumvented by the simple process of alleging that the primary purpose of such mines is the destruction of combatants. (See Morris Greenspan, *The Modern Law of Land Warfare* (Berkeley, 1959), 364.

38. Marcel Fegizon and Michel Magat, "The Toxic Arsenal," in Nigel Calder, ed., *Unless Peace Comes* (New York, 1968), 130.

39. Ignorance of the law was not allowed as an excuse, though "it may mitigate punishment." *The Flick Case,* cited in M. Greenspan, *The Modern Law of Warfare,* 486.

40. Judgment of the International Military Tribunal, *Trial of the Major War Criminals* (Washington, D.C., 1947), I, 224; Leslie Stephen, *Digest of the Criminal Law* (1877), art. 31. Thus Sanford Levinson correctly observes that the threat of instantaneous execution for refusal to obey a questionable order (which *is* a defense) is "very different" from a threat "where the penalty was demotion in rank." Levinson, in Marshall Cohen et al., *War and Moral Responsibility* (Princeton, 1974), 144. Compare *United States* v. *Von Leeb,* 10 *Trial of War Criminals* (hereafter cited as *T.W.C.*) 1, 11 *T.W.C.* 509 (1948); and Principle IV of the Principles of International Law Recognized in the Charter of the Nuremberg Tribunal and in its Judgment, as formulated by the International Law Commission, June-July, 1950.

41. *United States* v. *Von Leeb,* 11 *T.W.C.* 543; *United States* v. *Yamashita,* 327 *U.S.* 1, 16 (1946); *United States* v. *List,* 11 *T.W.C.* 757, 1256 (1948); Trial of Kimura, II *Judgment of the International Military Tribunal for the Far East* 1175 (1948); all cited in Jordan Paust's fine essay, "My Lai and Vietnam: Norms, Myths, and Leader Responsibility," *Military Law Review* (1972): 180-83.

42. Trial of Kimura, *op. cit.,* 1176.

43. *United States* v. *Von Leeb,* 11 *T.W.C.* 543-44 (1948). Compare Arnold Fisch, "Field Marshal Wilhelm List and the 'Hostages Case' at Nuremberg: A Historical Reassessment," unpublished P.H. dissertation, Pennsylvania State University, 1975.

44. T. E. Holland, *The Brussels Conference* (London, 1876).

45. Paust appears to have transcribed incorrectly the date of the Brussels Conference in his notes, for he has the conference being held in 1847 (*op. cit.,* 130). Consequently, he errs in criticizing Telford Taylor's remark that it was the United States, in the Lieber Code, that "took the lead in reducing [the laws of war] to systematic, written form" (*Nuremberg and Vietnam* [New York, 1970], 21). The Lieber Code—which dealt with enemy property, noncombatants, prisoners of war, hostages, reprisals, safe-conducts, parole, and similar matters—was quoted by the field manuals of other nations as such manuals were created in the late nineteenth century. Holland, *op. cit.,* 14, 22.

46. Cited in Paust, *op. cit.,* 131.

CHAPTER 2

The Reasons Why: Violators and Observers

Obviously, there are several reasons why war crimes occur. Under certain conditions and settings, some of these are more likely to surface than others, as we shall see. But all are important, and there will be no attempt made to create a "rank order." Generally speaking, the causes can be separated into two basic categories: The first consists of values and attitudes brought into the military by individuals; the second is composed of conditions affecting individuals *because* of their military service. The first of these categories may be divided further into three sub-categories: (1) character and personality traits, (2) ethnocentricity, and (3) ideological proclivities. The second category may be similarly subdivided into three separate parts; (1) combat theater conditions, (2) the quality of leadership, and (3) the nature of the weapons involved. Obviously, interrelations and overlapping exist. Former Sgt. Peter Martinsen described the various impulses involved in the torture of enemy soldiers in Vietnam by American interrogators: "There is an innate capacity to do harm to your fellow man in proper circumstances, and these circumstances are provided by the war in Vietnam. It's so horrifying to recall an interrogation where you beat the fellow to get an effect, and then [recalling lost comrades], you beat him out of anger, and then you beat him out of pleasure."[1]

Nonetheless, these "types" are sufficiently distinctive to render such category analysis useful, and we shall commence such analysis in a moment. But first, let us consider an atrocity that has substantially and understandably engaged the public's attention for the past several years, in order to illustrate my point concerning the interrelations of the various impulses leading to the commission of war crimes.

The massacre of hundreds of defenseless persons at My Lai 4 and the subsequent courts-martial of Lieutenant William Calley and others have evoked controversial views from political figures, among them President Carter and former President Nixon. The issues inherent in the My Lai massacre informed the deliberations that now constitute two new Geneva Protocols, and there continue to be expressions of opinion throughout the world concerning the event. Hence it would seem an appropriate subject with which to introduce some of the issues that this book addresses.

THE MY LAI MASSACRE

On March 16, 1968, "Charlie" Company, 1st Battalion, 20th Infantry Regiment, 11th Brigade, 23rd ("Americal") Division, swept through several hamlets attached to the Vietnam village of Song My in Quang Ngai province. In one hamlet, My Lai 4, members of "Charlie" Company's 1st Platoon systematically rounded up and executed in a ditch some 400 to 500 unresisting men, women, and children. The brigade commander reported the killing of 128 "combatants," thus masking what had really happened. Soldiers who expressed distress at what had taken place were warned to keep their feelings to themselves.

Several days later, Ronald Ridenhour, a helicopter door gunner attached to another unit of the same brigade, flew over the ravaged hamlet and was struck by the "complete desolation." He learned from comrades of the massacre that had taken place and decided to press for a complete investigation of what appeared to him to be an atrocity of enormous proportions. His letters to prominent congressmen prompted a full-scale army investigation, and finally, in November 1969, some twenty months after the massacre, sixteen officers and nine enlisted men faced criminal charges ranging from dereliction of duty to premeditated murder. First Lieutenant William L. Calley, Jr., was the only one of those charged to be found guilty by a court-martial; several others received reprimands.

The massacre has been amply described in several works.[2] I shall try to avoid repeating the familiar details here but shall attempt to organize some of the evidence that has emerged concerning the massacre, in a way that may demonstrate the presence in My Lai of each of the several issues to be discussed in this chapter—character deficiencies, ethnocentricity, combat conditions, leadership, and the crisis of conscience.

Character Deficiencies

Lieutenant Calley and Warrant Officer Hugh Thompson may be said to represent two ends of a moral spectrum among those soldiers involved in My Lai 4.

Thompson (as well as several enlisted men) drew a sharp distinction between the inflicting of injury on armed, resisting combatants and the shooting of unarmed, unresisting persons in the custody of military personnel. His moral and professional sensibilities were inflamed by what he saw from his helicopter over My Lai 4. Consequently, he immediately reported to brigade headquarters several indiscriminate killings he had seen, landed his aircraft beside Calley and his victims, ordered his door gunner to fire at anyone who shot any more detainees, hastened to place himself between Calley and his victims, located nine survivors among those who had been cut down by Calley's fire, and shepherded them back to safety.

Calley drew no such distinction between the shooting of armed combatants and unresisting civilians on March 16. Later, during the court-martial proceedings, when trial counsel Captain Aubrey Daniel described in his opening statement what Calley had done, Calley looked up with a guiltless grin. In the judgment of many, he was morally deficient.

He appears to have been intellectually and operationally deficient as well. Calley never seems to have learned or to have achieved much of anything. He stood in the bottom quarter of his high school class. He failed junior college in his first year. He was unable to perform as a railroad freight train conductor and was eased out of that job. He stood in the bottom quarter of his class again in Army Officer Candidate School. Unable to read maps or to inspire confidence in his men, he was a poor platoon leader. One of his men remarked that Calley "didn't know what was going on half the time." Calley wanted badly to succeed, but he measured success amorally. He would do almost anything to gain the admiration of his men and of his superior, Captain Ernest Medina. Another veteran of his platoon remembered that Calley was always trying to look tough, especially when Medina was present.[3] At his trial Calley maintained that his supervising of, and participation in, the killing of hundreds of men, women, and children in the ditch at My Lai was entirely proper. He told John Sack, his biographer, that he could not understand why he was being persecuted. The fact that Calley, not Thompson, led the 1st Platoon that morning in 1968 made a great difference.

Ethnocentricity

It is also important to note that Calley and his men were decidedly ethnocentric. If, one of Calley's men remarked, the Vietnamese—variously referred to as the "gooks," "slopes," and "dinks"—were being treated "like animals" by the men of "Charlie" Company, it was in large measure because "a lot of the guys didn't feel that [the Vietnamese] were human beings." Michael Bernhardt, a member of Calley's platoon, recalled that Captain Medina had "no respect" for the Vietnamese. Gary Garfolo, another veteran of Calley's platoon, described the men as being on "an Indian[-killing] trip." Gary Crossley, another member, told an interviewer that the Vietnamese "don't care if they live or die."[4] Vietnam was simply too different from what the members of "Charlie" Company had known in the States for them to treat its inhabitants with the "fair usage" they might have shown to members of their own culture. (The hamlet they had destroyed was not even called by its correct Vietnamese name by 11th Brigade personnel, but was known as My Lai 4 or "part of Pinkville." The Vietnamese call it Xom Lang.)

Combat Conditions

Prior to the massacre, in three months of action in Vietnam, "Charlie" Company had lost a quarter of its complement to sniper fire, mines, and booby traps. Pfc. Ron Grzesik had come to Vietnam predisposed to like the Vietnamese, but his feelings changed with the loss of his comrades to unseen mysterious enemies. Fear and rage "just started building. I don't know why. Everybody reached the point where they were frustrated. We weren't getting any action, yet the only thing on our mind was survival. After Bill [Weber] got killed, I began to stop caring. . . ."

On March 14, 1968, an apparently booby-trapped shell killed Sgt. George Cox and blinded another man. As their incensed comrades returned from this sad scene to their base camp, a wounded woman was kicked mercilessly and then shot to death. Shortly after the killing of the woman, Greg Olsen, a Mormon who was a member of Calley's platoon, wrote his father: "Why in God's name does this have to happen? These are all seemingly normal guys; some were friends of mine. For a while they seemed like wild animals." The next day, Captain Medina spoke at funeral services for Cox and told the company of the mission they were to perform the following day. They were to sweep through a hamlet searching for elements of an enemy battalion believed to be in the area. Several men claim that Medina spoke of taking "revenge on these people." Everything living was to die. If enemy forces were encountered and any surrendered, no prisoners were to be taken. The next day, when the killing at My Lai 4 began, a kind of chain reaction ensued. Some later recalled the "satisfaction" in killing Vietnamese. Pfc. Paul Meadlo, for example, "Felt good" about it because he had "lost a good, damn buddy, Bobby Wilson. And it was on my conscience. So after I done it I felt good. But later on that day, it kept getting to me."

Meadlo went on to say that it would have been difficult for him to have refused to shoot while Calley was by his side giving him direct orders and firing straight into the huddled villagers. Meadlo was clearly distressed by what he was doing; several testified that he broke down several times in tears as he assisted Calley.[5] Similarly, Gary Crossley, whom I have mentioned previously, once remarked that he was "not to say" whether or not any orders received that day had been proper.[6] Orders were orders.

Leadership

Given this predisposition to obey, it seems evident that much depended on the quality of the orders given by those who sent "Charlie" Company into My Lai and on those who commanded its units while there. Leadership has always been central to enforcing the laws of war, and My Lai surely demonstrates this: It would appear that no instruction had ever been offered to "Charlie" Company personnel on the laws of warfare (see page 148). Assigned in Vietnam to a region essentially controlled by the enemy, they found that some of their platoon leaders believed that "we had political clearance to destroy everything in the area. This area was, in the general classification of the word, a free-fire zone." When the planner and commander of the My Lai raid, Lt. Col. Frank Barker, told Chaplain Carl Cresswell the night before of his orders to level the village if any resistance was encountered, the chaplain observed: "I didn't know we made war that way." Barker ended the conversation with the remark: "It's a tough war."[7] Barker's boss, the new brigade commander, Colonel Oran Henderson, had called for more "aggressive" use of the 11th Brigade's forces that same evening before the raid. Barker and Captain Medina got the message.

Medina's remarks that evening at the funeral services for Cox were unclear. Some remember him calling for the killing of all in the hamlets; others feel that the orders were more vague. Lieutenant Jeffrey LaCrosse recalls that Medina said something about the helplessness of the civilian inhabitants given the strength of the enemy in the area, and that he told the men to take it easy on them. But others did not recall Medina making such a distinction. As one man put it: "The orders could be interpreted in different ways [by] different persons according to their emotional structure." Medina's orders, and the imperfect example he had previously set in the field, may not have been so outrageous as to be responsible, in and of themselves, for what transpired, on the one hand, but, on the other, they were not sufficiently scrupulous to reduce its likelihood.[8]

On a lower and more critical level, the leaders of Calley's own platoon were also guilty of criminal behavior and poor leadership. As ex-Pfc. Harry Stanley put it, the members of the platoon knew that "if they wanted to do something wrong [to prisoners of war or civilians], it was always all right with Calley. He didn't try to stop them." Ex-Pfc. Charles Hall offered a similar verdict: "On the lower level, squad leaders and platoon leaders didn't enforce the rule—like for beating people. This happened every day; every day there was disregard for the people. There were a few people who made a habit of this."[9]

Poor leadership was clearly at the heart of the My Lai massacre. Sadism, racism, frustration, and rage could all have been curbed by scrupulous, able field commanders, as they were elsewhere in Vietnam and human history. Calley's own abysmal leadership is central to our understanding of the tragedy of My Lai 4.

The Crisis of Conscience

How did Calley's more scrupulous subordinates cope with his orders? We shall see (in the final pages of this chapter) that soldiers have dealt with unconscionable and illegal orders in several ways—among them, by protesting, "fudging," or refusing. Calley's men were no exceptions in this regard. Robert Maples and Ron Grzesik disobeyed direct orders from Calley to shoot civilians. When Michael Bernhardt did this, Calley threatened him; thereafter, Bernhardt chose to "fire and miss on purpose." Herbert Carter appears to have preferred a self-inflicted wound to further service that morning at the scene of the carnage.[10] Warrant Officer Thompson had caused the guns of his helicopter to be trained on Calley to prevent further bloodshed. But Thompson, who was attached to the 123rd Aviation Battalion, was neither subordinate to nor the daily associate of Calley. Calley's men found it impossible to intervene in the fashion of Thompson. In a real sense, they were victims too—trapped by their military roles and by the dynamics of the situation.

Let us now turn from the single case of My Lai to our universe of cases, and to a separate consideration of each of the several reasons that appear to be the causes of war crimes. We shall begin (somewhat arbitrarily) by considering the role that the values and attitudes soldiers acquired before their military service appear to have played in the shaping of some war crimes.

VALUES AND ATTITUDES

Much has been said of the ways that military service and war alter the character and values of individuals. We are told that veterans acquire toughness, authoritarianism, self-discipline, callousness, psychoneurotic disorders, and numerous other traits.[11] Most recently, the mother of My Lai veteran Paul Meadlo made the point in concise tones: "I gave them a good boy and they made him a murderer."

To be sure, there is much truth to many of these claims; military service—especially combat service—clearly does affect many individuals in profound and often enduring ways. And stressful combat experiences can lead to a breakdown in military discipline and a disregard for standing orders regarding the treatment of prisoners and noncombatants—to acts born of fear, revenge, and frustration-aggression—as we shall see. But one cannot blame all war crimes on militarization, combat stress, and battlefield conditions alone. All men who serve in combat do not commit atrocities. Indeed, within a single unit, one can find some who behaved brutally and others who checked and prevented outrages. If the evidence of changes wrought by military service is substantial, so is the evidence that differences in values and behavior displayed by military personnel often reflect values that such persons brought with them into the service—values often acquired in childhood.[12] If some are "socialized" by their military experience, others are "presocialized" (as some sociologists have put it). Soldiers may possess a strong, ideological sense of commitment to religious or political values that (they may be led to believe) are being threatened by the enemy; they may be predisposed to look upon the enemy as racially or culturally inferior; or they may (for a variety of reasons) be less able or less willing to control aggressive or even sadistic impulses than others entering the service. We shall explore separately the relationship between such propensities and violations of the laws of war.

1. Character and Personality Traits

We know very little of the personality traits of war criminals and their more scrupulous counterparts from the distant past, and we have an imperfect knowledge of those of more recent days, but our information is sufficient to confirm some "commonsense"[13] views that many hold of war crimes: Many occur simply because the persons who commit them are brutal to begin with. In medieval France and England the feudal armies often contained substantial numbers of ex-brigands, murderers seeking pardons, and unprincipled sadists. The Flemish, English, Gascon, and Brabant mercenaries who "swarmed" into England during the mid-twelfth century struggle between Stephen the Norman and Geoffrey the Angevin were men of "evil hearts—affected neither by bowels of compassion nor by feelings of human pity." They were guilty of "crime and outrage," of pillaging the goods of the poor," of "murderering men in every quarter." Similarly, many of the knights who offered their services during the Albigensian Crusade were sinners seeking pardon. And many of the *routiers* (mercenaries) of that crusade who broke into Beziers in 1209 before the main French force and ran amok, slaughtering priests, women, and children as well as "heretics," were of this caliber. So were the group of 120 murderers pardoned by the Black Prince in 1357 (in order that they might serve in his Continental campaign), the "evil" English force stationed on the Scottish border in 1380, and certain cruel and unruly Swiss pikemen of the fourteenth and fifteenth centuries.[14]

In more modern times, such cutthroats could be found on both sides of the Mexican-American War and the American Civil War. In the former war many of the western and southern volunteers were "renegades" from the law officers of their own states. And in the Civil War both sides employed volunteers without regard to their criminal records. On the western front the North's 7th

Thomas Nast created this gruesome illustration of the bloody raid of Quantrill's guerrillas on Lawrence, Kansas, for *Harper's Weekly* in 1862.

Kansas Volunteers, "Jennison's Jayhawkers," had nearly as many ex-convicts in its ranks as had the South's "Quantrill Gang." And these irregulars committed robbery, murder, and arson with abandon. To the east, savage guerrilla warfare raged in that western portion of Virginia that had broken off from the rest of the state in 1862, and, once again, the chief actors were "ferocious beasts" who killed "for the sake of killing." Among the more notorious was "Devil Bill" Parsons, a rebel "bushwacker" of "low instincts," "filthy in appearance," whose "ferocious" deeds included the mutiliation of Union dead and the pillaging of farms.[15]

Some twentieth-century warriors were equally disposed toward sadism, be they German, American, British, Croatian, Japanese, Russian, Indian, Pakistani, Bengali, Vietnamese, or Spanish. One veteran of the Philippine Insurrection recalled that the more ruthless U.S. Volunteers were "of a very low type" with "no ideals beyond gratifying their animal appetites." General Matthew Ridgeway recalls that "in World War I [some American GIs] would cut off the ears [of the Germans] and string them around their necks," and other accounts confirm this gruesome practice. One doughboy promised to bring his mother a "German's teeth for you, don't be afraid I won't, that will be an easy thing to get." Brig. F. P. Crozier described with revulsion the sadism of the British veterans of the war who joined his "Black and Tan" counterinsurgents in Ireland. Colonel Draja Mikhailovich's Chetniks and Hitler's SS units each contained disproportionate numbers of sadistic men. And there were clearly a number of such persons in the World War II armies of Japan and the Soviet Union as well. More recently, the war in Bangladesh and the war in Vietnam bore witness to the enduring fact of the sadistic and unnecessarily aggressive behavior of some military personnel.[16]

What might explain this overly aggressive, sometimes sadistic propensity? Some, associating it with authoritarianism, point to the social backgrounds of the persons involved. According to this view, the lower on the social scale one goes, the more likely one is to find authoritarianism, aggressiveness, and other "antisocial" traits.[17] There is *some* truth in this. It would appear that some of the more brutal medieval brigands — *routiers*, Swiss pikemen, Austrian *landsknecht*, and Italian *conditerri* — were from peasant or Gypsy families. Those who were brutal in the American Civil War, the Indian wars of the American West, and the Philippine Insurrection were also disproportionately lower class. (Even General Jacob Smith, convicted of issuing criminal orders in the latter campaigns, was of more modest social origins than were his fellow commanders.) The Indian "untouchable" soldier has been very sadistic at times, and the same may be said of some lower-class combatants of the modern military of Greece, Poland, Austria-Hungary, Germany, and the United States. The *Waffen SS* and the *Einsatzgruppen* (Nazi extermination groups) were disproportionately of the lowest social classes, as were the guards in the concentration camps and the death camps. Bishop Hanno Lilje (a member of the German resistance) noted that his guards were lower-class soldiers who delighted in treating their captives (many of them of the upper classes) with a savagery "that gave a free hand to all their suppressed subaltern complexes."

Japanese sociologist Masao Maruyama makes a similar observation about Japanese atrocities in China and the Philippines.[18] When these atrocities are analyzed, he reports,

we are confronted with the unhappy fact that whoever may have been ultimately responsible, the direct perpetrators were the rank-and-file soldiers. Men who at home were "mere subjects" and who in the barracks were second-rank privates found themselves in a new role when they arrived overseas: as members of the Emperor's forces they were linked to the ultimate value and accordingly enjoyed a position of infinite superiority. Given the nature of Japanese society, it is no wonder that the masses, who in ordinary civilian or military life have no object to which they can transfer oppression, should, when they find themselves in this position, be driven by an explosive impulse to free themselves at a stroke from the pressure that has been hanging over them. Their acts of brutality are a sad testimony to the Japanese system of psychological compensation.

Former Sp4c. James Henry explained that in Vietnam GIs

all of a sudden find themselves with the power of life and death in their hands, and they have never had this power before, and they have never had *any* power before. I mean, they just get out of high school and all of a sudden they have all this power, and it does something to them. Plus I don't think they have anything in the way of real moral strength by the time they get over here. Some do, quite a few do, the older ones do, but most of the average guys you know, they haven't considered what they are doing.

Former Sgt. Peter Martinsen offered a revealing judgment on his comrades-in-arms: "If you encounter a man who likes to shoot water buffaloes, you may ask him, 'Why do you like to shoot water buffaloes?' and he says, 'Because I like to shoot water buffaloes.' It's so absurd. I remember a man who was a helicopter door-gunner and he liked to kill people on the ground, but only playing with them like a cat with a mouse with his machine gun, chasing them around, etc." Other Vietnam vets (including some who were themselves of low socioeconomic background) described some of their more brutal comrades-in-arms as the "dregs," "dropouts," and "real fuck-ups"; and they clearly associated their more humane comrades with college, the "middle class," or "good homes."[19] And this correlation of education and social standing, on the one hand, and humane observance of the laws of war, on the other, would appear to have some support. General Richard Taylor, CSA; Colonel William Peters, CSA; and Major Henry Hitchcock USA, were well-educated, cultured members of the Louisiana, Virginia, and Missouri elite (respectively) who earned fame as scrupulous observers of the laws and usages of war. Peters, for example, a professor at the University of Virginia before the war, was the officer who refused to obey orders to burn Chambersburg in 1865, "preferring to risk any consequences that disobedience might involve," rather than to harm defenseless inhabitants." In 1900 General James Parker protected and then released a Filipino prisoner on parole because he had reason to believe that the man could be trusted; Parker, a man "well-born," believed in "chivalry in war." He was "in favor of carrying on war like a gentleman." So were those aristocratic *Wehrmacht* officers in World War II who, revolted by the "unjust" and atrocious character of the war, protested, obstructed, and (in over 100 instances) finally sought to destroy the Nazi *apparat*. Colonel Henry Cummings, USA, won the praise of the Italian writer Curzio Malaparte both for the fact that "intellectually he was a man of culture and refinement," "noble," "a Christian gentleman," and for his refusal to allow members of the Potente Partisan division to execute summarily several young persons accused of being fascist snipers. ("The law must decide," Cummings told the partisans as he virtually took the prisoners from them at gunpoint.)[20]

Persons low in socioeconomic status also appear to be more willing to obey illegal, atrocity-producing orders than persons higher in socioeconomic status. It is not necessary that they be sadists themselves if they are willing docilely to obey orders that have the same result.[21]

However, all of this class-related evidence *must* be viewed in the proper perspective. Yes, persons low in socioeconomic status may be more likely to display aggressiveness than others. But how could one expect it to be otherwise? Lower-class children often have to contend with a brutal and brutalizing environment.[22] Perhaps soldiers from low socioeconomic backgrounds more docilely obey orders to kill noncombatants and prisoners. But, again, if this is the case, is it not understandable, given their sense of status and self-esteem? As Herbert Kelman and Lee Lawrence have put it:

Individuals low in socio-economic status tend to be socialized [to adhere to rules]; obedience to rules is all that is really expected of them; they are not taught to view the system as their own, one they can manipulate, one whose actions they can assess in the light of certain values to which authorities are supposed to live up. . . . Higher education and the occupations that depend on it are generally prerequisites for independent action and a sense of participation in our society. Thus, it is not surprising that individuals low in SES [socioeconomic status] and in education—given the way they are socialized and the realities they confront—tend to see themselves as pawns rather than as origins.

Educated, more fortunate young men, on the contrary, are "bound to the system" by virtue of the fact that they share internally "some of the basic values on which the system is established." When confronted with illegal orders, such persons are more willing to test such orders against these values and to reject orders inconsistent with them. Stanley Milgram found that those willing to refuse to obey the inhumane commands given in his experiment were better educated, had more developed moral senses (on the Kohlberg scale), and were more frequently members of more egalitarian religious organizations than were those who had obeyed these orders.[23] This helps to explain why the typical resister to illegal orders tends to be an educated, more culturally enriched officer, and the typical *performer* of such commands is an enlisted man from a more authoritarian, less comfortable, less "open" background.

But it only *partly* explains such a dichotomy. Yes, Lt. (jg) Edward Mason, a middle-class college graduate, *did* resist the orders of his commanding officer to fire on persons who were soon found to be innocent noncombatants. Yes, most of the enlisted men of Lieutenant Calley's platoon—several of them from "culturally deprived" backgrounds (low income, little education, broken families, etc.)—did obey their orders. Yes, Tsarist and Soviet officers *do* appear to have been more likely to observe and enforce the laws of war regarding prisoners and noncombatants in the Crimean War and World War II than were more modestly placed enlisted men.[24] But there are reasons other than cultural deprivation that may explain these phenomena. Officers are more likely to feel that they have more "leverage"—that is, status sufficient to enable them to *challenge* improper orders— than enlisted men. And, they *can alter* such orders as they transmit them to *their* men in order to reduce the likelihood that violations of the law will occur. Moreover, officers are more likely to be "professionals"—with more training, more of a sense of responsibility, and perhaps more experience—with all the differences in behavior that such professionalism can make. (We shall explore such effects later in this chapter.)

There is still another, more important reason to distrust as too narrow and simplistic claims relying on the socioeconomic variable. Several sophisticated studies concerning aggression in young men point to more idiosyncratic factors than are revealed in crude variables such as socioeconomic status. Parental rejection or acceptance of the child, the level of family discord, the presence or absence of punitive discipline and consistent behavior, the measure of responsibility allowed the child, and the degree of control "over deviant impulses" appear to be the critical variables in explaining why some boys grew to "hurt or injure" others and some did not.[25] In a nutshell, the child of irresponsible, uncaring, brutal parents is likely to be irresponsible and brutal himself. W. H. Auden captured the essence of this process:[26]

> A ragged urchin, aimless and alone,
> Loitered about that vacancy; a bird
> Flew up to safety from his well-aimed stone:
> That girls are raped, that two boys knife a third,
> Were axioms to him, who's never heard
> Of any world where promises were kept,
> Or one could weep because another wept.

Socioeconomic status is mildly correlated, to one degree or another, with these other variables, it is true, but it is hardly a perfect fit. Families in economic distress are more *likely* than others to experience family discord, punitive discipline, parental rejection of children, and so on, but upper-income families can have these traits as well.

In any event, there is evidence that a number of the war crimes explored in this study were committed by young men who came from backgrounds comparable to those that social psychologists have identified as potential producers of aggressively "antisocial" behavior. Quantrill's childhood certainly contained enough disruption and brutal relatives to contribute to his socialization in violence. The same may be said of several Vietnam-era soldiers, about whom we have enough information to suggest such a correlation of background and behavior.[27] A few examples: Pfc. W____ G____, the seventh of thirteen children from a deprived and disorganized one-parent home, quit school in the eleventh grade, joined up, and was sent to Vietnam in 1968. He became paranoid and aggressive to all, shot a Vietnamese civilian, was arrested, and then killed a fellow prisoner for a minor affront. A court-martial found him guilty of unpremeditated murder.

Sgt. S___ B___, a "highly strung" person who "tended to overact in response to suspected aggressive action," had some of the background traits we are considering. He decided that men working on a pagoda in a nearby village were dangerous to him, led a unit up to the pagoda, and falsely reported by radio that his unit had been fired on. This fabrication helped him, of course, to get permission to fire on the pagoda, which he did, killing a civilian worker. A court-martial found him guilty as well.

Pfc. J___ L___'s parents were divorced, and his father (who raised him) remarried, and then obtained another divorce. Poor, he had but seven years of schooling and a low AFQT (intelligence-achievement test) score. Court-martialed for knocking Vietnamese civilians from their bicycles as his vehicle passed them and for shooting two other noncombatants, he was found guilty as charged. Expert testimony was offered regarding his "extremely immature" personality and "marked aggressive tendencies."

Sgt. D___ G___ came from an impoverished family. His father deserted his mother. With few parental guidelines or controls, the boy developed few self-restraints, ceased to attend church services and became aggressive toward his friends and classmates. He enlisted and was sent to Vietnam, where his aggressive traits initially served him well. He impressed his superiors and was increasingly given combat responsibilities. Eventually he was made a sergeant, and one day was told to take four men out for five days to set up an ambush on a hillside several miles away from the rest of his unit. As soon as the squad had left the camp, he told the men assigned to him that he intended to "find a woman" for them in a nearby village to serve as their packbearer and to gratify their sexual desires. He found a girl in one home, forced her to accompany them, raped her, and then murdered her (ordering the others to fire at her as well). One of his more willing accomplices in the rape and murder, Pfc. C___ G___, was also from a deprived, morally underdeveloped background. He could not understand why the army would want to court-martial any of them for what seemed to him an inconsequential act, given all of the rest of the violence in Vietnam. The trial counsel cross-examined him:

T.C.:	You feel that the government has done you a grave injustice in bringing you here today for trial? You feel you are not involved in any way?
Pfc. G.:	Yes, sir, I feel that way.
T.C.:	You shouldn't be on trial?
Pfc. G.:	Well, yes, sir.
T.C.:	As a matter of fact, you have complained [from the stockade] that your promotion is being held up?
Pfc. G.:	I wrote to my senator. I told him I was being wrongly brought to trial.

Vietnam veteran Jan Barry, who clearly understands this moral underdevelopment in some GIs, has written a poem, "Thap Ba":[28]

> The old Cham temple of Thap Ba,
> the locals say it's a thousand years
> old,
> older than this stilted Anglo-
> Saxon language I use
>
> Older they say than the use
> of bullets, ballots, and the printing
> press
> older than the airplane and the bomb
> older than napalm
>
> was hit yesterday by a twenty-year old
> helicopter pilot
> fresh from the states
> Who found it more ecstatic than
> the firing range
> for testing his guns

Navy Corpsman R____ W____ grew up with three sisters and no brothers and an inconsistent father. Throughout his childhood he repressed resentment toward his father, a farmer who had worked him hard. Navy psychiatrist Herman Langer feels that when "Bob" got pleasure from shooting a wounded Vietnamese farmer instead of treating him, his background may have helped to structure the act.[29] The same may be said of Lieutenant William Calley. His basic insecurity and desire to appear "manly" in the eyes of his platoon and his company commander helped shape his behavior at My Lai.

Psychiatrist Charles Levy interviewed "a veteran from New York" accused of the murder of his girl friend. The "New Yorker's" childhood had been a relatively brutal and disorganized one, and he had evidently been brutal in Vietnam:

I didn't have to just sit back and take abuse from people and all that bullshit. In 'Nam, there was no law. I mean there was laws, but you didn't pay attention to them. 'Cause you knew when it came right down to it you were on equal terms with everyone. There was nobody that had odds against you. 'Cause everybody had a gun, and everybody had a right to kill. . . .

When I first started using a gun over there, it was like someone saying to me, "We're here. This is your right to fucking do whatever you want, whatever you think is right." 'Cause all my life I was always on the receiving end of abuse and everything. And here I was given the chance to fucking make up my own mind. Like who's got the right to live and who's got the right to die. And there was a lot of times it came down to the point where people on my own side deserved the right to die for the things they do. Maybe I was being self-righteous. But I was looking at it from my point of view. 'Cause I was always on the receiving end. And I guess only a person on the receiving end would understand what it's like—who really has the right to live or die. I mean, a person who never got fucked up or beat up by a brother or sister, or picked on because he was small or the smaller guy, wouldn't understand that. They'd think you were fucking nuts or you don't know what you're fucking talking about. But a guy that's on the receiving end all his life, he knows what the hell he's talking about. He knows who the bullies are and who deserves the right to go on living. That's the way I always looked at it. So when I got that gun, it was just like saying, "Well here, use your own judgement."[30]

Another Vietnam veteran, K____ C____, had a politically reactionary father who died a year to the day before he enlisted. C____'s childhood was rough and disorderly: "I had an an inferiority complex from getting pushed around a lot in gangs. I was looking for a way to prove my manhood." In Vietnam he deliberately directed an artillery strike on a placid village and destroyed it.

"George Ryan," a veteran interviewed by Murray Polner, had a blue-collar father who drank and a mother with nine other, younger children to care for. He maintained that he was the "only one of the family ignored by the parents": "They never took the time to talk with me. They never knew how scared I was and what kind of crap I had to take all the time. There were always new babies, new jobs for my father, new [activities] for my mother." Only 5 feet 4 inches tall, "George" lacked self-confidence in high-school; he "couldn't find the strength or the discipline to face up to anything demanding." Seeking to "prove himself," he enlisted in 1965. In Vietnam his unit came upon a wounded enemy soldier after a fire fight:

... my platoon sergeant said I should finish him off with my .45. I went up to where he was lying and moaning and waited for about thirty minutes, hoping he'd die first; then I closed my eyes, fired—and missed. I didn't want to kill him. I remember very well just sitting there looking at him. And he wouldn't die. Finally, the sergeant came up and said I'd have to do something. Was I chicken? So I fired.

When I walked back to the other men, they were all proud of me. It was a big thing to kill a North Viet in battle and this, so to speak, was in battle. It's not how many you kill but what your friends think. My buddies told me I did a good job and that made me happy. He was an enemy and we didn't even have enough copters to take out our own wounded. It was in battle. Everyone said I was a good soldier.[31]

Polner asked "George" what he had thought the consequences would have been had he refused to obey the order: "If I had said that—and I never would have—but if I had said that to my sergeant, I wouldn't have been court-martialed but I would have been blacklisted, put on KP back at base camp, and labeled a coward. That I couldn't take."

Conversely, soldiers with well-developed moral sensibilities, self-discipline, and self-respect tend to be more observant of the laws of war than those we have just considered. Many sixteenth- and seventeenth-century French officers were said to have known "very well how to lead their men when their conscience as citizens rejected the orders they received in their capacity as soldiers." Deneys Reitz was the son of a lawyer who was the last president of the Orange Free State in South Africa. His childhood was comfortable, his parents loving, and his education good. When the Boers and the English began to fight, young Reitz joined up and served to the end, but he retained his moral composure, sense of "legalism," and disapproval of acts causing unnecessary suffering throughout.

As a guerrilla, Reitz could not see "a great deal of difference between killing a man with an explosive bullet" (just made unlawful by the Hague Conventions of 1899) "and smashing him with a lyddite [artillery] shell" (a measure that remained legal). Nonetheless, he refused to use explosive cartridges, because he respected the rule of law.

Captain Mikhail Koriakov, a Soviet infantryman, was a religious person, despite his status. During the Soviet advance through Europe, he vigorously defended German women from Soviet soldiers (some of them drunken men) bent on raping them, at some risk to his own life. Similarly, many of the *Wehrmacht* officers who resisted the unlawful rules set for them by the Nazi leadership were deeply moral men. It was not their aristocratic origins or officer status alone that explained their relative scrupulousness. Their aristocratic background may well have ensured them a moral education, and their training certainly counted in their resistance (as we shall see), but it was their moral sensibilities — *not* just class consciousness or professional pride — that drove many of them to acts of resistance. General Ludwig Beck and Colonel Hans Oster, for example, were profoundly ethical men, both the sons of evangelical clergymen. Admiral Wilhelm Canaris, another resistor, was also religious and intensely moral and utterly intolerant of any abuse of prisoners or noncombatants. Generals Ulex and Blaskowitz, and many of their troops, were disgusted by the "absolutely incredible lack of human and moral feeling" displayed by SS and SD personnel in Poland. They called upon the High Command to remove and punish the local SS and "all its highest leaders" and to take steps to end the "brutalization and moral decay." Colonel Helmuth Stieff's letters from the Russian front are filled with his loathing for the "shameless," "savage" acts of the SS and SD there. They were "beasts." They observed no "rules of humanity or of the simplest kind of decency." Stieff began to speak of his "duties before God" and joined plotters who sought to kill Hitler and halt the war. When the attempt failed and the plotters were seized and condemned, many left notes for their families, explaining their behavior in moral and religious terms.[32]

Many examples of the importance of strong moral guidance in men who scrupulously observed the laws of war may be found in the American military experience as well. This, after all, was what lay behind the behavior of Generals Taylor and Parker, Colonels Peters and Cummings, and Major Hitchcock, noted previously. It also explained the refusal in World War II of philosopher-intelligence officer J. Glenn Gray to obey an immoral order. And it explained the behavior of many morally alive Vietnam GIs. Pfc. Rocky Bleier had attended Notre Dame and possessed a well-defined set of moral values. He described an incident that occurred while on patrol in Vietnam:

Three of us went off to find water and suddenly came across a little man, less than five feet tall. He seemed to come out of nowhere. . . . It was a man about 30. My two colleagues grabbed him by his black pajamas.

"You VC? You NVA?"

He said nothing.

"Papa-san, you VC? You VC?"

We didn't know what to do with him.

The point man said, "Hell, let's kill him. I should have killed him right away. Then we wouldn't have to worry."

The other guy said, "Maybe we should tell him to di di [get out of here]. Then we can shoot him as he's running away."

The point man replied, "Let's just tie him to a tree and shoot him right here."

It was a few incredulous moments before I realized what they were saying. "What are you guys talking about?" I said, "We can't shoot this guy. Let's take him back to the lieutenant."

"No," the point man said. "The lieutenant said he doesn't want any prisoners. What's he gonna do with him? We'd just have to watch the gook and take him with us on the march. The lieutenant doesn't want to be bothered with him. We can't take him back."

I said, "Let's take him back and let the lieutenant decide. If he wants to kill him, that's his business."

"Well, I don't know. The lieutenant might be sore because we brought him back. He said he doesn't want any prisoners. He's gonna be sore."

"Well, let him be sore," I said. "We can't shoot him. He doesn't have a weapon. He hasn't tried anything. He just showed up."

Finally, we took him to the lieutenant, who checked him out and freed him.

Pfc. S____ J____, the soldier who reported Sgt. D____ G____'s rape and murder of a Vietnamese girl while on patrol, and Sgt. Michael Bernhardt, the soldier who helped Ronald Ridenhour to bring about the investigation that finally resulted in the full disclosure of the My Lai massacre and the prosecution of several of those involved, both had stable, morally sound childhoods and strong religious training and had acquired an active ethical code. At My Lai, Bernhardt *did* feel an impulse drawing him toward the violence. After all, he was one of the only ones altogether unwilling to participate; his comrades *expected* him to participate. But he *resisted* the impulse: "It's a matter of controlling it, you know, saying, Well . . . no, I can't do that. That's not right. . . .' "

Cpl. Tom Michlovic had also acquired a strong ethical code in modest but warm and moral surroundings. He served in Vietnam, returned, and was outraged by the outpouring of sympathy and support for Lieutenant Calley:

As a veteran of that horrible "theater of the absurd," I strongly object to the implications:

That I lost my moral responsibility by my symbolic "step forward";

That a soldier has no conscience, and acts only under orders;

And that if subjected to the same circumstances, I too would have coldly slaughtered those villagers.

I, like Mr. Calley, am an individual; and if during my sojourn as an infantryman in Vietnam I lost all sense of moral perspectives, it was my fault, not the military's and certainly not my country's.

Gary Garfolo, a My Lai veteran, was surely overstating, but he was still close to the mark when he told Richard Hammer, "I never did anything over there I didn't *want* to do."[33]

Other examples might be given, but perhaps these will suffice to illustrate the causal link that exists between personality traits and the commission of, or prevention of, war crimes.

Other values acquired before military service can also contribute to the making of war crimes — among them, ethnocentric and ideological points of view.

2. Ethnocentricity and Ideology

Ethnocentric attitudes have been at the roots of brutality in warfare for millenniums. I have already mentioned the ruthless manner in which many primitive tribes treated persons foreign to the tribe. This localistic tendency of societies to identify negative reference groups consists at times of racism (the dividing of so-called superior and inferior groups along racial lines), at times of fanaticism (the dividing of "good" and "evil" persons along religious lines), and at times of ethnocentrism (the dividing of "civilized" and "uncivilized" peoples along lines of language, culture, or political boundaries). In each case, this tendency is one of the more enduring causes of brutality in war — one that the laws and customs of warfare have not succeeded in subduing. Significant cultural differences, along technological, religious, or organizational lines, can cause the militarily dominant society to regard itself as superior, "above" keeping to the same norms that it observes with societies of comparable development. And the process is accentuated if the differences include racial ones. The tendency of Chinese, Greek, Roman, British, French, German, American, and other developed civilizations to define less developed societies as "barbarians" and "savages" has often led them to relax whatever rules of warfare they were observing with others. Modern examples of this might include the seventeenth-, eighteenth- and nineteenth-century American Indian wars, the various eighteenth-, nineteenth-, and twentieth-century French and British wars of empire, the Philippine Insurrection, and the Vietnam War (where the MGR, or "mere gook rule," prevailed). The remarks of Jacob Dowling, an attorney from New York who served as an officer under Colonel

Chivington during the Sand Creek massacre of Southern Cheyenne in 1864, may illustrate the point. Dowling told an investigating committee that he had offered no quarter, but had "killed all I could, and I think that was the general feeling in the command. I think and earnestly believe the Indians to be an obstacle to civilization, and [feel they] should be exterminated."[34]

Formal relaxation of rules occurs less often in wars between peoples of different ethnicity, religion, or race if their nations are on similar levels of technological and legal development, but *informally* the rules may still be ignored by those combatants who are particularly racist, fanatical, or ethnocentric. Christians sometimes treated captured Muslims brutally in the Middle Ages. Similar brutality has been displayed during the sixteenth-century wars of religion in France, the Thirty Years' War, the French Revolution, the Franco-Prussian War, the war between the United States and Japan, the Korean War, the Arab-Israeli wars, the Nigerian Civil War, and the wars on the subcontinent of India. During the sixteenth-century wars of religion in France, for example, Huguenot forces killed Catholic priests in sanctuaries; Catholic leaders planned assassinations and sacked Huguenot towns, drowning their inhabitants. Catholic Generals D'Aumale, Somarine, and Monluc were far from being scrupulous in their observance of the sixteenth century's usage of warfare. Religious fervor could produce war crimes, as did racism. During World War II, American soldiers were asked to comment on their feelings about the enemy after they had actually seen German or Japanese prisoners (see Table I). They were also asked to comment on how badly they wanted to kill enemy soldiers. Six times as many said they would "really like to kill" Japanese soldiers as Germans. Over half wanted to destroy Japan entirely. Only 13 percent felt the same about Germany. In short, American GIs were unmistakably less disposed to observe the laws of war in the Pacific theater than they were in Europe. And this is true despite the fact that the percentage of combat troops in the Pacific who said they had witnessed *enemy* violations of the laws of war was the same (13 percent) as that of European theater combatants. To be sure, the process of relaxation is understandable if "barbarians" have not, in fact, adopted any such laws of war themselves—if

TABLE   1

Reaction to Seeing Enemy Prisoners Among Veteran Enlisted Infantrymen in One European and Three Pacific Divisions, November 1943, March–April 1944

QUESTION:
How did seeing Japanese (German) prisoners make you feel about Japanese (Germans)?

	All the more like killing them	Miscellaneous answers	No feeling one way or another	They are men just like us; it's too bad we have to fight them
Europe	18%	12%	16%	54%
Pacific	42	16	22	20

Source: From Samuel A. Stouffer et al., *Studies in Social Psychology in World War II, Vol. II, The American Soldier: Combat and Its Aftermath* (copyright 1949 © 1977 by Princeton University Press), published for Social Science Research Council, Chart XI, p. 161. Reprinted by permission of Princeton University Press.

their manner of warfare is still that of *bellum internecium,* total war, or war without quarter. Racism explains at least part of this difference in the views of American GIs in Europe and the Pacific, but part is due to the behavior of Japanese soldiers observed by veterans of the Pacific theater. Many Japanese were simply unwilling to surrender when confronting certain defeat and death. Their codes and training often led them to suicidal measures. General A. A. Vandergrift, commanding the U.S. Marines at Guadalcanal, explained to his superior that he had "never heard or read of this kind of fighting: These people refuse to surrender. The wounded will wait until the men come up to examine them and blow themselves and the other fellow to pieces with a hand grenade. You can readily see the answer to that. . . ."

"The answer," as Vandergrift later observed, "was war without quarter."[35] Given the circumstances, he can hardly have been blamed. After the first several wounded Japanese had killed Americans, one simply took whatever measures were deemed necessary to protect one's men. But, if understandable in cases like these, such a relaxation of the rules is still regrettable when it is not urgent. Reprisals inflicted on prisoners or noncombatants, for example, accomplish nothing unless the side guilty of first violating the laws responds satisfactorily to the first one or two thoroughly justified, carefully explained, proportionally calculated acts of reprisal. Continual retaliation may gratify the soldier's lust for vengeance, but it does not serve any useful military or strategic objectives and may well be detrimental to attaining such objectives, as we shall see.

Although ethnocentric and racial differences among combatants can mean that war crimes are more likely to occur, the absence of such differences clearly explains why war crimes are not as frequent in some wars as in others. The American Civil War, between English-speaking persons of similar ethnic origin and cultural background, was not nearly so brutal and ruthless as (to give but a few examples) the Vietnam War or some of the recent wars on the Indian subcontinent. "Billy Yank" and "Johnny Reb" were perfectly capable of brutality on occasion, to be sure (especially when "Johnny Reb's" victim was black), but they were also quite capable of acts of compassion, empathy, and camaraderie. During the "infamous" March through Georgia, acts of kindness abounded.[36] The same may be said of the Boer War. The Dutch and British had serious differences, and the fighting was intense, but, comparatively speaking, the war was not a very ruthless one, largely because the two cultures had much in common. "I never hated the English," Deneys Reitz explained. He himself observed the laws of war scrupulously and was pleased to say that the "English soldiers, both officers and men, were unfailingly humane. This was so well known that there was never any hesitation in abandoning a wounded man to the mercy of the troops, in the sure knowledge that he would be taken away and carefully nursed, a certainty which went far to soften the asperities of war."

This was partly due to the professionalism of the British forces, to be sure, but these were the same British units who had brutally exterminated Afghan villages a decade before. Cultural affinity, cutting across religious and ethnic lines, could also cut *across* racial lines. Private Fred Louderback was outraged by the be-

havior of his companions at Sand Creek in 1864, when hundreds
of inoffensive Indians were slaughtered. He told his commanding
officer that he intended to charge him with murder, and when
that officer warned him to keep his mouth shut, Louderback
"told him I enlisted as a soldier, and I considered my tongue my
own, . . . [and] could use it whenever I wanted to." What especially
incensed Louderback was the fact that his comrades had murdered a "half-breed" friend of his. Seventy-eight years later, after
the final collapse of American forces in the Philippines, a Japanese officer returned property stolen from an American prisoner
who was a graduate of Notre Dame with the remark: "I graduated
from Southern California in '35." As Stanley Milgram has demonstrated, persons who are close to others are less likely to inflict
pain on them than persons who are more detached, separated,
distant from their victims. What I am claiming here is that the
process is the same whether the "closeness' is physical, cultural,
racial, or ideological.[37]

Another negative reference group is the political enemy. He
may be ethnically, racially, and religiously quite similar to his
foe, but if his *political* culture is sharply different, he is quite
capable of treating his opponent on the battlefield atrociously.
Ancient Greece and Rome witnessed brutality of this kind during
periods of alliance realignment or colonial revolts.[38] More recently
during the American Revolution, loyalists and rebels often gave
no quarter to one another, so desperate had some become. David
Ramsay, a contemporary, noted that "the passions of both sides
were kept in perpetual agitation and wrought up to a degree of
fury which rendered individuals regardless, not only of the laws
of war, but of the principles of humanity."[39] The rebels hanged
captured loyalists in New Jersey, Pennsylvania, and South Carolina or shot them as they surrendered like "wild beasts, that are
to be slain on sight, and without warning." A British major with
Cornwallis regarded certain southwestern "mountain men" to be
"more savage than Indians," with "*every one* of their vices, but
not one of their virtues": "I have known one of them to travel
two hundred miles through the woods, never keeping any road or
path, . . . to kill a particular person belonging to the opposite
party."

If the rebels were at times brutal, they were no worse than their foes. Colonel Banastre Tarleton's dragoons were infamous for their treatment of prisoners. And most of Tarleton's men were Tories from New York.

Many British commanders were outraged by the conduct of men on both sides, to be sure, but some, like Tarleton, Mackenzie, and Lord Rawdon, approved. Mackenzie was delighted by the brutal treatment by the British and their Indian allies of Wyoming Valley (Pennsylvania) inhabitants, "spreading terror and dismay, . . . burning and destroying their property. . . ." Rawdon, for example, felt that the British should "give free liberty to the soldiers to ravage it at will, that these infatuated creatures may feel what a calamity war is." The British officer who ordered that stables be burned at Frenchtown, Maryland, during the War of 1812 was of the same mind as Lord Rawdon. "The question we generally ask when we go to any place," he told the owner, "is: how you voted at the election [of the Congress that voted the declaration of war]."[40]

Brutality displayed in the French Revolution, the war between the United States and Mexico, the border areas of the American Civil War, the Philippine Insurrection, the Mexican Revolution, the Russian Revolution, the Spanish Civil War, the Greek Civil War, the Korean War, and the Vietnam War was often a function of the political and ideological character of the wars themselves.[41] The Texans in General Taylor's army in 1846 were particularly ruthless in northern Mexico, giving Mexicans their own "Alamos." Filipinos remember the crimes committed by American troops on Samar, and crimes there were. But American veterans had their own memories of Filipino atrocities, and there were many of these as well.[42] Indeed, the Filipino massacre of the U.S. Marine detachment at Balangiga that provoked General Smith's illegal orders to American troops on Samar was itself a violation of the laws of war. One soldier participating in the Philippine campaign wrote a satiric poem, "The Gentle Filipino," popular with his comrades-in-arms, which describes the behavior of some Filipino *independencias:*[43]

> With a white flag on his shanty, hanging there to catch your eye;
> And his rifle ready for to plug you bye and bye, . . .

He's as playful as a kitten, and his pastime as a rule
Is to shoot the flag of truce man, as a sort of April Fool.
And if he can find a tree top and get up there with his gun
And pick off all of the wounded, then he knows he's having fun.

The Filipinos had good cause to fight their American oppres-
sors — no doubt about *that*. They had every right to engage in
ruses, hit-and-run raids, and other legitimate acts of war, but the
Filipino soldier who shot at badly wounded men was not serving
his cause well, and was just as reprehensible as the American
who used the "water cure" to obtain information from Filipinos.

The resentments aroused by colonialism and racism, the
passions that inspire the "class conscious volunteer," the "freedom fighter," the nationalist, socialist, or fascist revolutionary
are often ingredients of atrocity-producing situations. Wars
of *revanche* are also prone to become unduly violent. Recall
that it was such warfare that Emmerich Vattel had in mind
in *The Laws of Nations*. He and other jurists hoped to reduce the
brutality of such wars in order to eliminate one cause of their re-
currence. Twenty years after *The Laws of Nations* had appeared,
Colonel Charles Stuart made the same point concerning the war
in America. The "barbarity" engaged in by some of the British
troops had simply caused "irrecoverable hatred" for them. Colonel
Stuart was quite sure that these "acts of severity" would never
"cause these people to submit." Count Pier Luigi Bellini, the Lake
Como district partisan commander in World War II was no less
anxious than Stuart to see his partisans use restraint: "To answer
evil with evil will only do harm to our cause and bring us down to
the same level as our enemies." Fidel Castro's scrupulous observance of the laws of war in the treatment of captured government soldiers during the Cuban Revolution certainly did his
side's cause no harm.[44] Restraint, even in ideological conflicts, is
entirely reasonable and appropriate. But, unfortunately, reason
rarely presides over such conflicts.

Cultural impulses and values, then — be they exhibited in
personality traits, racism, ethnocentrism, fanaticism, or ideolo-
gies — can produce potential war criminals. But they are not
the only producers. Combat conditions, poor leadership, and

certain types of weapons—external forces—contribute to crimes too. Obviously, an overly aggressive, fanatical soldier led by a brutal, insensitive commander in an ill-defined, stressful battlefield setting is particularly prone to commit atrocities. But given a sufficiently stressful setting, inhumane leader, or "blind" weapon, even the more temperate, self-disciplined soldier is capable of war crimes. Let us now consider these external forces.

EXTERNAL FORCES

1.The Combat Environment

Thus far we have considered crimes that appear to have been committed by overly aggressive, unstable, fanatical, racist (in short, personally predisposed) individuals. Some of the acts we shall consider in the next few pages may have been committed by such persons, but many were not. Many were committed by reasonably stable individuals whom one would never have imagined to be capable of brutality. Why did such "decent" persons violate the laws of war? One reason is that several severe stresses produced by combat—fear, frustration, rage, guilt, the desire for revenge—all can lead men to illegal behavior.

The socializing ritual by which units of men going into battle tend to prepare themselves for danger may lend itself to the creation of atrocity-producing situations unless the process is carefully monitored by conscientious professionals. Soldiers about to fight have fears that can be reduced or controlled if they are satisfied that they and their comrades are at least as tough, "mean," deadly, and capable as the enemy. The "bull session" is the forum and vehicle for the socializing of those unbathed in bloodshed. A few examples of what can transpire at such sessions may suffice. In 1809 a British regiment embarked for Wellington's Peninsular campaign. Its men began to discuss the prospects before them. One private wrote home: "What a funny drole set of beings the old soldiers of the Regt. are. They are continually relating such marvelous tales of murders, rapes and robberies that would frighten the Old Devil Dunk himself. . . . I listen to these tales with some degree of interest. . . ."[45]

A century and a quarter later, in 1942, U.S. Marines prepared themselves for a landing on Guadalcanal. Richard Tregaskis was among them:

> While working over their weapons, the marines passed their inevitable chatter, "shooting the breeze" about the girls they had known here or there, their adventures in this or that port, a good liberty they had made here or there. But now, a large part of the chatter deviated from the usual pattern. A lot of it was about the Japs.
>
> "Is it true that the Japs put a gray paint on their faces, put some red stuff beside their mouths, and lie down and play dead until you pass 'em?" one fellow asked me. I said I didn't know. "Well, if they do," he said, "I'll stick 'em first."
>
> Another marine offered: "They say the Japs have a lot of gold teeth. I'm going to make myself a necklace."
>
> "I'm going to bring back some Jap ears," said another. "Pickled."
>
> The marines aboard are dirty, and their quarters are mere dungeons. But their *espirit de corps* is tremendous. I heard a group of them, today, talking about an "eight ball," which is marine slang for a soldier who disgraces his fellows because he lacks their offensive spirit. This eight ball, said one lad, was going to find himself in the water some day. Somebody was going to sneak up behind him and push and him overboard. Others agreed, and, looking around at them, I could see that they meant it.

Sgt. F____ R____ was in an infantry unit Vietnam in 1967. He recalls that he and his comrades steeled themselves for the dangers before them with "Wild West talk ... Y'know: 'Gonna get me a fuckin' gook,' or 'All them V.C. need is a little 'Willie Peter' [a phosphorus grenade]. Everybody was trying to outdo the next guy in sounding mean." As Roy Grinker and John Spiegel put it: "The combat soldier can become a killer without guilt in spite of his past training by virtue of his identification with the group."[46]

Sounding mean, however, is not the same as being mean. Despite their talk, many men go into battle reluctant to kill another human being. Later, after engaging with the enemy and seeing the dead and dying, the soldier's inhibitions about killing, very real before the baptism of fire, may begin to dissipate.[47] One Vietnam veteran recalled feeling differently about life and death after seeing casualties for the first time: "All over the place you see guys with legs blown off, gooks with their heads blown off and their chests wide open and all kinds of shit. You just say, "Man, is that all there is to it? Is that all there is to it?" Just, you're dead. And no more. And you get the attitude that people are just matter. It's just something you begin to live with."[48]

Another GI's letters from Vietnam illustrate his transformation:[49]

5 February

We have been fighting hard for two days, and it looks bad for us. We have lost some ten or fifteen out of our company. . . .

I got a 45 off a M-79 Gunner, stuck it to one of the people that was a prisoner, and had the interpreter tell him if he didn't stop giving so much trouble, I was going to blow his guts out. He kept on squirming around trying to get away and co-operating none at all, so I blew him away. The other prisoner we had co-operated very quickly. . . .

We just got through pushing all the civilians out of the town to a close-by secure area. There, we can keep an eye on them, and at the same time, have them out of the way in case we get into it again. They also can't be trusted; it is a little hard to tell them apart, VC or civilian. . . .[50]

6 February

People wonder why a guy comes back from a place like Vietnam and acts like an animal. Well, I myself have changed just in the last three days. I'm hard on the inside, and as far as I'm concerned, if anyone stands between me and my job, I'd just as soon kill 'em. Life isn't worth much anyway, besides, some of those people are better off dead. . . . Sometimes I just don't know whether I give a damn if I die or not. A lot of guys here feel the same as I do.

The feeling you get when walking through rice paddy after rice paddy, never getting that well-earned rest, is the wish for a sniper to shoot at you, or for a little action of any sort. . . .

24 February

Every time we kill a Cong, we cut his left ear off. I tried it once, but after I did, I couldn't stomach it. That is, doing it to someone dead— alive, Ok, dead, No! I didn't think I would have the stomach to watch or let someone else do it, but I have acquired a stomach for that much. Some of the men get their kicks by safety-pinning their combat patch to the forehead of the ones they kill. Boy, does war change a man's ideals!

This particular soldier may well have possessed traits that pre-disposed him to react as he did. (After returning from Vietnam he shot and killed his wife's boyfriend, albeit that act may have been made possible by either his pre-Vietnam value system or his Vietnam experience itself.) But predisposed or not, the combat experience surely helped precipitate both his shooting of a prisoner and his comrades' other brutal acts. Sgts. Donald Duncan and Peter Martinsen, both veterans of Vietnam, described the phenomenon well. According to Duncan:

> There was a certain psychological effect; it took place after a battle: these people had been very scared. It was perhaps a method of regaining their manhood; it's a vengeful thing; it's a number of factors; and of course I suppose these acts become easier and easier to the individual the more often he goes into combat, the more often he is scared.

And according to Martinsen:

> None of us ever thought that we would actually torture, or even beat a prisoner. There was not much force used—coercion and harassment, yes—but not much physical force until after members of the detach-ment were killed and death became a reality. You see, we knew, other people were dying, but when one of our friends was killed, death became a reality, and we realized that a certain amount of force does work.[51]

The brutality displayed by numbed or vengeful or frustrated combatants is as old as war itself. Frustration and vengeance may explain the behavior of the soldiers of Marcellus, who dis-obeyed their commander's orders and sacked Syracuse after its capitulation in 212 B.C. (albeit booty was an independent motive in that age.) They may also have been behind the refusal at Phocaea and Loca of similar Roman legions to obey their com-manders (mentioned in the introduction). The desire to revenge Carthage for such acts of Roman cruelty inspired Hannibal's famous oath. The Gascon soldiers who reduced Forcha di Penne to ashes in 1528 were "animated to revenge" by casualties they had incurred in the seige of that town. Their commander sought to check them, but they could "not be made to leave their slaughter." The English and French forces contesting for Rouen in 1591 began with acts of chivalry and generosity toward one another. As they sustained more and more casualties, they slowly drifted toward more and more atrocious behavior.

During the American Revolution, revenge was a familiar impulse. It appears to have inspired the British forces under Benedict Arnold, who massacred 80 defenders of New London's Fort Griswold after that garrison's stubborn resistance had ceased. (Fort Griswold's fire had caused 193 British casualties.) The behavior of forces such as those of Arnold and Tarleton led one member of the Continental Congress, John Mathews of South Carolina, to propose that orders be given "to the officers commanding our troops to put to death all persons found in arms against these United States" if "any further acts of inhumanity be perpetrated by the British armies." Mathews's resolution received no support; it died and was never printed. But it may serve as a measure of the rage felt by some soldiers; this member of the Continental Congress, though from a state that had suffered greatly at the hand of Tarleton's dragoons, was still removed both in time and place from the scene of the atrocities themselves. How much more bitterly must soldiers who witnessed the scenes of these events have felt. Some such witnesses may have been present later at King's Mountain, when a combined Patriot force overwhelmed Colonel Patrick Ferguson's British and loyalist troops. Lynn Montross describes the aftermath:

> The loyalists raised handkerchiefs on their ramrods, but after the surrender a stray ball mortally wounded a patriot leader, Colonel James Williams. His men revenged themselves horribly by firing into the huddled mass of prisoners until the officers put an end to the slaughter.
> The victors, who had only 28 killed, burned the British wagons and retired with their plunder and wounded. On the march the 600 miserable loyalist survivors, loaded with burdens, had several men shot down for disobedience or trying to escape. Their charges of cruelty seem to have been well founded, judging by the astonishing order issued by Colonel Campbell on October 11th, "I must request the officers of all ranks in the army to endeavor to restrain the disorderly manner of slaughtering and disturbing the prisoners."

To the north, in New Jersey, Pennsylvania militia angered a Hessian *jäger* unit by first pretending to surrender and then, as the *jägers* approached, firing into their ranks, killing an officer and several men. "The Hessians retaliated later by bayoneting the Rev. John Rosbrugh, a sixty-three-year-old Pennsylvania militia chaplain, after robbing him of his watch and money."[52]

During the War of 1812, acts of vengeance were again reported. Some of these served only to inspire counterretaliations. When Virginia militiamen fired on some British troops clinging to their capsized boat during a landing, the British retaliated with acts of pillage and rapine in Hampton. These acts, in turn, "highly inflamed" the Virginia militiamen, and the brutality continued to feed on itself in this circular fashion. Similarly, to the north, the British defeated a force of Americans near Detroit and captured several hundred men. Many of the wounded were slain by Indians allied to Britain and by "their more savage allies," the British themselves. Upon being paroled, several of the survivors related frightful tales, some of which were repeated by an angry Major Daniel McFarland to his brother:

Yes Brother the wounded and number of Prisoners were KILLED IN COOL BLOOD after they had surrendered; far be it from me to wish a war of extermination, but with a nation whose honour is violated faith, whose humanity is savage ferocity I ask no quarter nor will I give it; the sword of Vengeance is Drawn and I trust in God it will not be sheathed till it is glutted. Retaliation however painfull will alone insure that respect which humanity calls for.[53]

During the Civil War, Confederate troops under Nathan Bedford Forrest overcame the garrison at Fort Pillow, Kentucky, and because the garrison was partially composed of black soldiers, the rebels massacred the entire unit. Consequently, when an Iowa regiment with Sherman's Army of the Tennessee later charged and overran a Confederate rifle pit, the Iowans asked the twenty-three surrendering survivors if they "remembered Fort Pillow" and killed all twenty-three. Pvt. John Brobst, who related the incident to his wife, added: "When there is no officer with us, we take no prisoners. We want revenge and we are bound to have it one way or the other. They must pay for their deeds of cruelty. We want revenge for our brother soldiers and we will have it.[54]

Later, when President Lincoln had been assassinated, two Confederate prisoners of war at the Pilot Knob stockade foolishly expressed their satisfaction with the deed, whereupon their guards held a drum-head court-martial and voted twenty-five to five to shoot the two. Majority rule prevailed.[55]

Neither the Iowans nor the Pilot Knob guards were able to exact vengeance on the actual wrongdoers themselves. Thus they took out their aggressions on the first enemy soldier to annoy them. This form of frustration-aggression is common in warfare. It was behind Captain Edwin Bookmiller's decision to let the survivors of the Balangiga massacre kill some twenty natives the relief party found in the area. It was behind the savage attacks on German-speaking Poles by irregular Polish soldiers and mobs after the collapse of the Polish defenses in 1939. It was behind the massacre of the Greek village of Distomo in 1944 by a German unit that had just been mauled by *andartes* (partisans). And it was behind the brutal behavior of many Soviet troops as they advanced into Eastern Germany in 1945. The Soviet Third Army's commander, General Rybalko, for example, had lost a daughter to German marauders. As his men advanced into Germany, he is said to have told his men: "the hour of revenge is at hand! We all have personal reasons for revenge: my daughter, your sisters, our Mother Russia, the devastation of our land!" His men were particularly ruthless.[56]

Frustration-aggression more recently explains the behavior of British troops on Cyprus in 1956. A bomb was detonated by Grivas' men during a soccer match at Lefknonico, killing several British soldiers. Their comrades went on a rampage, beating residents of the village and smashing windows, giving vent to their anger for several hours before they could be brought under control.[57] It may also go far to explaining several violations of the laws of war in Vietnam. Marine Lance Corporal F___ S___ was placed in charge of a four-man ambush squad one night in late August 1966. He had just lost two close friends in combat and had just returned from a visit to another friend who had been wounded in the same fire fight. Unable to trap any enemy soldiers by morning, he moved into a nearby village "to kill a gook," took a man from a home, tore up the man's identification card, and shot him. At his trial he explained: "I had to kill him. I had to kill a VC. . . . I had to help those guys that were dead. I had to do something for them."

Sgt. C____ H____ was attached to a unit that was ambushed during a sweep through the "Iron Triangle" in June 1967. His platoon leader and several comrades were killed. Only two enemy bodies were found. The sergeant ran up to them with an axe and decapitated the corpses. At H____ 's trial the executive officer of his unit testified that he "was probably moved by either momentary rage . . . or a desire to revenge what had just happened." A fellow sergeant observed: "I don't think anybody that hasn't been to Vietnam could really appreciate it."[58]

A helicopter crew member wrote home from Vietnam to his father about the casualties helicopter crews had sustained and added:

Dad, now more than ever I am determined to do everything possible to wipe these rotten bastards off the face of the earth. I have a long time here, and heaven help anyone of them, man, woman, or child, that crosses my path. Total and complete destruction is the only way to treat these animals. I never thought I could hate as much as I do now.

Tell Mom I'm all right, happy and busy. And with the help of God I'll be back in a year.[59]

Soldiers sufficiently angry and vengeful, who are frustrated in their efforts to retaliate against the enemy itself, sometimes vent their aggressions on whoever is available.[60] Their desire for revenge is keenest when the comrade lost has been a close friend, of course. Army psychologists and psychiatrists reported in World War II that the primary group (one's "buddies," one's rifle team, squad, or, at most, platoon or company) were terribly important to the typical GI. The primary group was the GI's circle of friends, his confidants in moments of stress, his comrades-in-suffering, and his most visible vehicle for his own survival. Conversely, he was *their* comrade, *their* vehicle for survival. He was their "responsibility" and they were his. Time and time again, soldiers have indicated their sense of guilt upon separation, however temporary, from their comrades.[61] And time and time again, they have revealed their profound sense of loss and anguish at the loss of "buddies."[62] This sense of loss unquestionably lies at the root of many war crimes.

Needless to say, units that cannot readily identify the enemy—especially those units engaged in counterinsurgency operations, units that are sniped at, harassed by booby traps and mines, ambushed in apparently tranquil terrain, and so on—are more likely to feel vengeful, to display frustration-aggression, than are those units engaged in more conventional warfare. This is why, as Maj. W. H. Parks has pointed out, the 1st Marine Division in Vietnam had substantially more courts-martial for violations of the laws of war in Vietnam than did the 3rd Marine Division; the 1st was essentially engaged in counterinsurgency operations against NLF units, while the 3rd fought a largely conventional war against NVA forces.[63]

Nonetheless, many potential war crimes—be they inspired by one's character, values, or anguish—can be, and often are, averted by professional, responsible leaders responsive to the laws and customs of warfare. And irresponsible leaders can, as easily, bring them about.

2. The Quality of Leadership and the Nature of Weapons

The laws of war are only as strong as those who insist that they be observed. Wellington insisted that he sincerely intended the *ius belli* be obeyed, but he complained that his subalterns were simply not enforcing his orders concerning the treatment of non-combatants and prisoners: "I may order what I please, but if they do not execute what I order, or if they execute with negligence, I cannot expect that British soldiers will be orderly and regular."

Junior officers and noncommissioned officers are charged with the training and supervision of their men with regard to the laws of warfare and the "rules of engagement," but they have at times failed to fulfill these responsibilities. A congressional committee complained in 1813 that British officers (some of whom may have recently served with Wellington) were not making significant efforts to restrain their men, but were, on the contrary, tolerating their excesses: "That troops who had been instigated by the example of their officers to plunder the property and burn the houses of unarmed citizens should proceed to rape and murder, need not excite surprise, however, it may inspire horror."

During the war between the United States and Mexico, General Winfield Scott claimed that the volunteer regiments had "committed atrocities—horrors—in Mexico, sufficient to make Heaven weep and every American of Christian morals *blush* for his country," and that "sometimes" these acts had been committed "in the presence of acquiescing, trembling volunteer officers." Few, if any, of these crimes had been punished, he maintained, because the volunteer officers were "afraid of their men."

During the massacre of Black Kettle's tribe on the Sand Creek in 1864, some of the *enlisted men* were unable to prevent (or to stomach) their *officers'* bad conduct. Lt. Harry Richmond of the 3rd Colorado Volunteer Cavalry Regiment killed and scalped some three women and five children who were in the custody of a squad of men. As the women and children were shot, "screaming for mercy, . . . the soldiers in whose charge these prisoners were shrank back, apparently aghast." He had not stopped Richmond, but, at substantial risk, Cpl. Amos Miksch, one of the men, later told an investigating committee that Lieutenant Richmond's act was "disgusting to me." Other officers present also killed and scalped noncombatant Indians. More significantly, none sought to check these acts. Sgt. Lucian Palmer could not recall hearing any orders from officers to stop the murders or scalpings, which was not surprising, inasmuch as he testified that he had seen these officers scalping Indians themselves. Maj. Scott J. Anthony's responses to Mr. Loan, counsel for the Joint Committee on the Conduct of the War investigating Sand Creek, are pertinent:

Loan: Had the officers control of their men . . . ?
Anthony: There did not seem to be any control.
Loan: Could the officers have controlled their men or were the men acting in defiance of their officers?
Anthony: I did not hear any orders given but what were obeyed. As a general thing the officers and men were doing just what they saw fit to do.[64]

Later, during the Philippine Insurrection, a company of the 27th Nebraska Volunteer Infantry Regiment was ordered from its tents in the middle of the night by a drunken lieutenant and told to fire upon a nearby village. The lieutenant had heard a shot fired from the village, or so he said. Neither the company commander nor any other officer senior to the lieutenant was on hand. Some 3,000-4,000 rounds were fired, according to one corporal who was present, and the next morning the company found that it had killed a woman and a young boy in the village.

At the Battle of the Bulge, a company in Col. James Woolnough's regiment captured fifty Germans after a fierce fire fight. The company commander was shot by one who had not surrendered, and the angry men shot the other fifty. Colonel Woolnough regarded that as "natural." "I don't think anybody considered they were covering things up when this wasn't reported. . . . I didn't think it was necessary to report that. I thought that was part of war."

Such a vengeful act surely was a regrettable "part of war." But it was also a violation of the laws of war, and it went unreported, thus leaving no official stain, and also no official notice to those ultimately responsible, that such acts were occurring.

Official notice *was* taken, however, of some acts of rape and assault in early 1945 as the U.S. Army raced into Germany. There were only 32 rape trials in January and February, prior to the breakthrough. But as the German lines collapsed, American units overran their objectives and small units often became separated from their commanders for a day or two. Due more, perhaps, to this *void* in leadership than to anything else, self-discipline declined. Some 128 rape trials convened in March; another 259 in April.

Unclear commands can be just as pernicious as no commands at all. Sgt. D____ served with a unit in Korea that had taken some North Korean prisoners. When he and some others delivered the prisoners to the officer in charge of the receiving station, the officer told them to "take care" of the prisoners. The prisoners did have some wounds, but the orders were too vague, and Sgt. D____ and his colleagues interpreted them to mean that the prisoners were to be shot. When they told the officer-in-charge what they had done, "his only reaction was to say: "Well, go get some more; we need info.' "[65]

Some soldiers preparing for Vietnam combat assignments drilled in camps where one popular marching cadence taught to the troops by drill sergeants was:

> I Wanna Go To Viet-Nam
> I Wanna Kill A Viet-Cong
> With A Knife Or With A Gun
> Either Way Will Be Good Fun
> Stomp 'Em, Beat 'Em, Kick 'Em In The Ass
> Hide Their Bodies In The Grass
> Airborne, Ranger, C.I.B.
> Nobody's Gonna Fuck With Me

A Ranger company commander in Vietnam posted this message in a prominent place:

> if you kill for pleasure
> you're a sadist . . .
> if you kill for money
> you're a mercenary . . .
> if you kill for both
> you're a RANGER!!

The precise effects of these commonplace slogans and epithets upon the GIs are, of course, unclear, but, obviously, they could hardly have helped soldiers to learn the importance of observing the laws of land warfare.

The evidence of misconduct on the part of officers and non-commissioned officers in Vietnam is sketchy, but there is enough of it to warrant our attention. Pfc. David Parks had a sergeant in Vietnam who mutilated an enemy corpse, and a platoon leader (a lieutenant) who made "an old woman crawl through the mud with his gun pointed at her head." Neither was a very impressive model of behavior (though the battalion commander was, inasmuch as he punished the platoon leader for abusing the woman).[66] Pvt. M____ S____, Pfc. W____ H____, and Lance Corporal M____ K____ volunteered to serve as a night ambush team shortly after the death in combat of several members of their company. Their platoon leader, 1st Lieutenant A____, told them to "shoot first,

ask later," and to "pay these little bastards back." A more sea-
soned veteran, Sergeant M___, called the team leader aside
after the lieutenant's remarks and tried to clarify this open-ended
invitation to vengeance. They were "not to kill just *anything* that
moved" but to "do their job." Unfortunately, either the sergeant's
remarks were not as clear and forceful as the lieutenant's illegal
orders, or the team leader was predisposed to follow the lieutenant's lead, for the men killed thirteen women and children in
a nearby village after being unable to trap any enemy soldiers
that night. In June 1968, a company of Americal Division troops
swept through part of the "Dragon Valley." It took some casualties and captured two NLF nurses. Capt. L___ G___, the company commander, and 1st Lt. W___ D___, a platoon leader,
stood by as the two women were repeatedly raped and sodomized.
Aware that they might be in trouble if their behavior was reported, the officers murdered one of the two, as her vagina and
rectum were bleeding, and they feared that medical personnel at
a receiving station might initiate an investigation.

Pfc. U___ W___ came from a broken home. He had left high
school before completing his eleventh year of education. His
AFQT score was low, but he would probably not have conducted
himself as he had in Vietnam were it not for the criminal behavior of his platoon sergeant, H___ B___, who challenged the
new replacement to show that he was as "mean" and tough as
other blacks in the unit by killing a "gook" and cutting off the
corpse's fingers and ears.[67]

Sometimes noncommissioned officers and junior officers *try*
to enforce the laws of war only to be undercut or overruled by
indifferent, irresponsible, or downright sadistic superiors. A few
examples: In 1861 a body of New Mexico Volunteers under the
lax, free-wheeling command of one Colonel Chaves massacred a
number of inoffensive Navajo Indians who were attending horse
races at Fort Fauntleroy. Sgt. Nicholas Hodt tried to stop the
killing, which had begun spontaneously upon the unexpected
firing of a shot:

> Every man then ran to arm himself. Companies did not regularly form,
> but every man ran wherever he saw fit. . . . The Navajo, squaws and
> children, ran in all directions and were shot and bayoneted. I tried my

best to form the company I was first sergeant of, and succeed in forming about twenty men—it being very hard work. I then marched out to the east side of the post. There I saw a soldier murdering two little children and a woman.

I hallooed immediately for the soldier to stop. He looked up but did not obey my order. I ran up as quick as I could, but could not get there soon enough to prevent him from killing the two innocent children and wounding severely the squaw. I ordered his [cartridge] belts to be taken off and [ordered him] taken prisoner to the post. On my arrival [there] I met Lieutenant Ortiz with a pistol at full cock, saying, "Give back this soldier his arms, or else I'll shoot you, God damn you'—which circumstances I reported to my company commander, he reporting the same to the colonel commanding. . . ."

The answer he received from the colonel was, "that Lieutenant Ortiz did perfectly right and that he [Colonel Chaves] gave credit to the soldier who murdered the children and wounded the squaw."

In Vietnam, Pfc. F____ R____ angrily reported the cold-blooded murder of a POW to his sergeant. He was told to keep his mouth shut. He then went to two officers, who backed up the sergeant: "Whatever the gunny [gunnery sergeant] says, that's what goes. . . . Be cool." Lt. Mark Lenix participated in a "routine search and destroy mission" in the "Wagon Wheel" area northwest of Saigon. Helicopter gun ships circled overhead to be called in if enemy troops were flushed out. None was, and soon

the gun ships got bored. So they made a gun run on a hootch with miniguns and rockets. When they left the area we found one dead baby, which was a young child, very young, in its mother's arms, and we found a baby girl about three years old, also dead. Because these people were bored; they were just sick flying around doing nothing. When it was reported to battalion, the only reprimand was to put the two bodies on the body count board and just add them up with the rest of the dead people. There was no reprimand; there was nothing. We tried to call the gun ship off, but there was nothing you could do. He just made his run, dropped his ordnance, and left.⁶⁸

Many of these officers were probably not *particularly* sadistic or racist. They were simply not sufficiently scrupulous. Many must have known the difference between what was lawful and what was not, but were more concerned with vengeance or with their own careers (with keeping "the boat from rocking") than they were with upholding the laws of war. Lt. Edwin Anderson, USN, commanded a gunboat during the Philippine Insurrection. He wrote home of his distress at the brutal treatment that the American forces were displaying toward Filipinos, "well-disposed" and "evil" alike. He was disgusted by the "water cure" torture. But he commanded several amphibious raids of Filipino coastal villages during which homes were burned, crops destroyed, and tortures used. He apparently did so because he recognized that his superiors expected him to carry out his orders, which happened in this case to be those of Gen. Jacob Smith. Never mind that the orders were repugnant. Smith was often on hand, praising Anderson for "my good work." "He would see that I got recognition," the young Annapolis graduate wrote his wife. Recognition was what motivated SS General Von dem Bach as well. He knew the difference between what was allowed in warfare and what was not, for at times he punished men under his command for violations of the laws of war. But his desire to acquire a Knight's Cross caused him to drive his men to produce high numbers of dead partisans, despite the consequences that this pressure on his subordinates had upon the fate of noncombatants and prisoners.[69] Similar pressures existed in Vietnam. The demand for a high "body count" was frequently mentioned by veterans as a cause of war crimes. Inasmuch as it was viewed as one of the more important inputs to one's efficiency report, the unit's "body count" could become very important to career-minded battalion and company commanders. Col. David Hackworth's charge in this regard is well known, and well confirmed by peers:

. . . [T]he controversial body count has been a means for officers to advance their careers and thus is also a symptom of what ails the military in Vietnam. How a man is rated generally as a commander from company up is by how many enemy he killed. Great pressure was placed on this, one of the key things for advancement.

Add to pressure from an ambitious battalion commander the "cover-your-ass" caution of a career-minded company commander, and one has a potential for a real leadership shortfall. Pfc. A____ B____ witnessed the rape and murder of a Vietnamese girl mentioned previously and reported it to his company commander. But as Daniel Lang put it, "the Captain was in a bind; that is, he was torn between the dictates of his conscience, which condemned the crime, and concern for his Army career, which . . . the battalion commander—who outranked [Captain] 'Vorst' and who was also a 'lifer'—was in the habit of admonishing the Captain had to bear in mind."

But B____ persisted:

Three times I saw the C.O. about [the rape] and three times he used [the expression]: 'I'll handle everything,' 'I'll handle everything,' 'I'll handle everything.' Maybe he did, but not in a way that had anything to do with anyone's making amends." At his meeting with "Vorst" the day of the Captain's return, he went on, he noticed that the company commander failed to deplore the murder, and instead stressed its potentialities as a scandal. . . . Captain "Vorst" stated, . . . "I guess you realize how serious this incident is, and that it could cause an international issue."[70]

(Eventually B____ saw a chaplain who put him in touch with Criminal Investigation unit officers.)

"Cover-up," then, had become the name of the game for more than a few officers who were confronted with ugly facts concerning the behavior of troops under their command.[71] As Gen. James Woolnough put it, career-minded officers had to "keep their finger on their number" on the promotion list. "I don't blame them," he added.[72]

On the other hand, officers and noncommissioned officers have *prevented* at least as many war crimes as they have caused (or failed to prevent). Good leadership *has* made a difference, and it may be useful to look at several examples of such good leadership in order to demonstrate this to the doubtful.

One might begin with an example from the colonial American past. Captain James Oliver was a "hawk" in 1675, but he knew the *ius belli,* and he consequently refused to countenance the lynching of several Indians suspected of treachery during the war between the Massachusetts Bay Colony and the Narragansett

Bill Mauldin's "Willy" and "Joe" are held in check in this cartoon by a company commander responsible for the rights of noncombatants. Drawings copyrighted 1944, renewed 1972, Bill Mauldin; reproduced by courtesy of Bill Mauldin.

Indians (King Philip's War). His action saved their lives. Later, during the American Revolution, the Civil War, and the nineteenth-century Indian wars, junior officers often took steps to prevent atrocities. The same may be said of German, British, Polish, and Russian officers during the Crimean War, World War I, World War II, and the Cyprus conflict. Bill Mauldin apparently knew of at least one American company commander in the European theater during World War II who would not allow soldiers to steal from local noncombatants (see illustration). And Anthony Herbert, a noncommissioned officer in Korea and an officer in Vietnam, guarded the "safety of the civilian populace" and would "allow no abuse of civilians or prisoners."[73]

Herbert is the officer who is best known among those who scrupulously observed and defended the laws of land warfare in Vietnam, but there were many others, less known, who were just as scrupulous and whose efforts surely counted. One GI wrote home, complaining that "we just aren't given a free hand to work. Always have to watch how the people are treated. . . . if you rough up the civilians to get info about hidden weapons and [enemy troops] you stand a good chance of being shafted by the Old Man [a battalion commander who appears to have been one such scrupulous leader]."[74] Lieutenant Sam Bunge, a 101st Airborne platoon leader, spoke at the "Winter Soldier Investigation" hearings of war crimes he knew had been committed in Vietnam, but in the process he described his own conduct as a new platoon leader and gave an excellent (if inadvertent) picture of how leaders should (and often did) behave:

When I first took over my platoon, we were on a sweep action and we received a couple of rounds of sniper fire from a village in an area that we knew had a lot of VC. The civilians weren't terribly sympathetic to them or to us. So we went over to the village to check it out, to look for weapons, to see what was in there. We'd been there several times before but after we reached the center of the hamlet (it wasn't a very big place), I noticed that a couple of haystacks were on fire in an area that we'd already come through. I asked the squad leader of the 3rd squad back there why that was and he said, "Well, that's SOP [Standard Operating Procedure]." And I said, "No, it's not." He said "Well, the other lieutenant (referring to my predecessor) said that if we ever get sniper fire from a village we were supposed to burn it down." So after we got the village secure, I called all the squad leaders together and changed the policy. The point here is, that in a war like Vietnam where small unit commanders have such autonomy (lieutenants and captains to a large degree run the show), an individual can make a big difference. If a man wants to burn villages, he can do it.[75]

As his own testimony indicated, however, if a platoon leader did *not* want villages burned, he could generally *stop* those who did. Given the firepower and rapid deployment that small units could expect, such units were often widely dispersed in Vietnam, and consequently junior officers often *did* make "a big difference." And they will continue to make a difference.[76]

Thus far we have restricted ourselves to the leadership displayed by enlisted men, noncommissioned officers, junior officers, and field-grade officers below the rank of colonel or brigadier general. Obviously, generals have committed or prevented war crimes too. And so have their civilian chiefs. We must now consider cases involving these more senior officers and officials.

We need not range far back into the distant past to provide ourselves with sufficient cases for analysis. Let us begin with two seventeenth-century cases. The first is that of the 1622 war between the Virginia Company and the Indians of Virginia. Before the Indians (fearful of the loss of land and game) attacked the Virginia settlers, the company felt constrained to treat the local native inhabitants equitably, in general accord with established rules and customary practices. But the Indian attack gave them a "way of conquering" these bothersome neighbors, made "much more easy" than treating them "by faire means," the company secretary wrote, "because our hands, which before were tied with gentleness and faire usage, are now set at liberty." Retaliation was swift and severe; the Indians were treated like rebellious subjects, and noncombatants as well as warriors were slain.[77]

Our second seventeenth-century case again involves English colonial leaders and Indians. In 1623 Thomas Weston's fur-trading station near the Plymouth settlement was imperiled by natives who claimed that Weston had cheated them. The commander of the Plymouth Plantation's garrison, Capt. Miles Standish, sallied forth with the sanction of the settlement's leaders and killed five natives, none of whom was clearly identified with the threat to Weston's station. The spiritual head of the Separatist Pilgrims, Pastor John Robinson, wrote to the plantation's leaders from Leyden, complaining of the harshness of this act of retaliation:

Oh, how happy a thing had it been, if you had converted some before you had killed any! Besides, where blood is once begun to be shed, it is seldom staunched of a long time after. You will say they deserved it. I grant it; but upon what provocations and invitements by those heathen-ish Christians [Weston's men]? Besides, you being no magistrates over them were to consider not what they deserved but what you were by necessity constrained to inflict. Necessity of this, especially of killing so many (and many more, it seems they would, if they could), I see not. Methinks one or two principals should have been full enough, according to that approved rule, The punishment to a few, and the fear to many. Upon this occasion let me be bold to exhort you seriously to consider of the disposition of your Captain, whom I love, and am persuaded the Lord in great mercy and for much good hath sent you him, if you use him aright. He is a man humble and meek amongst you, and towards all in ordinary course. But now if this be merely from an humane spirit, there is cause to fear that by occasion, especially of provocation, there may be wanting that tenderness of the life of man (made after God's image) which is meet. It is also a thing more glorious, in men's eyes, than pleas-ing in God's or convenient for Christians, to be a terrour to poor barbarous people. And indeed I am afraid lest, by these occasions, others should be drawn to affect a kind of ruffling course in the world.

Colonial leaders had simply ignored customs and usages in making war on the "poor barbarous people" who had helped these colonists survive in the wilderness. Our next case, that of the British efforts to quell the revolution in America a century and a half later, involved the use of Indians *against* colonists in a *bellum internecium*. Gen. John Burgoyne's ill-disciplined Indian troops were placed under the command of Colonel La Corne St. Luc, whose strategy was as clear as it was atrocious: "We must unleash the savages against the wretched rebels in order to impose terror on the frontiers. . . . It is necessary to make the whole business brutal."

Governor William Tryon of New York, in forwarding this advice to the Crown, said that he was "exactly of opinion with Colonel La Corne St. Luc." During the War of 1812, Governor William Woodbridge of the Michigan Territory, displayed leadership just as deficient as that of Governor Tryon. Angered by the behavior of some British troops and their native American allies, he called for "an active, exterminating war."[78]

We have already noted the failure of company- and regimental-level volunteer officers to enforce the laws of warfare during the war between the United States and Mexico and during the American Civil War. We must also note the apparent failure of some senior officers to do the same. Lt. George Meade wrote home from the front in northern Mexico, annoyed that Gen. Zachary Taylor had displayed "neither the moral nor physical force to restrain" these same volunteer troops. A unit of Kentucky volunteers had shot a boy cutting cane in a field. When "this poor little fellow, all bleeding and crying, was . . . laid down in front of the General's tent," Taylor had warned the regiment that it would be sent to the rear if it was not more careful in the future, but nothing more was done about this or similar incidents. Gen. James Lane scolded his Kansans in late 1861 for their excesses in September 1861, but the scolding had little effect, possibly because Lane himself was known to have pillaged. Indeed, later, after Quantrill's raid, Lane called from the U.S. Senate for a "war of extermination" in Missouri.[79]

The most interesting Civil War case is that of Gen. W. T. Sherman and his March through Georgia. Sherman maintained that he had "never ordered the burning of any dwelling." He had "been 3 years fighting [his own army's] stragglers" and insisted it was harder to keep them from violating the laws of warfare than it was "to conquer the enemy." He blamed the excesses of his Army of the Tennessee in Georgia on the laxness with which junior officers enforced his orders, and it must be remembered that Sherman did sometimes post guards before churches and other obviously nonmilitary buildings, that he did punish some soldiers caught entering private homes, that he was not amused or gratified by acts of pillage or arson, and that by the time his army had swung north again into North Carolina, it had ceased the plundering and razing of communities. Moreover, at least two of his corps commanders, Maj. Gen. J. C. Davis and H. W. Slocum, were thoroughly repelled by the looting and arson. And it is also true that instructions no. 14, 15, and 16 of General Order 100 (Francis Lieber's 1863 "Code") could be viewed by the Union army commanders to sanction acts that might not appear to some to conform to the Principle of Proportionality, were "military necessity" to dictate such measures.

However, by the time that Sherman's army reached Atlanta, very few officers or men believed that Sherman was serious about Lieber's Code. According to General Davis, "the belief in the Army is that General Sherman favors and desires [pillaging and arson] and one man when arrested told his officer so." Sherman had authorized (Special Field Order No. 120) units to "forage liberally" when in need of food or fuel. On one occasion he rode by one party ransacking a storeroom. " 'Forage liberally!' " one man shouted to him, "and general laughter thereat." (The general remained "sober as a judge.") Sherman made it clear to the mayor of Atlanta that his order for all civilians to leave Atlanta must be obeyed. Hardships would have to be endured as the price of rebellion and military necessity. Sherman explained that "the utter destruction of [Georgia's] roads, houses and people will cripple their military resources." As with the British in 1775, the line separating the vigorous suppression of treasonable and rebellious behavior and the illegal abuse of protected noncombatant residents of a legitimately warring power was not entirely clear, but Sherman appeared to have crossed it more than once. He clearly expected his men to "make the rebels yell," and expressed satisfaction with the "ingenuity" displayed by junior officers who ordered acts that "in a well-ordered and well-disciplined army" would be "deemed irregular."[80]

General Sherman did not *invent* total war. Indeed, his was a gentle army compared to that of Ghengis Khan or Hitler; his strategy was humane compared with the nuclear deterrent strategies of the United States and the USSR. But his March may be said to have been portentous. The mechanization and universalization of war in the past century inexorably affected the status of noncombatants and their property as leader after leader has opted to set aside "the niceties" of the *ius belli* in order to prosecute the war to his satisfaction. Rarely has anything been gained by such measures,[81] but much has been lost. The blockade of Germany during World War I extended, according to the *ius gentium* and the Hague Conventions, only to contraband of war, but Sir Edward Grey interpreted contraband to include food-stuffs, inasmuch as the German populace, having submitted to food rationing, had surrendered their protected status and had become "combatants, differing [from front-line troops] only in the weapons they carried." Front-line German troops continued to be fed, but several hundred thousand residents of the Central Powers are said later to have died of diseases associated with undernourishment in the last years of the war.[82]

More striking was the atrocious behavior and criminal leader-ship of the Japanese military and the German government in World War II. The Japanese "rape of Nanking" and the bombing of Shanghai appear to have been sanctioned by senior com-manders who knew that their troops were not obeying the laws of war. An American diplomat in Nanking described at length in his diary the brutal and virtually unrestrained conduct of the con-quering Japanese troops. On more than one instance he ob-served that the cruelty of Japanese soldiers was not entirely checked by the appearance of a superior officer: "If a soldier is caught by an officer or M.P. he is very politely told that he shouldn't do that again." John Toland suspects that the troops "could only have been incited by some of the more radical offi-cers," and although we do not know enough about the "rape of Nanking" to say that he is correct, it seems likely that he is close to the mark at least.

In Europe, Hitler personally prohibited "any leniency or hu-mane attitude towards war prisoners," and treated the "supply-ing of food to local inhabitants of conquered areas and to prisoners of war" in Eastern Europe as "unnecessary humanitarianism." "I shall shrink from nothing," he wrote: "No so-called international law, no agreements will prevent me from making use of any advantage that offers. . . ."

Hitler was also guilty of bomber attacks upon London, Coven-try Cathedral, and other nonmilitary British communities; but

Sikh prisoners, used as live targets for rifle practice by their Japanese captors in Singapore. From Lord Liverpool, *Knights of Bushido* (London, 1958).

here he was not alone. The British Prime Minister, Winston Churchill, authorized the bombing of German cities the day after he became the first minister, apparently in order to distract the German bombers from their raids on Royal Air Force bases. In this regard he was successful, but after the German air attacks had been blunted, Churchill ordered raids upon German cities to "make the German people taste and gulp each month a sharper dose of the miseries they have showered upon mankind."[83]

In 1918 Secretary of War Newton D. Baker had said that the United States would never participate in an air attack "that has as its objective the promiscuous bombing upon industry, commerce, or population in enemy countries." Later, when the Japanese dive-bombed Shanghai and Spanish Fascists did the same to Guernica, President Roosevelt and Secretary of State Cordell Hull expressed their sense of outrage. During World War I, President Wilson had deplored the German unrestricted use of the submarine, and in 1928 the commander of the U.S. submarine force told the Secretary of the Navy: "It is inconceivable that submarines of our service will ever be used against merchant ships as was done during the World War." Yet both "inconceivable" measures became quite unremarkable in World War II. Immediately following our declaration of war, the Chief of Naval Opertions ordered unrestricted attacks on all shipping in the vicinity of enemy waters. By 1944 we were fire-bombing cities. And in August 1945 President Truman displayed a lack of concern for the niceties of the laws of warfare in announcing the use of the atomic bomb on Hiroshima:

> Having found the bomb, we have to use it. We have used it against those who attacked us without warning at Pearl Harbor, against those who have starved and beaten and executed American prisoners of war, against those who have abandoned all pretense of obeying international laws of warfare. We have used it in order to shorten the agony of war, in order to save the lives of thousands and thousands of young Americans.[84]

Truman's remarks are particularly interesting, for they appear to combine several different self-exculpations regarding the bombing of cities: vengeance or retribution, tu quoque (the other

Fascist bombing of the undefended Basque town of Guernica provoked Pablo Picasso to create this mural in 1937. *From the Metropolitan Museum of Modern Art.*

side committed war crimes too), military exigencies, and the imperiousness of weapons deployment. In fact, the first of these (revenge) is clearly prohibited by international law; the second (*tu quoque*) was deemed an insufficient defense at Nuremberg; the third (military exigencies) is limited by Hague, Geneva, and national laws to targets sufficiently military to satisfy the Principle of Proportionality (which means that all or most of the attacks on Hamburg, Dresden, Tokyo, Hiroshima, Nagasaki, and other largely undefended cities could be called illegal); the fourth ("Having found the bomb, we have to use it.") is obviously more of an explanation than any defense. But it was used again, more recently, by high U.S. officials concerning the use of force in Vietnam, as we shall see.

In the early 1950s and the period from 1965 to 1973 the United States bombed Korea and Indochina severely. Hundreds of thousands of noncombatants were killed in both wars by these air strikes, and millions were made homeless. In addition to air strikes with high explosives, directed by forward air controllers and troop commanders upon specific, apparently military targets, other attacks with naplam and (in Indochina) with tear gas, herbicides, and antipersonnel ("cluster") bombs took place, as did some relatively undirected raids with high explosives. General Emmett O'Donnell, the Far East Bomber Command's chief in 1951, reported that "almost the entire Korean Peninsula is just a terrible mess. Everything is destroyed. There is nothing standing worthy of the name." Operation Rolling Thunder, the area bombing of Vietnam from scores of B-52s in the mid- and late 1960s, was no less devastating, albeit it was later found to have been of little or no military value.[85]

The impersonality and "blind" character of such a modern weapons delivery system as the jet bomber make it a ready vehicle for war crimes, both when the bomber is commanded by an irresponsible pilot *and* when it is assigned an improper mission by an irresponsible leader. Such a leader may be guilty of violating the laws of war through improper deployment of airborne firepower for one or more of a number of reasons: Firstly, he may simply "not give a damn" about the laws of war. In this regard he would, of course, be comparable to the morally underdeveloped officers and men discussed earlier. He may feel that the use of bombing is legitimate, even if noncombatants suffer, in order "to change the will of the enemy leadership" (Maxwell Taylor). But if this pragmatic objective overrides the Principle of Proportionality, it becomes criminal. That appears to be what happened in 1966. According to Chester Cooper:

> As the weeks wore on, the bombing expanded in scale and intensity and became part of the overall military campaign, rather than a separate war. Nonetheless each "package" of targets was carefully reviewed not only within the Pentagon, but in the State Department and White House as well. This review process eroded by late 1966, and it became more and more difficult to get sensitive targets stricken from the list. By then the White House threshold of discrimination had been so lowered that the military would have had to suggest an absolutely outrageous target for the President's staff to veto it. Guidance on bombing restrictions was now derived from broad instruction rather than target-by-target examination.

Secondly, our leader may seek to save blood with treasure— that is, he may regard these and other weapons (correctly or incorrectly) as a means of reducing U.S. military casualties. "We're going to trade fire-power for men," President Johnson explained in 1965. More recently, General Westmoreland praised "machines and technology" for "permitting economy of manpower on the battlefield" as "in the factory." In the future, Westmoreland predicted, the United States would "take advantage of its technology—[and the public would] welcome and applaud the developments that will replace wherever possible the man with the machine."[86]

It is understandable that an affluent, developed society would seek to increase a unit's firepower in the hope that casualties to one's own men would be reduced. What is tragic about the phenomenon is that the process appears to take place independent of any serious consideration of the Principle of Proportionality. This will no longer be possible, inasmuch as this Principle will be *codified law* once the present Geneva Protocols are adopted.

American leaders (and those of other nations as well) are apparently willing to sacrifice the lives of combatants to save the lives of their own nation's noncombatants, or those of one's allies, but many improperly draw the line at "enemy" noncombatants. In early 1972 the author and several students sent a questionnaire to several hundred military and civilian officials in the Pentagon (as well as to members of the Council on Foreign Relations and a random sample of the public). In addition to more conventional questions, a number of hypothetical situations were posed, among them:

Enemy forces are advancing on a vital position. You estimate your forces can halt the enemy with 50 or 60 casualties to your company. By calling in air strikes you would substantially reduce your casualties to approximately a dozen. However, there is a strong possibility that the air strikes would endanger hundreds of civilian lives. Would you:

_____ Call in the air strike

_____ Fight without the air support

_____ Other _____

The hypothetical situation was deliberately vague, but it was still surprising to find that many respondents wrote: "Whose civilians? Ours or the enemy's?"[87] Many civilian and military senior officials who should have known that noncombatants are noncombatants, no matter *where* they live, did not appear to realize this. One may well say, "I can understand why they might have drawn such a distinction," but one should not accept such a distinction nor excuse others for having failed to make it, for the distinction is illegal and immoral. Protected persons under the *ius belli* are protected from harm from *all* quarters, not simply from the firepower of their own country's soldiers.

Thirdly, a leader may feel (especially if he is in a position of command in an air force) that air power must be used because it is there. The fact that Lt. Gen. Sam Williams was an air force officer helps to explain why he recommended the bombing of North Vietnam's dikes in 1965 "to put Hanoi under a couple of feet of water . . . and hurt them badly." Service loyalty explains many instances of moral legerdemain. Adm. William Leahy had been highly critical of a proposal to spray chemical and biological agents on Japanese crops in 1944. It would "violate every Christian ethic I have heard of," he remarked, "and all the known laws of war." But he was not particular about a blockade that might have produced a comparable incidence of serious malnutrition. In 1949 Admiral Radford made much of the "immorality" of the air force's recommended mission for the proposed B-36. Strategic bombing of enemy cities with nuclear weapons was simply illegal and unethical: "I don't believe in mass killing of noncombatants. . . . I am against indiscriminate bombing of cities." Radford preferred the navy's more ethical supercarriers. Later, however, when the navy developed Polaris, Radford became an *advocate* of "massive retaliation," and it was the *air force's* turn to object on moral grounds to the *navy's* new nuclear delivery system. The air force's ICBMs were bigger and more accurate, and thus could (at least theoretically) be used in a "counterforce" role against small, "hardened" military targets such as enemy ICBM silos, whereas Polaris was good enough only for the unethical "countervalue" (city-targeting) mission.[88] Air force pilots temporarily assigned to ground missions told Fred Branfman in 1968 that they longed to participate in bombing raids such as those over Laos and Vietnam: "You become a part of the machine as you [bomb]. Guys who fly [on such missions] keep their professionality. That's why as we phase down here the air force will want to bomb. . . . I haven't bombed for three months and I really feel out of shape."

Finally, the leader who orders the improper application of airborne firepower and other sophisticated modern weapons may be a captive of his own "Pentagonesque" world (a world with nice-sounding but dangerously defective phraseology such as "surgical strike" and "search and clear"), a captive of his physical and mental distance from the battlefield. He may *think* that bombing raids are adquately governed by rules of engagement, and may not realize that some of the Forward Air Control pilots who call in such raids believe that they can distinguish a combatant from a noncombatant by "the way he walked" or "the way he looked." The leader may believe "the technology is solid" and not sense that minor technical errors, such as inadequate estimates of wind velocities, may send B-52 bomb loads down on the wrong targets. Actually, one high-ranking officer,

Gen. John Deane, allowed that the "electronic battlefield *might* make a mistake" in sorting out combatants and noncombatants; he told a House committee looking into the new concept in 1970 that he *was* aware that on-the-spot assessment officers and field commanders would have to use their "best judgment." But he felt that their "best judgment" would suffice. Two officers assigned to the monitoring of such electronic devices dropped into sensitive areas of Vietnam were not as sure. They told CBS newsmen that

there's no checking as to who you're firing at, because the [evening] curfew covers our conscience on that. . . . If you pick up somebody moving at night, that's it. . . . *You* don't have to look and see whether it's men, women or children [whom you have hit after you clear for firing]. *You* don't have to go up there and clean it up.

Pressed, the officers granted that one *could* call on the area ground command to inspect the area itself before authorizing fire on the persons whose movements had been detected, but if one wanted "good credit on your record," one would "want to [clear for] fire right away."[89]

General Deane was probably not trying to be devious. He was just too far removed from day-to-day battlefield conditions to realize that the electronic sensors and monitoring equipment were not being used as carefully as he had led the committee to believe. One might well argue, though, that he *should* have realized this. The very notion of an electronic battlefield brings to mind blind, impersonal devices, subject to simple mechanical or personal errors. The creators and deployers of such devices *should* sense their potential for evil. But, if they do, they are not saying so.

Perhaps cognitive dissonance explains in part this failure to admit the drawbacks in a new weapons system. One who becomes committed to a particular innovation finds it very difficult to admit, regardless of the weight of the evidence, that the innovation has serious shortcomings. Erich Wulff, a physician who served at Hue for six years, describes a similar kind of cognitive dissonance of an American official in Vietnam whom I knew pretty well. He knew very well what was going on. But then he became one of the chief advisors of Ambassador Lodge, and in this position, he repeated and believed what he was told. So, the higher up you get in the hierarchy, the less informed the Americans are—all the more able they are to blindfold themselves and to feel only what they want to feel.

This kind of self-deception that persons practice once they have committed themselves to a particular policy or course of action is precisely what took place in the circle around Lyndon Johnson between 1965 and 1968 (a phenomenon described by Townsend Hoopes, Johnson's Undersecretary of the Air Force, in *Limits of Intervention*).[90] Self-deception hardly constitutes a war crime in and of itself, but the self-deception of war leaders in certain settings can clearly lead to war crimes.

Not all instances of command error may be attributed to callousness or self-deception, of course. Most errors are ones that leaders would very much like to avoid making. But a leader's distance from the everyday realities of combat can sometimes lead to tragic misperceptions. Recently, there was an "Officer Responsibilities Symposium" held at the Army's Command and General Staff College. The college's student officers (captains, majors, and lieutenant colonels) had virtually all seen action in Vietnam. At one point they were asked by the college's instructors to discuss a hypothetical "Cobra Strike" (see Appendix 1), a situation in which they were asked to imagine themselves to be "Cobra" helicopter gunship pilots ordered to fire on a village that they had reason to believe was undefended. In fact, several *had* been "Cobra" pilots, and had been confronted with similar dilemmas. Their response was straightforward: One never allowed one's self to get close enough at a slow enough speed to a target to tell whether the target was legitimate or not in terms of the formal rules of engagement. "You pick an access and an escape route, go in, hit, and get out. You never know who's there." It's not that they didn't *want* to know. They simply knew that if the village *were* defended, they would themselves be imperiled were they to approach too closely or too slowly. Significantly, the instructors who designed the otherwise intelligent "Cobra Strike" exercise did not appear to realize that rather crucial fact.[91]

Lt. Col. Franklin Hart has argued that

It is unfortunate but not illegal if the commander unintentionally erred in his judgement about the size of the force he faced and caused excessive civilian casualties. Precise estimates of enemy strength are extraordinarily difficult in fighting guerrillas in or near villages. . . . The natural tendency of battlefield commanders is to take steps to avoid excessive casualties to their own units through the employment of all firepower means available to them. . . .

But Capt. Jordan Paust disputes Hart: "An unintentional error in judgment can still amount to a dereliction of a criminal nature in certain circumstances. Furthermore, a 'disproportionate' use of firepower does not result in an 'incidental' or noncriminal injury to civilians but a war crime."[92] Paust's critique appears to be sound. A commander who fails to use good judgment by ordering "excessive" fire in populous areas is guilty of dereliction of duty, at the very least, and often of murder as well, and so is the commander who "should have known" that his orders would lead to unnecessary injury to protected persons and/or property.

How do bomber pilots and bombardiers feel about missions in which noncombatants are sometimes slain in numbers far out of proportion to any legitimate military-related damage done? Why do they not simply behave like Yossarian and drop their bombs on unpopulated areas if and when they sense that their targets are not ones allowed under the Hague and Geneva Conventions? To begin with, the question as posed assumes that pilots and bombardiers have a clear understanding of these conventions, or of their own country's rules of engagement, and many do not. It also assumes that they have an opportunity to learn the true character of their targets, an opportunity that, as we have just said, they often lack. But the question is still useful, for many bombardiers *do* sense what they are doing before they do it. Psychiatrists Grinker and Speigel reported in 1944 that "many a bombardier tosses in his bunk at night to think what his bombs may have done to the civilians miles below his plane. . . ." Lt. Allan Kass, an artist-turned-copilot of a B-24 wrote to his wife in 1943:

You know what makes me feel funny? We go on a mission, bent for destruction. We are, no doubt, party to the slaughter of many innocent people. Yes, we've probably murdered some kids. We have a grand time. We were a little nervous at first, but now we delight at danger. It's exciting. It's even fun! And when we return from destroying, we relax to the most soulful music in the world, the creation of man's Godlike side. We *drown* ourselves in the creative. Could it be our conscience?

Most bomber crew members, however, have largely been un-affected by what they were doing to those below them. Staff Sergeant H____ served as a radioman on a B-24 based in North Africa in 1943. He gave little thought to the persons affected by the bombing raids, as he was "awed by the equipment, by its capabilities."[93] Lt. Howard Zinn, a bombardier who participated in the fire bombing of Royan was "completely unaware of the human chaos below." One air force general who *was* aware of the damage done by the new incendiary bombs had one over-riding reaction: "They were marvellous!" Some high-ranking officials later dismissed the havoc wrought by these raids as the inevitable (if "regrettable") consequence of modern warfare, but, as Zinn has pointed out, they cannot shrug off the guilt they own as the knowledgeable persons responsible for the initiation and execution of the orders for such raids.[94]

Stanley Milgram has demonstrated that modern man is capable of using a machine to harm an innocent person, even when personally troubled by the process, if given straightforward orders by an authority figure. He also discovered that one's willingness to obey such orders varied inversely with the social distance between one's self and the victim of one's actions.[95] The farther the social distance between one and the innocent victim, the more likely one is to obey an order to harm the latter. B-52s and fighter-bombers are never close, in any sense, to any noncombatants they may harm. "The key," one pilot told Fred Branfman, "is to be able to bomb without really thinking about it, automatically, . . . instinctively." Jon Floyd had been a marine A6A "Intruder" pilot operating out of Chu Lai. He described the war "from the pilots' standpoint" as "very impersonal."

You fly. You see flak at night. That's about as close to war as we get. . . . you don't see any of the explosions. You can look back and see 'em, but you don't see any of the blood or any of the flesh. It's a very clean and impersonal war. You go out, fly your mission, you come back to your air-conditioned hootch and drink beer or whatever. You're not in contact with it. You don't realize at the time, I don't think, what you're doing.

Another pilot remarked: "It's a job. The plane is not something anyone can fly. I'm like any professional—I know how to put the thing where it's wanted, and I trust the senior officers who told me to put it there because I know they are professionals too." But he granted that thoughts of harm to noncombatants bothered him at times: "Sure. It's grim; I know. But I don't think the people who trained me, acquired these [sophisticated machines] and wrote 'the book' [the Rules of Engagement] would then send me out there to kill innocent people." This particular pilot found the accounts of the devastation inflicted on the Plain of Jars (*Voices from the Plain of Jars*, compiled by Fred Branfman) shocking but difficult to believe. Once again, cognitive dissonance may have been at work. One of Buck Brown's cartoons is to the point in this regard. He depicts a B-52 pilot, in the act of discharging a load of bombs high over Vietnam, in conversation with a conscience-stricken copilot: "Hell, do as I do, kid; pretend there's no one down there." As Julius Stone has said, the impersonal character of much modern warfare "may yet render the principle of humanity as archaic as the principle of chivalry may already have become."[96] The imperious nature of the design, development, and deployment of modern weapons leaves much to be desired; we must, then, simply insist on that which is "to be desired" and not accept uncritically whatever comes down an assembly line.

One does not need to misuse modern gadgets in order to commit war crimes, however. More conventional weapons systems are perfectly capable of doing the job, given the wrong set of ground rules. American forces in Vietnam were given the wrong set. "Free-fire" zones were designated. Intermittent "harassment and interdiction" artillery fire was authorized. "Search and destroy" missions were undertaken. "Operation Phoenix" assassination teams of CIA men were dispatched, with army escorts and covering units. Other unmentionable "dirty tricks" were ordered, and military personnel knew that all of these orders had not exactly originated with their company or battalion commanders. What kind of example was set for the army personnel who escorted "Phoenix" assassins into Vietnamese villages and saw these CIA personnel shoot suspected NLF officials in cold blood? What kind of judgment was being used by the editorial staff of an important military journal when it chose to accent a defense of American commanders in Vietnam against charges of irresponsibility and war crime complicity by printing the words of the convicted war criminal, Gen. Jacob Smith: "No civilized war, however civilized, can be carried on on a humanitarian basis"?[97]

Pacification Director Robert Komer is said to have remarked that "if we can attrit[98] the population base of the Viet Cong, it'll accelerate the process of degrading the VC." From such a view of "pacification" it is only a short step to another one, expressed by a Cobra pilot in the delta: "Terror [is the answer]. The Viet Cong have terrorized the peasants to get their cooperation, or at least to stop their opposition. We must terrorize the villagers even more, so that they see their real self-interest lies with us."[99]

The architects of many of America's Vietnam policies, therefore, used atrocious (as well as simply immoral) judgment. But we do not wish to overstate the case. If some of our Vietnam policies inevitably led to (and sometimes themselves constituted) violations of the laws of war, there were many war crimes committed by U.S. forces in Vietnam that cannot be laid at the foot of America's politico-military leaders. After all, Secretary of Defense McNamara, on orders from President Johnson, *did* issue several self-restraining "Rules of Engagement," and General Westmoreland, head of the U.S. Military Assistance Command in Vietnam, *did* issue several directives regarding the treatment of prisoners and noncombatants, the proper and improper use of firepower, and the reporting or war crimes. Nearly all GI's *did* receive some instructions in the laws of war, and on arriving in Vietnam all received copies of "The Enemy Is in Your Hands" (see Appendix 2). The Criminal Investigation Division *did* investigate and recommend prosecution of at least fifty violations of the laws of war, most of which resulted in convictions and sentences.[100]

These ground rules were not simply window dressing. In many sectors they were treated quite seriously. Pfc. David Parks and Sgt. George Carver were annoyed by the restraints. Parks complained that

It sometimes takes the mortars ages to come in when we call for help. There are too damn many channels. . . . They have to check with Air Control, Army Control and ARVN headquarters before they can fire a single round. What kind of war are we fighting anyway?

And Carver added in the same vein: "We have a 'code of ethics' over here. . . . Don't shoot at them unless they shoot at you first. Just great isn't it! I sometimes wonder who we are trying to impress over here. . . ."[101] Apparently *their* commanders were following the rules.

The decentralized character of the fighting in Vietnam, however, made it difficult for conscientious commanders to oversee every activity of their men, and some soldiers found their own ways to circumvent the rules. CWO Dennis Caldwell of the 1st Aviation Brigade described such circumstances:

As far as clearance to fire went, my first three months I never heard of the term "clearance to fire." If there was somebody that we thought might be VC by his actions, by running or hiding, he was a dead man.

Ninth Division were people that we supported mainly when I first got to Vietnam. We had pretty much our own show. We didn't have to ask anybody what to shoot. We didn't have to ask for clearance. After that we worked closer to Saigon. We worked probably within a 30- or 40-mile radius of Saigon in all directions, and we had extreme trouble receiving clearance to fire. An air force forward controller, who coordinates air strikes from jets, told me another time, "If you have trouble obtaining clearance to fire, just holler out that you're receiving fire and we'll send jets in to bomb the hell out of the place, whether or not you actually receive fire, or whether or not there are any weapons in the area at all."

Peter Martinsen spoke of a comparable phenomenon—that of "lip service":

We had received word from Westmoreland earlier that "It has come to my attention that prisoners are not receiving rights due to them under the Geneva Convention, according to article" etc., etc. "This must immediately stop." The major just read it off to us. And the next week he was rapping a prisoner on the head with his M-79 grenade launcher.

Col. Jack Broughton piloted a fighter-bomber on raids into North Vietnam. When aircraft such as the ones he had been flying (the "Thud," or F-105) were attacked by MIGs, the pilots found it necessary to jettison all bombs in order to acquire sufficient speed for evasive maneuvers. They had orders to avoid populated areas and certain protected areas, such as cultural sites and dikes. Broughton describes for us in frank language what happened one day when MIGs attacked his formation:

I decided the bombs had to go. We had already used so much fuel that we would have little time, if any, to look for a good target once we managed to haul our fannies out of there. We had covered a fair amount of sky at 600 knots and, lo and behold, there was a slight break in the clouds and wonder of wonders, one of the forbidden sanctuaries sprawled beneath us. This one came off the protected list some time later, but I claim the first load of bombs into the middle of that baby doll.[102]

No one would ever have been able to demonstrate that Broughton had deliberately violated the Rules of Engagement had it not been for his candor, for he was truly "out of sight, out of sound." Given his independence from any authorities supervising his conduct and the peculiar circumstances surrounding the incident, it seems difficult to imagine how any of Broughton's superiors could have been expected to prevent his bombing the unnamed forbidden target or to prosecute him for disobeying orders. Yet, to some, that bombing must have appeared to have been carefully planned by higher authority.

"Higher authority" was the villain at the Russell "War Crimes Tribunal" in 1967. In their efforts to acquire evidence that would brand U.S. commanders as war criminals, members of the tribunal elicited the testimony of ex-U.S. servicemen who had served in

Vietnam. But the transcript of those hearings reveals contrary evidence of individual, lower-echelon initiatives in the circumventing and ignoring of the *ius belli,* the *Law of Land Warfare* manual, and the Rules of Engagement. Carl Oglesby and Peter Weiss questioned an ex-infantryman, David Tuck, and a former POW interrogator, Peter Martinsen:

Oglesby: How did you first find out that it was standard practice to take no prisoners?

Tuck: Well, you see, shortly after we got over there we heard from these other outfits, the First Air Cavalry, First Brigade, 101st Airborne, they told us that would be our policy. That we weren't going to take any prisoners unless we happened to capture an officer and then there was an American officer there to decide that he should be saved; otherwise we were to get rid of him. . . .

Oglesby: You mentioned a field manual on interrogation which you said was classified. I can't ask you for its contents, but could you answer this question? Can you explain to the Tribunal, in general terms, what could be classified in a manual on interrogation?

Martinsen: I don't know why the manual was classified. It was fairly general and I can tell you it did not specifically advocate the use of torture.

Oglesby: What are the ways in which you learned how to torture?

Martinsen: The ways were there.

Oglesby: It was passed on by word of mouth?

Martinsen: Everyone is subject to violence in our society. Everyone can think of some nice fiendish ways to torture people, I think.

Oglesby: How did you learn to use a field telephone?

Martinsen: A field telephone is part of the equipment of the interrogation team.

Oglesby: How did you learn to use the field telephone in the interrogation process as an instrument of torture?

Martinsen: I heard it before I went to Vietnam. I asked others, "How do you interrogate people?" I asked people who had been in World War II and Korea, people who had performed interrogations under combat conditions. They said, "You get a little field telephone, and you ring him up and he always answers." That was an overstatement; it's very untrue, but it's a common belief, that pain can elicit information promptly. . . .

Weiss: Were you taught that the Vietnamese people were of less value than the Americans, for example, or the people of Western nations?

Martinsen: The general view point of the American troops was that the Vietnamese were apathetic, ignorant, dirty and were really not worthy of our efforts to be there. That was the general feeling.

Note that the *questions* sought information regarding official training practices and doctrine ("Were you taught . . . ?"), whereas the *answers* indicated that much of these practices had been "learned" via mere peer socialization. Ex-Sgt. "Nick D'Allesandro" told Murray Polner of torturing two POWs, but added: "It was me and a sergeant. Now, get this right: we weren't encouraged by anyone to do so—we were in charge of this whole operation ourselves. It was all pretty much local."[103]

Ex-Lt. (jg) Donald Thompson served ashore with the U.S. Marines in 1965. He maintained that the ground rules, such as they were, were vague and inadequate and that this was why the men tended to violate the laws:

There were never any instructions from the top on how we were supposed to sort out the good guys from the bad guys. So, over the course of the next year, we invented our own rules like: if it runs, kill it; if it moves by night, kill it; if you find a booby trap, destroy the house closest to it. . . . The My Lai massacre came as no surprise to those of us who were there; it was an extreme example of an everyday occurrence—the inevitable result of troops formulating their own rules of engagement.

Lieutenant Thompson was right about one thing: Those commanders in Washington and Saigon were not any better at sorting enemy combatants from noncombatant civilians than were the "grunts" in the field. But *their* "Rules of Engagement" were the *lawful* ones. The ones invented by the lieutenant's marine comrades were not. And, as Thompson himself observed, these "rules," inspired as they were by fear, frustration and anger, "created far more VC than they ever pacified."[104] It is not surprising that among those Vietnam veterans interviewed by John Helmer, some of whom had witnessed the shooting of Vietnamese women and children, those who had also experienced poor leadership and were attached to units with high incidences of disciplinary actions and "fragging" incidents were over twice as likely as those who had experienced good leadership in units with low incidences of disciplinary action to have witnessed such war crimes. We do not know whether the problem with these men's units was chiefly a matter of the quality of leadership or one of the character of the men themselves, but the correlation of allegedly poor leadership, high incidence of disciplinary problems, and war crimes is certainly worth noting.[105]

We have said something of the poor and reprehensible leadership displayed by some senior officers and civilian policy makers. Just as we have noted instances of both poor and good leadership displayed by junior officers, we shall now briefly examine the actions of their senior counterparts, for, clearly, some senior officers and civilian leaders have often demonstrated that they want the laws of war to be observed. They may not always be able to ensure compliance; Aemilius Regillus and Scipio Aemilianus, for example, appear to have been unable for some time to halt the slaughter their men were engaging in. But they eventually did stop the killing and thus did save lives. In 1704 Marshal de la Colonie observed the foraging rule that his sovereign and the Holy Roman Emperor had agreed upon in 1692, holding his officers and sergeants "responsible for such as could not return to camp with the rest," and "by such precautions" he "stamped out most of the deeds that these brigands [his men] were in the habit of committing."[106]

During the French and Indian wars, Gen. Sir Robert Pigot impressed the citizens of Newport, Rhode Island, where his forces were garrisoned; and when the British withdrew, Pigot was praised for "the strict and positive orders he gave for the observance of the most exact regularity and discipline during the evacuation. . . . The men were in no wise chargeable at their quitting the island, with any wanton cruelties, or needless destruction, or with an unjust seizure of property."[107]

More famous for such conscientious behavior than Amherst or Pigot is Robert E. Lee. His orders to the Confederate forces moving into Maryland and Pennsylvania are worth reproducing at same length here. He expressed first his concern for "the yet unsullied reputation of the army" and then explained that

the duties exacted of us by civilization and Christianity are not less obligatory in the country of the enemy than in our own. The commanding general considers that no greater disgrace could befall the army, and through it our whole people, than the perpetration of the barbarous outrages upon the innocent and defenseless and the wanton destruction of private property that have marked the course of the enemy in our country. Such proceedings not only disgrace the perpetrators and all connected with them, but are subversive of the discipline and efficiency of the army and destructive of the ends of our present movements. It must be remembered that we make war only on armed men, and that we cannot take vengeance for the wrongs our people have suffered without lowering ourselves in the eyes of all whose abhorrence has been excited by the atrocities of our enemy, and offending against Him to whom vengeance belongeth, without whose favor and support our efforts must all prove in vain.

The commanding general, therefore, earnestly exhorts the troops to abstain with most scrupulous care from unnecessary or wanton injury to private property, and he enjoins upon all officers to arrest and bring to summary punishment all who shall in any way offend against the orders on this subject.[108]

Not all of Lee's forces were as scrupulous as their commander, but his example and leadership surely reduced the amount of harm done to noncombatants by Confederate forces in his theater of the war.

More recently, the Kennedy brothers appear to have displayed some scruples in their handling of the Cuban missile crisis. To be sure, President Kennedy dispatched naval forces to the Caribbean to blockade Cuba and readied air and missile forces for possible war with the Soviet Union, but he seemed quite anxious to avoid nuclear war, conscious as he was of the devastation that would result. His brother Robert spoke out specifically against the "surgical" air strikes that General Curtis Le May proposed against Cuban missile sites. Such strikes "would

have brought death to thousands of innocent Cuban civilians,"
the Attorney General maintained. A surprise attack against
Cuban targets would have been "inhuman, contrary to our traditions and ideals, an act of brutality for which the world would
never forgive us."[109] Other policy makers might not have hesitated
to savage Cuba with bombs.

High-principled leaders can prevent barbarous acts that violate
the laws of war. And this is so whether they be leaders of democra-
cies, monarchies, oligarchies, socialist states, or guerrilla movements. Let us briefly consider the effect of guerrilla leadership
on the conduct of their men.

Guerrilla leaders who sanction acts of terrorism, cruelty, and
brutality are clearly responsible for the criminal behavior of their
men. The Mau Mau standing order to "cut into small pieces any
enemy captured in a fight" was patently atrocious, and only the
moral sensibilities of individual Mau Mau guerrillas explain the
fact that this order was infrequently observed.[110] Many Mau Mau,
Vietmihn, Palestinian, and Cypriot leaders seemed to feel that,
given the sacredness of their cause, they were simply above the
laws.[111]

Communist revolutionary leaders have sometimes displayed
the same trait. Inasmuch as communists believe that the struggle
of the proletariat to gain control over the means of production is
natural, inevitable, and thus proper, some of them see nothing
sacred about moral or legal principles that don't facilitate this
process. In fact, the laws of warfare do not stand in the way of
socialist victories, even if a few socialist leaders may appear at
times to believe they do. The Geneva Conventions of 1949 provided that guerrilla forces who subject themselves to the leaders
of the revolutionary movement, wear distinctive designations,
and observe the rules of warfare are themselves now protected
by those laws. But some do not accept the supremacy of the *ius
belli*, unless those laws coincidentally sustain the revolution's
momentum. Soviet jurists have argued that inasmuch as anti-
imperialist partisan warfare is "just" warfare (in the dialectical
sense), the actions of such partisans are, ipso facto, just. Similarly, imperialist combatants are waging unjust war and are thus
inherently behaving unjustly (e.g., the mercenaries tried by revolutionary law in Angola).[112]

Other socialist leaders accept rules if they remain "practical." Mao Tse-tung's "first law of war" was "to preserve ourselves and destroy the enemy," a rule that is echoed in the words of the American communist leader Henry Winston: "The door should be wide open to any new and effective forms of struggle forged in the fires of the freedom fight. The only test for tactical weapons of the freedom struggle should be: Will they advance or set back the struggle?" Mao counseled his forces to protect enemy captives, to care for enemy wounded, and to honor the rights of locals, but only as part of "the propaganda directed at the enemy's forces."[113]

Fidel Castro does not appear to have begun his revolutionary career predisposed to jettison the laws of warfare whenever they seemed "impractical" or "counterrevolutionary." He had attended law school and had clearly internalized something of a legalist's way of thinking. In 1955 he rejected terrorism: "To set off bombs . . . can only be the work of scoundrels without conscience."

He treated wounded Batista soldiers humanely after fire fights at La Plata and El Uvero, released hundreds of government prisoners unharmed because of his inability to guard them in the mountains, disciplined both his own forces and any bandits found to be posing as rebels, and provided attorneys to those facing court-martial. Batista's officers were often guilty of violating laws that Castro scrupulously observed, and the consequences of these divergent policies seemed clear. As Fidel himself noted: "Killing [prisoners and suspects] has made *them* weak; refusing to kill has made *us* strong. . . . only cowards and thugs murder an enemy when he has surrendered. . . . The rebel army cannot carry out the same tactics as the tyranny which we fight."

As a guerrilla leader, then, Castro insisted that the laws of war be observed, and this behavior may well have been of value in gaining support for his movement. Unfortunately, it appears that his scruples took on a decidedly different color once his troops had destroyed the *Batistano* regime. In March 1959 he put forty-four *Batistano* air force officers on trial, and when they were acquitted for want of sufficient evidence of criminality, the judge was murdered, several witnesses were jailed, the defense lawyers lost their jobs, and the officers were retried, convicted, and sentenced to long jail terms. "Revolutionary Justice," Castro explained, "is based not on legal precepts, but on moral conviction. . . . Since the airmen belonged to the [criminal Batista] air force . . . they are criminals and must be punished."[114] These pilots may well have been guilty of war crimes, and, as we have said, it is difficult to gather evidence against crimes committed during acts of air warfare. But the international laws of war extend to all, and it is unfortunate when socialism is read by some as a justification for incarcerating POWs without due process.

One final observaiton on leadership appears to be warranted by the evidence: The professional soldier, for all else one might charge him with, appears to have been more interested in observing and enforcing the laws of war than his less professional counterpart. Professional soldiers, be they medieval knights, Renaissance mercenaries, "Old Order" aristocrats, or modern West Point "ring-knockers," have in common a concern for (and often a devotion to) the customs, rules, traditions, and mores of military service. The ability to command, maneuver, and fight does not make one a professional, for professionalism includes a sense of responsibility to society for one's actions. Hence Genghis Khan does not qualify; an able warrior, he did not appear to sense any responsibility toward any but himself and his tribe. The truly professional soldier learns his responsibilities early in his career and is reminded of them throughout. General Macarthur put it well:

The soldier, be he friend or foe, is charged with the protection of the weak and unarmed. It is the very essence and reason for his being. When he violates this sacred trust, he not only profanes his entire cult but threatens the very fabric of international society. The traditions of fighting men are long and honorable. They are based upon the noblest of human traits—sacrifice.[115]

Temporary citizen officers are often just as high principled as officers from West Point, Sandhurst, and St. Cyr, and many inform themselves fully of what is expected of them and of their men under the laws of warfare. But some citizen soldiers do not understand the need for restraints. "All's fair," they have heard it said, "in love and war." The enemy's population must pay taxes, raise sons, observe rationing regulations, and grow food. Why do they warrant the attention of a busy and imperiled artillery spotter, a rootin'-tootin' tank commander? Why are the enemy's non-combatants protected by so many rules? Are they not "filthy Huns, "untermenschen," "fascist pigs," "mere gooks"? Why all the fuss?

This difference between professional and citizen soldiers is as old as the profession of arms itself. "Good wars" have always been preferred to "bad wars" by those whose trade is fighting. Whether one considers ancient Greece, the noble Saladin and his Saracens, the fifteenth-century *conditerri*, or the more modern English, French, Germans, Japanese, and Americans, one cannot fail to notice the relatively more brutal ways of the amateur, citizen soldier. Not every professional descendant of a samurai was a noble soldier in World War II, but such descendants were generally more scrupulous than the typical Japanese citizen soldier. Not every regular Soviet officer tried to check the ravaging of those in the Red Army who were brutal or bent on revenge, but many did. The military's journal *Red Star* criticized the vengeful language of citizen army correspondents such as Ilya Ehrenburg in early 1945:

"An eye for an eye, a tooth for a tooth" is an old saying. But it must not be taken literally. If the Germans marauded, and publicly raped our women, it does not mean that we must do the same. This has never been and never shall be. Our soldiers will not allow anything like that to happen—not because of pity for the enemy, but out of a sense of their own personal dignity. . . . They understand that every breach of military discipline only weakens the victorious Red Army. . . .

Not every *Wehrmacht* career man was scrupulous about the laws of war, not by any means, but compared with the Nazi party's citizen army (the SS) the *Wehrmacht* appeared to be saints in arms. Over 800 Soviet citizens who had endured the brutal German occupation of their communities were asked, "Who among the Germans you saw behaved best?" Their responses left no doubts:

Front-line troops	545
Civilians	162
Garrison troops	69
SS, SD, Gendarmerie	10
Others	23

The *Wehrmacht* sometimes served as the chief occupying presence. Its administrators were "almost invariably reported to have been more popular" than either those of "civil government or the SS."[116]

Professionals were more law abiding and humane than citizen soldiers in the American South and West. Brigadier General John Wool found Alabamans to be atrocious in their treatment of the Cherokee. "With these people it really seems to be no crime to kill an Indian," Wool wrote to the Secretary of War. "They do not look to the probable consequences." He made the same point later with regard to the treatment by citizens of Oregon and Washington of the Walla Walla Indians. The leaders of two local volunteer cavalry units had "murdered the chief when he appeared under the flag of truce, and sent bits of his scalp, his ears and his hands 'as trophies to their friends.'" It took two companies of Wool's regulars to protect some 400 peaceful Walla Walla from the "inhuman and barbarous" attacks of "the citizens."[117]

Other regulars had similar feelings of revulsion for the "cowardly and brutal" behavior of western white settlers. Gen. Alfred Sully, Ethan Allen Hitchcock, George Crook, Edward Canby, John Pope, James Carleton, Nelson A. Miles and Oliver Otis Howard, to name but a few, were careful to observe the laws and usages of warfare in fighting Navajos, Seminoles, Pigeans, Mescaleros, Apaches, Cheyenne, and Nez Perce, something that generally could not be said of their counterparts in the Colorado, New Mexico, California, and Montana Volunteers. In early 1864 an adventurer named King Woolsey led a mob of territorial volunteers through Indian communities in the Arizona Territory, killing and burning. Gen. James Carleton expressed his outrage at the treatment of women and children, but Woolsey replied: "It sir is next thing to impossible to prevent killing squaws in gumping [sic] a rancheria even were we disposed to save them. For my part I am frank to say that I fight on the broad platform of extermination." General Carleton, however, insisted on more scrupulous behavior. In fact, on one occasion, when he learned that treachery was employed against Indian foes, he ordered the return of all that had been seized if the encounter were found to have violated the *fides* principle, if it was "not fair and open." A few hundred miles to the north, the Sand Creek massacre by Colorado Volunteers of Black Kettle's village distressed many regulars, especially inasmuch as the commander there had ordered no prisoners to be taken. General Pope was consequently led to remand the "atrocious" orders of another commander in order to prevent another Sand Creek.[118]

The regular enlisted man may well have been just as circumspect. In 1880 an eastern adventurer, who wanted to "get him an Indian," murdered a Ute in southern Colorado. The men of the 23rd Infantry turned him over to the Utes, who executed him. The heirs of Colonel Chivington's Colorado Volunteers were probably shocked. "White men" simply did not do such things to "white men."

"White men" were not only capable of doing such things (if they were sufficiently professional), but they were also capable of praising alien nonwhites who displayed similar professional traits. Maj. Matthew Bateson had kind words for Macabebe (Filipino) scouts: "For discipline and observance of the rules of war they can give our own soldiers many pointers." The Macabebe scouts were probably as professional as they appeared to be to Bateson because they had served for years in the Spanish Colonial Army of the Philippines, whereas the American troops with whom Bateson had compared them were largely irregular volunteers.[119]

There were many American professionals in the, twentieth century who scrupulously observed the laws of war, whose conduct may be contrasted with that of irregulars who did not. Several examples of this divergence are scattered throughout this book and will not be repeated here. But we have not as yet mentioned the ostracizing by regulars of airmen who strafed enemy pilots parachuting from their aircraft, nor the anger displayed by Lt. Col. Anthony Herbert when his call for "medivac" care of a wounded enemy soldier was ignored by a medivac pilot who was unwilling to go to the aid of a "dink," and an *enemy* "dink" at that. "I have a wounded soldier," Herbert barked into the radio. "I say again: a *soldier.*"[120] We might also note that, though our survey of American policy makers and the public indicated that the military elite was variously more militaristic and "hard line" when compared with the various civilian subsamples, on a question relevant here, that same group displayed considerably more restraint than the random sample of adult males. All were asked to imagine themselves to be

in charge of a military detachment protecting a U.S. Embassy in a lesser developed nation. An anti-American demonstration has begun which, according to intelligence reports, could be eventually dangerous to embassy personnel and property. Local law enforcement agencies have yet to arrive or have lost control of the situation. The following is a representation of the rising activity of the crowd. Please indicate the orders which you would give your detachment in response to each of the crowd's activities.

passive sit-in _____

crowd rowdy, shouting insults _____

crowd arming with non-firearm weapons _____

crowd using the above weapons _____

sniper fire _____

crowd armed with firearms _____

crowd using firearms_____

crowd rushing embassy_____

The critical points in time in this scenario appeared to the typical respondents to be the first use of nonlethal weapons and the first sign of sniper fire. When the responses are disaggregated by group and weighed according to the extent of force each was willing to authorize his men to use in response to the threat that the crowd appeared to pose, it becomes clear that the professional officers, conscious of the proper "book" methods of crowd control, responded with more temperate orders than those offered by randomly sample adult males from Pennsylvania. The responses given (higher number = less restraint) when sniper fire was being received, for example were: military officers, 3.62; random sample of Pennsylvania adult males, 3.87.

The numbers are, of course, only suggestive, for these are simply expressions of opinion. But the behavior of ill-trained irregulars belonging to Michigan and Ohio National Guards units during the Algiers Motel shootings in Detroit (1967) and the killings on the Kent State campus (1970) may be contrasted with the more professional, self-restrained behavior of the 82nd Airborne units trained in crowd control who relieved the Michigan National Guard in Detroit.[121] Professionalism appears to facilitate self-restraint in armed forces.

THE PROBLEM OF ILLEGAL ORDERS AND THE CRISIS OF CONSCIENCE

We have said something of the behavior of troops and the leadership displayed by their commanders, but we have dealt only peripherally with the problem that officers and enlisted personnel alike may face—the illegal order. Needless to say, an order that may *appear* illegal to one who receives it may not, in fact, *be* illegal. But we can restrict ourselves for the moment to examples of *actually* and *obviously* illegal orders. How have combatants responded to the receipt of illegal orders?

The question implies that all those who receive illegal orders experience a crisis of conscience. That is clearly not the case. As we have seen, some soldiers are all too willing to violate the laws of war. And many others overcome their distress at the thought of participating in an unjust war or committing war crimes by transferring personal responsibility to the official who issued the order. Shakespeare's Henry V disguises himself as a common soldier on the eve of Agincourt and speaks with his men. The English "cause," he remarks is "just" and "honorable." "That's more than we know!" one responds. "Ay, or more than we should seek after," says another, "for we—are the king's subjects. If his cause be wrong, our obedience of the king wipes out the crime of it for us." This view was sufficiently popular in Elizabethan England to justify dramatic presentation, and it was to be heard two centuries later, when General John Burgoyne told his fellow members of Parliament:

Sir, in foreign wars, the conscience of the quarrel belongs to the state alone. The soldier draws his sword with alacrity; the cause in which he engages rests between God and his Prince, and he wants no other excitements to his duty, than such as the glory of his country, personal honour, and just ambition will suggest.

Admittedly, Shakespeare's actor-soldier and George III's real one were speaking of the "just war" question—not a question of the *ius belli*. But their deference to authority is at least suggestive of how they may have reacted to illegal orders, and it is a deference that is very much alive today. Stanley Milgram found the subjects of his 1960-vintage experiments to be pliable and deferential, willing (however reluctantly) to give what they believed to be intensely painful electric shocks to distressed innocent victims. They regarded the orders being given them by Milgram's "leader" to be immoral, but his white coat, his professional demeanor, and the momentum of the situation drew them on. "I refuse to take the responsibility for what might happen to that man!" one remarked. Assured by Milgram's "leader" that "the responsibility is mine," the reluctant subject continued to give increasingly painful shocks. Asked later why he had not refused to give these shocks, he responded: "He [the "leader"] wouldn't let me!" Another obedient subject told Milgram, "I had to follow *orders*!" General von Blomberg told Hitler's Economic Minister Schacht: "I have no responsibility when [I] carry out the Fuehrer's orders. That is precisely where his greatness lies—that he has taken all the responsibility upon himself alone." A German noncommissioned officer explained the willingness of many German soldiers to carry out outrageous killings:

[They were] ordered from above.... Those who ordered [such acts] must have had their important reasons. By now we have been educated in such a manner that we no longer discuss such orders but obey them without question.... I would [not] have had fun doing it—not the least little bit. But I would [have carried out the order].[122]

Many members of modern industrial society are predisposed to obey without serious challenge all orders that appear to come from legitimate, "superior" sources.[123] For such persons the crisis of conscience, sad to say, is not as serious a problem as it is for those who are less disposed to obey such orders without questioning their legality and morality.

The first option available to one who concludes that a military order is illegal is to protest to whoever gave the order, or to that person's superior, that the order is dangerously vague, or that it is clear enough, but appears illegal, and cannot be carried out without further clarification or explanation. Sometimes this will suffice. In March 1919, Lord Plumer, the general commanding the British Army of the Rhine, protested to his government the continuation of the blockade of Germany. His men were "unable to endure the spectacle of starving children." The blockade was relaxed. During World War II, *Wehrmacht* Colonel Edward Wagner complained of the behavior of *SS Gruppenführer* von Woyrsch and his unit in the Polish occupation zone, and the Gestapo agreed to relieve von Woyrsch and evacuate his group. In 1941 Field Marshal von Kluge, distressed by the character of the German occupation leadership in Russia, issued orders condemning plundering, in order to "evidence some consideration for the indigenous population." Other officers managed to defuse orders from Hitler to shoot all captured Soviet commissars and Allied airmen.[124] In Vietnam, Sp4c Randolf Porter's protests to his platoon and company commanders regarding their orders concerning two captured enemy nurses appears to have saved the life of one of the women.[125] Other examples could be offered, but perhaps the point is so obvious that no further laboring is necessary. Soldiers have protested illegal orders, and many of these protests have prevented war crimes.

In the event, however, that a soldier's protest fails to accomplish its purpose, the soldier might ignore the order while reporting that he has carried it out, he might stall, delaying the execution of the orders, or he might fail to carry out the orders in an efficient manner—any one of which courses of action could prevent the war crime from occurring. Maj. R. L. Bullard complained of American officers who hampered effective control of the Philippines because they were not "in sympathy" with the policies of their superiors regarding the pacification of the islanders. Field Marshal von Bock often quietly ignored orders from

Hitler's command headquarters regarding the brutality with which conquered peoples in the East were to be treated. Captain Peterson, a *Wehrmacht* officer on General Gehlen's staff, behaved comparably during an inspection of a camp housing Russian POWs, and wrote to a friend: "When one is, officially, conforming to orders from above, action at the behest of one's own private conscience must be so devised that it does not come to notice and yet attains its aims."

Colonel Imai, a hero of the Bataan campaign, received orders to "kill all prisoners and those offering to surrender." He demanded a written order and in the meantime ordered his staff to release all prisoners after advising them of the best means of escaping from the area. According to John Toland:

> His staff stared at him. Imai yelled at them to execute his command and not stand around "like so many wooden-headed dolls." More than a thousand prisoners were released. As Imai watched them go into the jungle he argued with himself that no Japanese general would have issued such an inhuman order. But if it was true, he would have to pretend that the prisoners had escaped on their own.

In Vietnam at least two forward "spotter" officers were criticized for the degree of circumspection they displayed in the calling of air and artillery strikes on targets such as populated communities suspected of harboring enemy troops. They took these "chewing out" sessions in stride, "yessir-ed" their commanders, returned to their posts and continued to discriminate carefully between targets that they regarded as legitimate according to the Rules of Engagement and those that they did not. Neither was ever promoted to 1st lieutenant, and one was eventually reassigned, but as neither contemplated a career in the service, neither cared: "No sweat."

Other GI's in Vietnam avoided the atrocity-producing and casualty-producing situation during the "Vietnamization" stage of the war, as battlefield discipline deteriorated, simply by refusing to "move out." Retired U.S. Marine Col. Robert Heinl confirmed the situation for the *Armed Forces Journal* in early 1971.[126] Everything was coming apart at the seams, and the number of violations of the laws of war were declining along with every other battlefield statistic.

Deliberate and open disobedience of orders was risky, of course, especially when one could not disguise it.[127] Gen. Robert de Saint-Vincent, commanding Vichy's 14th Military District, risked Nazi wrath when he refused to supply military assistance during the entrainment of foreign-born Jews in August 1942.[128] General Dietrich von Cholitz would have been in very grave trouble had he somehow fallen into the hands of Hitler's police after failing to obey Hitler's orders to put the torch to Paris in August 1944. The young German officer who protested the order to execute several hundred civilians on the Russian front was "warned that the penalty for disobedience is death." He begged for "ten minutes time to think it over" and finally "carried out the order with machine-gun fire." This officer obtained leave and procured a change in assignment in order to avoid such an order in the future, but, faced with a threat to his life, he had carried out the executions. J. Glenn Gray and Arvid Fredborg tell of other German soldiers who, when faced with similar orders, refused to carry them out and were shot. A similar fate befell the Chilean soldier who refused to participate in the patently criminal terrorizing of the populace that transpired upon the overthrowing of President Salvatore Allende.[129] Neither the three Dutch marines who refused to burn Javanese villages in 1947[130] nor the several American soldiers distressed by apparently illegal orders in Vietnam were *shot* for following their conscience, but several were court- martialed and imprisoned. One veteran of Vietnam explained what went through his mind after he had heard men talking about the atrocities that were being committed:

If they were true, it meant my company had murdered people; it meant I had helped by making sure the weapons worked. . . . if I decided not to do my job anymore I would be sent to jail and court-martialed. It meant a lot of people would think I was a traitor to my country because I didn't believe in the war anymore; it meant some of the people in the company and outside the Army would hate me because they wouldn't understand why I had changed my mind; it meant I would get a dishonorable discharge; it meant I would find it hard to get a job; it meant losing the privileges of the G.I. Bill for schools and hospital care; it meant hardships on my parents. It meant a lot of bad things I didn't want to think about, based on stories I wasn't sure were true. So I decided to forget about it.[131]

But some soldiers whose duties brought them daily into atrocity-producing situations were less able to "forget about it." If they could not overcome the problem by protesting, if they were uncomfortable about disobeying orders, they might still choose to resign, and, if such course of action was not available, they might simply desert.

For some the solution was even simpler. The "half-pay" reserve officer in eighteenth-century Britain could decline the offer of an active service commission. Sensing a moral dilemma, Lord Cavendish, the Earl of Effingham, and Admiral Keppel all refused to serve in the American Revolution, as did Maj. John Cartwright, who when offered a post in the fleet, told Lord Howe: "Thinking as I do on the most unhappy contest between this kingdom and her colonies, it would be a desertion of my principles . . . were I to put myself in a situation that might probably cause me to act a hostile part against them."[131]

Officers already on active duty found this course of action much more difficult—either because resignation was not a remedy that their superiors made readily available or because resignation would have marked the end of a promising career, a comforting social position, and a secure livelihood. During the Second Seminole War, Gen. T. S. Jessup displayed considerable distress with his role as a military commander. He disagreed with the "total war" policies that he had been ordered to pursue and asked to be relieved. But when he found himself subjected to criticism and suggestions of cowardice, he reversed himself and issued the desired "no quarter" orders to his men. Lts. George Deas, George Meade, and U. S. Grant, and Cols. J. S. Kinney and Ethan Allen Hitchcock were all shocked by their nation's "wicked" declaration of war on Mexico. Grant later remarked that he could not imagine "a more wicked war than that waged by the United States on Mexico. I thought so at the time, when I was a youngster, only I had not moral courage enough to resign."

Hitchcock had felt similar qualms about "the proceedings in the Southwest" as early as 1836. He noted in his diary that he was "averse to being an instrument for these purposes." In 1841 he confessed "to a very considerable disgust in the service" he was performing during the Seminole Campaign. General Zachary Taylor's move to the Rio Grande in 1845 provoked more censures, and precipitated an extended debate that Hitchcock conducted with himself in the pages of his diary:

[Spring 1846] if I could by any decent means get a living in retirement, I would abandon a government which I think corrupted by both ambition and avarice to the last degree.... We ought to be scourged for this aggression.... My heart is not in this business. I am against it from the bottom of my soul as a most unholy and unrighteous proceeding; but, as a military man, I am bound to execute orders....
[Summer 1846] I am losing everything valuable in my profession [by not being with my regiment at the front because of my illness]....
[Fall 1846] I am very much disgusted with this war in all of its features. I am in the position of the preacher who read [David] Strauss' ["higher"] criticism of the Gospel History of Christ [which characterized Christian beliefs as "myths"]. Shall he preach his new convictions? Shall he preach what his audience believes? Shall he temporize? Shall he resign? Here the preacher has an advantage over the soldier, for, while the latter may be ordered into an unjust and unnecessary war, he cannot at that time abandon his profession—at all events, not without making himself a martyr.... Now, ... as the war is going on, it must, as almost everybody supposes, be carried on by us aggressively, and in this I must be an instrument.... I am convinced that no contingency connected with this war can affect that in me which, by its nature, is immortal, and the end must be the same be my passage to it what it may. As a matter of taste and choice, I should prefer a more quiet career, and one in which I could pursue my favorite studies, of philosophy. But this is not to be.

Hitchcock had finally managed to persuade himself that he could insulate his soul from the moral dilemma and that he could remain within the military with full rank and status. Hence off he went, with General Winfield Scott, to Mexico. Eight years later he was at it again, contemplating resignation in order to avoid service if war was to be declared against Spain in order to annex Cuba. He was still in the service when the Civil War began.

His temporizing was hardly frivolous. Hitchcock was a conscionable man whose agonizing was very real. But the army was his life; he was a career officer, not a ninety-day volunteer. Resignation would have cut him off from too much of what had become vital to him.[133]

His nephew, Maj. Henry Hitchcock, was no careerist. An attorney, he was a volunteer officer during the Civil War, attached to General Sherman's staff. He faced the same crisis of conscience. Sherman was countenancing crimes—Major Hitchcock had no doubts about that. What was he to do about it? What were his responsibilities? He protested the burning of the Marietta Court House. Sherman heard him out and then attempted to justify the deed. Hitchcock did not agree with Sherman's view, but he was unable to dissuade his commander, and so he let the matter drop. His job was done. He noted in his diary: "H. H. [that is— Henry Hitchcock] has said all he could to restrain this destruction, and is not guilty of any, even what is *legitimate* by laws of war." Later he complained about the retaliatory burning of a blacksmith's house and shop. Once again Sherman defended the action. Hitchcock disagreed but restrained himself:

I shall quit discussing this matter. I am but a staff officer, to obey orders. To volunteer advice to [the] General I have neither right nor duty, and 'tis but policy also to wait till asked. I have not volunteered any to *him*, but even to discuss or criticize his actions is not my place, and would only weaken my influence hereafter. No doubt to a certain extent he was right—some things can be reached only in that way—hence it is right to retaliate for murder of prisoners by killing in return etc., etc. But war is war, and a horrible necessity at best: yet when forced on us as this war is, there is no help but to make it so terrible that when peace comes it will *last*.[134]

Major Hitchcock wished to remain with Sherman, and he felt that further criticism "would weaken my influence."[*] He soon fell silent altogether and began to adopt Sherman's defenses of pillaging and burning.

In Vietnam many American officers faced similar crises of conscience. Some spoke out; a handful resigned prematurely.

Many, like the Hitchcocks, could not bring themselves either to challenge authority or to resign. Most of these were regular officers whose professional ethics were checked by their career anxieties. Many of the officers with whom I spoke were conscious of and troubled by these careerist pressures—pressures that they generally identified with the imperious efficiency report. When asked by Command and General Staff College instructors to discuss the hypothetical "Cobra Strike" (see Appendix 1), the air attack ordered on what appeared to be an undefended village, most frankly agreed that the typical officer would "fudge" by declaring a malfunction or a low-fuel state and that he would ignore the final outcome (which in this case was realistically said to be the calling in of artillery fire by the ground commander as an alternative). Few actually *advocated* such "fudging," but all honestly confessed that they would dread the consequences of the exercise of their own judgment in refusing to fire. Were they to have been incorrect in their judgment that the attack violated "the rules of engagement and the rules of land warfare," the refusal to fire could well have endangered the lives of men in the ground unit. But the majority argued that the typical officer would be more troubled by the effect such a refusal might have on his career than anything else. As one put it, "It's a case of 'cover-my-ass.'"

Colonel Hitchcock would not have appreciated the suggestion that he was behaving as if his scruples were less important than his career, that his was "a case of 'cover-my-ass,'" but such a verdict would be at least partially justified. His greatest fear, like Jessup's, was the loss of "face"—not the efficiency report. But "face" and efficiency reports are two sides of the same coin; each was terribly important to the nineteenth- or twentieth-century "careerist" soldier. This explains why some officers may "look the other way." Obviously, it does not *justify* their doing so. Sanford Levinson correctly observes that the soldier who obeys an illegal order because his life is threatened is to be distinguished from one who obeys such an order in order to avoid a lesser penalty, such as a demotion in rank.[135] But the fact is that many career soldiers know that a single negative comment on an efficiency report can end their chances of promotion, and that knowledge sometimes informs the way they treat illegal orders.

Most regular officers, then, are not willing to sacrifice their careers when they find their orders morally repugnant. But a few are. During the Second Seminole War, the rate of resignations from the U.S. Army rose from an average of about 25 per year (prior to 1836) to as many as 117 in 1837, and some of these were probably the acts of men selectively objecting to the war on conscientious grounds. We are not sure of this, however, for few of the letters of resignation offer reasons. But there is no doubt about several more recent resignations of professional soldiers. Brig. Gen. Franklin P. Crozier, for example, spoke of officers in the Royal Irish Constabulary who resigned in 1920 in disgust over the reluctance of the British government to curb the brutality of the "Black and Tans." Indeed, Crozier resigned himself for that same reason.[136]

Several *Wehrmacht* officers resigned in the late 1930s protesting the orders and conduct of the Nazi leaders. Gens. Ludwig Beck and Johannes Blaskovitz were probably the more famous to offer this type of resistance. In 1935 Hitler ordered Beck, Chief of the General Staff, to prepare contingency plans for invasion of Czechoslovakia. He did so but warned in his letter of transmittal that he would be "compelled to resign" were Hitler to order the plans into motion. Later, when Hitler *did* order the army to prepare to attack Czechoslovakia, Beck called on other officers to listen to their consciences. The officer who carried out orders, Beck maintained, was "co-responsible" with the official who gave them, and: "History will burden those military leaders with blood guilt who fail to act according to their professional knowledge and their conscience."

Beck resigned, but, tragically, he allowed Hitler to keep the resignation secret from the army during the critical month of September 1938. Hence his act was robbed of any exemplary qualities it may have possessed.[137]

General Blaskovitz, Commander in Chief of the German Army during the Polish campaign, was disgusted by the atrocities committed by the SS in that country. He first protested the slaughtering of Jews and Poles. Such slaughter was criminal; it was also counterproductive, making such groups "much more dangerous than they would have been if we had acted in a considered and practical way." But "the greatest harm" done was "the extreme brutalization and moral degeneracy" that was settling on the German people as a result of these acts. This "plague" had to be stopped by subjecting "those criminals and their following instantly to military command and military jurisdiction." Blaskovitz was ignored, and subsequently he resigned.[138] If he could not bring about a change in policy, he would at least remove himself from a position of authority in order to avoid further personal association with these crimes.

Some officers took the same step in the Vietnam era. Six percent of all 1967 army graduates of officer candidate school (OCS) who later resigned their commissions did so because of moral dilemmas they found themselves in as a result of the war. But military men found resignation to be much more painful and final (as, indeed, it was) than civilian (NSA, AID, USIA) officials whose bonds to their organizations were not as strong as were those of West Pointers with ten or fifteen years of service.[139] Some career enlisted personnel resigned as well, but, as with the officers, the time lag between the moment when their conscience demanded that they resign and the moment when they were actually released from the service was sometimes as great as one or two years.

Consequently, some officers and men confronted with orders they deemed illegal have chosen to appeal to appropriate forums for relief on the grounds of conscientious objection,[140] and others have deserted from the military altogether. Substantial numbers of common soldiers in the Fourth Crusade deserted when it became clear to them that their leaders were committing them to morally repugnant campaigns. German soldiers began deserting to Sweden and Switzerland as early as 1940, and many of these men were acting out of revulsion with orders regarding the treatment of Polish and Russian residents of occupied areas. One German resident of Yugoslavia, for example, joined the SS *Prinz Eugen* division in order to "fight the Bolsheviks." Repelled by SS brutalities in the Ukraine, he deserted and managed to get as far as Hungary before he was captured and sentenced to death. American GIs who deserted from units bound for Vietnam in the late 1960s and early 1970s were somewhat more fortunate. None of those who fled to Canada, Switzerland, Japan, and Sweden, and who later surrendered themselves or were caught, suffered the death penalty. But many endured long periods of self-imposed exile because they would not allow themselves to be forced into, or returned to, atrocity-producing situations, and because they found no more legitimatized alternative available.[141]

When one's protests were ignored and no other relief was available, desertion at least removed one from personal responsibility and guilt. But, inasmuch as desertion was generally not undertaken as a concerted action involving several persons—in other words, since it did not usually carry the impact of collective action—it had little effect on those who were issuing the orders that violated the *ius belli*. Those who hoped to change those orders, to stop the violations, were compelled to take more positive measures than resignation or desertion. In some circumstances soldiers sought to oust from power those violating the laws. In other cases some simply went over to the enemy. Needless to say, their consciences did not lead them to such extreme measures easily. Nor was there any guarantee that their consciences had led them to a correct view of the situation. Ex-Confederate soldier Carleton McCarthy described sympathetically the process by which he and his comrades came to the decision to join the Confederate army. The typical Confederate soldier, he explained, was, "above human law, secure in his own rectitude of purpose, accountable to God only."[142] McCarthy had not chosen to take up rebel arms because of any Union violations of the laws of war, to be sure. But his position may serve to illustrate the kind of "higher law" principle generally involved in measures properly styled treasonable if the actors were to fail in their purpose.

The most striking modern example of military men who sought to oust their leaders in part because of the atrocious orders of those leaders is that of the *Wehrmacht* officers who sought from 1939 to 1944 to end Nazi rule. The conspirators were, of course, primarily concerned both with the loss of lives in a war that they did not especially favor, and with Germany's fate after the inevitable defeat. But some were also gravely distressed by attacks on Jewish stores and persons in Germany (attacks like the

Kristallnacht) and by the treatment of Jewish and other religious and ethnic groups on the Eastern front.[143] They spoke often of the struggle raging in their consciences regarding the proper course of action to take.[144] Hitler dismissed them as "antique knights with dusty conceptions of honor," but these "antique knights" very nearly did him in. Hans Gisevius and Harold Deutsch tell us of at least five separate plots by *Wehrmacht* officers to destroy the top Nazi leadership. With the failure of the last of these, the dramatic "Stauffenberg plot," over fifty officers, half of them noble descendants of "antique knights," were executed.[145]

These efforts to overthrow the Nazi leadership were styled treason against those in high places (*Hochverrat*), whereas the measures taken by those who sought to aid the Allies in order to forestall or weaken Nazi aggression and brutality were styled acts of treasons against the German state itself (*Landesverrat*). For many it was one thing to attack criminal leaders, quite another to pass military secrets to enemy agents, for the latter course of action might well result in the death of a number of German comrades and the prostration of the fatherland itself. But for those who were satisfied that such a fate was all that Germany could expect, that justice demanded the country's defeat, collaboration with the enemy was deemed entirely appropriate, especially inasmuch as it did not appear that anti-Nazi plots were accomplishing anything. Gen. Walther von Reichenau protested the illegal character of Hitler's Low Country invasion plans in 1939 and was ignored. Therefore, he told Opposition officers to get word of the plans to the Allies in the hope that the latter would strengthen their defenses. Col. Hans Oster of the *Wehrmacht* intelligence service (*Abwehr*) met with the Dutch military attache Maj. Gijsbertus Sas and passed the plans on, as his "conscience will no longer allow him to continue to work for a band of gangsters." Later he told Sas of the plans for the invasion of Norway as well.[146] German enlisted men had less awesome information to provide, but after witnessing atrocities a few managed to go over to the enemy.[147]

Germans were not the first soldiers of course, to solve the problem of illegal orders by such final measures as these. The giving of aid to the enemy because of revulsion over the conduct of one's own forces was never a commonplace act, but we can find examples of it in the past. The Mexican Battalion of Saint Patrick in 1847 was composed in part of deserters from the invading U.S. Army, and fifty-five years later some U.S. soldiers (among them Cpl. David Fagin of the 24th Infantry and one Vance of the 37th Infantry) went over to the enemy during counterinsurgency operations in the Philippines.[148] Col. J. H. Patterson, Richard Meinertzhagen, and Orde Wingate all went against their orders and the policies of their government in aiding the Zionist cause in the 1920s, 1930s, and 1940s. French officers who ignored the orders of Marshal Petain in 1940, 1941, or 1942 and joined General De Gaulle and the Allies surely experienced a comparable crisis of conscience, as did those who joined the Russian Liberation Movement of General Andrei Vlasov while in German POW camps in 1942 and 1943.[149] We cannot say that all of those who joined the Filipino insurgents, the IRA, the Zionists, the Gaullists, or the anticommunist Vlasov necessarily did so because of the immoral or illegal character of any orders they had received. But some did "go over" for such a reason.

Going over to the enemy is a grim, sad, and dangerous business. So are plots, desertions, and the disobedience of orders. We surely ought to afford soldiers who are distressed by orders they consider illegal some recourse that will serve both to forestall measures such as these and to ensure justice as well. Defining such a recourse is one of the tasks we have taken on in chapter 3, wherein several measures designed to reduce the power of the various impulses that lead to war crimes are considered and recommended, and it is to these measures that we must now turn.

NOTES

1. John Duffett, ed., *Against the Crime of Silence* (New York, 1969). 435.

2. See especially Seymour Hersh, *MyLai 4* (New York, 1970). Richard Hammer, *One Morning in the War* (New York, 1970); Hammer, *The Court-Martial of Lieutenant Calley* (New York, 1971); Hammer, *Interviews with MyLai Veterans* (film); John Sack, *The Autobiography of William Calley* (New York, 1970); Martin Gershen, *Destroy or Die* (New Rochelle, 1971).

Since I wrote these pages, the report of the Peers Board of Inquiry came to my attention as well. In this regard see the summary of that board's findings, as proposed by its general counsel, Robert MacCrate, in *66th Proceedings of the American Society of International Law* (1972), 194. MacCrate quite properly lists one cause that I have not discussed in the preceding pages, with which I am in complete agreement—the tendency of N.L.F. military personnel to make themselves indistinguishable from civilians.

3. Hammer, *Court-Martial*, 57, 59, 78; Hersh, *op. cit.*, 20.

4. Hersh, *op. cit.*, 24, 30, 39n; Hammer, *Interviews*.

5. Hersh, *op. cit.*, 26-43, 55; Gershen, *Destroy or Die,* passim; Lifton, *Home from the War*, 54; Hammer, *Court-Martial,* 159.

6. Hammer, *Interviews*.

7. Hammer, *Court-Martial,* 42, 187, 246.

8. *Ibid.,* 187-89, 211, 250-38, 290-92, 314; Hersh, *op. cit.*, 30, 42.

9. Hersh, *op. cit.*, 24, 32.

10. *Ibid.,* 26-66; Hammer, *Court-Martial,* 114. In February 1968 a different platoon leader had been talked out of killing all the inhabitants of a village by his men, but they did shoot all the males of military age (Hammer, *Court-Martial,* 197-98).

11. See, for example, V. G. Kiernan's essay on military service and the industrial work force in M. R. D. Foot, ed., *War and Society* (London, 1972); Peter Bourne, *Men, Stress and Vietnam* (New York, 1970); D. Brody and L. Rappaport, "Violence and Vietnam," *Human Relations* 26 (1973): 735-52; John Helmer, *Bringing the War Home* (New York, 1974); American Friends Service Committee, *The Draft* (Philadelphia, 1969); Roy Grinker and John Spiegel, *Men Under Stress* (Philadelphia, 1945); Hans Toch, et al., "Readiness to Perceive Violence," *British Journal of Psychology* 52 (1961): 389-93; Nancy Phillips, "Militarism and Grass-Roots Involvement in the Military-Industrial Complex," *Journal of Conflict Resolution* 17 (December 1973): 625-55; Forrest Mc Donald, "The Relation of French Peasant Veterans of the American Revolution to the Fall of Feudalism in France, 1789-1792," *Agricultural History* 25 (January 1951): 151-61; and William Benton, "Pennsylvania Revolutionary Officers and the Federal Constitution," *Pennsylvania History* 31 (1964): 419-35.

12. See, for example, David Mantell, "Doves and Hawks," *Psychology Today* (September 1974); C. J. Lammers, "Midshipmen and Candidate [Royal Netherlands] Reserve Officers . . . ," *Sociologia Neerlandica* 2 (1965): 98-122; Edward Berger, et al., "ROTC, Mylài, and the Volunteer Army," *Foreign Policy* 1 (Spring 1971): 135-160; Jonathan Borus, *Archives of General Psychiatry* (April 1974); Y. Amir, "Kibbutz-born Soldiers in Israeli Defense Forces," *Human Relations* 22 (1969): 333-44; W. Cocker-

ham, "Selective Socialization: Airforce Training as Status Passage," *Journal of Political and Military Sociology* 1 (Fall 1973), 215-29.

13. I see nothing wrong in going to some length to offer confirmation of views that many hold to be "mere common sense." After all, until "commonsense" views are sustained by empirical evidence, they are not of much value. (Do "birds of a feather flock together," or do "opposites attract"?)

14. John Schlight, *Monarchs and Mercenaries* (Bridgeport, 1968) 16; Zoe Oldenbourg, *Massacre at Montségur*, trans. Peter Greene (New York, 1961), 90-116, 120; H. L. Hewitt, *The Black Prince's Expedition of 1355-1357* (Manchester, 1958), 164; John Barrie, *War in Medieval English Society* (Ithaca, N.Y.: 1974), 34, 44; Anthony Mockler, *The Mercenaries* (New York, 1969), 83, 86, 93. Compare James W. Thompson, *The Wars of Religion in France, 1559-1576* (1958 ed.), 154, 507-8; Walter Schaufelberger, "Der Alte Schweizer und sein Kreig," *Wirtschaft, Gesellschaft, Staat, Zurcher Studrein zur Allgemeinen Geschichte* 7 (Zurich, 1952): 109, 113 ff.

15. Lloyd Lewis, *Captain Sam Grant* (Boston, 1950), 159; William E. Connelly, *Quantrill and the Border Wars* (Cedar Rapids, Iowa, 1910), 100 ff. , 436-37, 454; Stephen Starr, *Jennison's Jayhawkers* (Baton Rouge, La., 1973), 20, 48, 100, 254, 342; Charles Lieb, *Twelve Months in the Quartermaster Corps* (Cincinnati, 1862), 126-27; "The Bushwacker's War," *Civil War History* 10 (1964): 420-23; W. W. Winthrop, *Military Law* (Washington, D.C., 1886), 11n.

16. Corporal John LaWall, "16 Months in the Philippines" (n.p., 1901), p. 103, Spanish-American War Survey, Military History Research Collection, Army War College; Ridgeway Oral Interview, I, 113, Senior Officer Debriefing Collection, Military History Research Collection, Army War College; *Our Soldiers Speak*, ed. Dixon Wecter (New York, 1941), 336; Crozier, *The Men I Killed* (London, 1937), 121; John Toland, *The Last 100 Days* (New York, 1965), 119: Helmer, *op. cit.*, 168; various personal interviews; Vietnam Veterans Against the War, *The Winter Soldier Investigation* (Boston, 1972), 27, 41, 106, passim.

General Ridgeway's World War I doughboys were not unique, of course. Seaman James Fahey left us a record of the propensity of some of his World War II shipmates to mutilate the bodies of downed Japanese *kamikazi* pilots: "One of the marines cut the ring off the finger of one of the dead pilots. . . . one of the fellows had a Jap scalp. . . . one of the men on our [gun] mount got a Jap rib and cleaned it up; he said his sister wants part of a Jap body. One fellow from Texas had a knee bone. . . ." (Fahey, *Pacific War Diary, 1942-1945* [New York, 1963], 225).

17. The subject is a complex one, and the literature vast, but one

might begin with Quincy Wright, *A Study of War* (Chicago, 1942), II, 1203 (citing C. K. A. Wang's study); Theodor Adorno, et al., *The Authoritarian Personality* (New York, 1950); S. M. Lipset, *Political Man* (Garden City, N.Y., 1960).

18. Joseph Schott, *Ordeal of Samar* (Indianapolis, Ind., 1964), 70; Colonel O. L. Hein, *Memories* (New York, 1925), 25; Arnold Toynbee, *The Western Question in Greece and Turkey* (London, 1923), 278 ff. (on the Greek and Turkish *chette* brigands and their more humane counterparts in the upper classes); Jesse Maris, *Remembering* (1951), 31, USMC Box, Spanish-American War Survey, Military History Research Collection, Army War College; conversation with reliable source (concerning "untouchables" in the Indian army); George Stein, *The Waffen SS* (Ithaca, N.Y., 1966), 13-15, 44, 141 ff., 259-63; E. Colby, "War Crimes," *Michigan Law Review* 23 (1925): 501 (on Austro-Hungarian "gypsy soldiers," guilty of various acts of pillage and rapine in World War I); H. Royce, E. Zimmerman, and H. Jacobsen, eds., *Germans Against Hitler* (Bonn, 1960), 172; Masao Maruyama, *Thought and Behavior in Japanese Politics,* ed. Ivan Morris (London, 1963), 19. Seaman James Fahey spoke to Filipinos who had experienced Japanese occupation and made diary entries similar to Maruyama's observations: Japanese soldiers were "a very poor lot; ignorant and uneducated. They had been recruited from the farms and rural areas of Japan. Whenever drunk, they committed obscenities unheard of before. They were like animals. The men in the Japanese Navy were of a better calibre, being educated, and their outrageous actions more limited" (*Pacific War Diary*, 307).

19. Mark Lane, *Conversations with Americans* (New York, 1970), 180; Murray Polner, *No More Victory Parades* (New York, 1971), 77-78; various veteran interviews.

20. R. Taylor, *Destruction and Reconstruction* (New York, 1968 [originally published 1879], 147-148; *Marching with Sherman: Passages from the Letters and Diaries of Major Henry Hitchcock,* ed. Mark De Wolfe Howe (New Haven, Conn., 1927), passim; Gen. John B. Gordon, *Reminiscences of the Civil War* (New York, 1903), 305-6; James Parker, *The Old Army* (Philadelphia, 1929), 314-16; Mother Mary A. Gallin, *German Resistance to Hitler* (Washington, D.C., 1961), 40; *Germans Against Hitler,* ed., H. Royce, et al., 176-78; Curzio Malaparte, *The Skin,* trans. David Moore (Boston, 1952), 10, 311. (The gesture made by Cummings, it should be pointed out, was quite spontaneous, and does not appear to have been ideologically inspired, as the more cynical among us might suspect.) See the discussion that follows for more on aristocratic *Wehrmacht* officers.

21. Herbert Kelman and Lee Lawrence, "Assignment of Responsibility in the Case of Lieutenant Calley," *Journal of Social Issues* 28 (November 1972), 204-7.

22. See, for example, Peter Townshend, ed., *The Concept of Poverty* (London, 1970); Belton Fleisher, *The Economics of Delinquency* (New York, 1966); Hans Toch, *Violent Men* (Chicago, 1969); David M. Smith, *The Geography of Social Well-Being* (New York, 1973); Alice Glazier, ed., *Child Abuse* (New York, 1971).

23. Kelman and Lawrence, *op. cit.*, 206-7; Stanley Milgram, *Obedience to Authority* (New York, 1974), 205.

24. Neil Sheehan, "The 99 Days of Captain Arnheiter," *New York Times Magazine* (August 11, 1968), 7-9, 69-75; Hersh, *op. cit.*, 18; K. S. Farquharson, *Reminiscences of Crimean Campaigning and Russian Captivity* (Edinburgh, 1883); *The Tragedy of Silesia*, ed. Johannes Kaps (Munich, 1952), 396, 406-7, 428; *Politics* (January 1946), 5; (October 1946), 319. Compare John Flanagan, ed., *The Aviation Psychiatry Program in the Army Air Forces* (Washington, D.C., 1948), 217, for evidence that enlisted airmen in World War II were more aggressive than officers.

For evidence of brutality among educated, upper-middle-class officers, see the *New York Times* (March 15, 1891), for an account of West Point graduate John Wickliffe's role in an anti-Italian massacre in New Orleans; Don Rickey, *Forty Miles a Day on Beans and Hay* (Norman Okla., 1963), 181, on the brutality of some late nineteenth-century West Pointers; and Peter Karsten, *The Naval Aristocracy* (New York, 1972), 210, 265-67, on the same phenomenon among Annapolis graduates.

25. See William and Joan McCord and Alan Howard, "Familial Correlates in Nondelinquent Male Children," *Journal of Abnormal and Social Psychology* 66 (1961), 79-93; S. and E. Glueck, *Unravelling Juvenile Delinquency* (New York, 1950); A. Bandura and R. H. Walters, *Adolescent Aggression* (New York, 1959); and Renatus Hartogs, "Who Will Act Violently: The Predictive Criteria," in R. Hartogs and Eric Artzt, eds., *Violence: Causes and Solutions* (New York, 1970), 332-37.

26. W. H. Auden, "The Shield of Achilles," in *W. H. Auden: Collected Poems,* ed. Edward Mendelson (New York, 1976), 455.

27. Conneley, *Quantrill,* 42-43. Earlier research that several of my students and I conducted probed the *attitudes* of Annapolis and ROTC officer candidates and other college males. Attitudes are not behavior, but it is at least worth noting here that those who offered the more belligerent responses also expressed greater willingness than others to obey morally repugnant orders (E. Berger, L. Flatley, J. Frisch, M. Gottleib, J. Haisley, P. Karsten, L. Pexton, W. Worrest, "ROTC, My Lai, and the Volunteer Army," *Foreign Policy* 1 [Spring 1971], 144).

28. In this and other discussions of many other courts-martial, I will generally not use the full names of the persons involved. I am not seeking to "protect the innocent," for all were found guilty. But I do not think there is any point at this point in time in subjecting these persons to further public disclosure. Nonetheless, I will list the court-martial (CM) numbers (all are available at the Federal Records Center, Suitland, Maryland) and (where relevant) the Court of Military Review opinion citations in order that the interested reader can consult the full record, thusly: *United States* v. *Pfc. T____ G____*, CM 420246; *U.S.* v. *Sgt. D____ G____*, CM 416161; *U.S.* v. *Pfc. C____ G____*, CM 416160; *U.S.* v. *Pfc. J____ G____* CM 416159. (The last 3 listed cases here served as the basis for Daniel Lang's vivid account, *Casualties of War* [New York, 1969]. Lang also disguises the names of the individuals involved. Barry's poem appears in the V.V.A.W. collection, L. Rottmann, ed., *Winning Hearts and Minds* [New York, 1972], 51).

29. Langer, "The Making of a Murderer," *American Journal of Psychiatry* (January 1971), 950-53; *Human Behavior* 1 (January-February 1972), 56.

30. Hersh, *op. cit.*, 19-21; Charles Levy, *Spoils of War* (Boston, 1973), 170-71.

31. *Esquire* (October 1970), 158; Polner, *No Victory Parades* (1971), 33, 35, 39-40.

32. A. Mockler, *Mercenaries* (New York, 1968), 19; Reitz, *Commando* (New York, 1930 ed.), 1-48, 137; Koriakov, *I'll Never Go Back* (New York, 1948), 93; M. A. Gallin, *German Resistance to Hitler: Ethical and Religious Factors* (Washington, D.C., 1961), 20, 40, 47; Harold Deutsch, *The Conspiracy Against Hitler in the Twilight War* (Minneapolis, 1968), 53, 185-88; "Ausgewaehlte Briefe von Generalmajor Helmuth Stieff," *Vierteljahreshefte fuer Zeitgeschichte* 2 (1954): 297 ff.; Royce, Zimmerman, and Jacobsen, *op. cit.*, 21 ff., 248.

33. J. Glenn Gray, *The Warriors* (New York, 1959), 188-95; Daniel Lang, *Casualties of War* (New York, 1969), 109; R. J. Lifton, *Home from the War* (New York, 1973), 53, 58, 177; Joseph Lelyneld, "The Story of a Soldier Who Refused to Fire at Songmy," *New York Times Magazine* (December 14, 1969), 32 ff.; "Rocky Bleier's War," *Sports Illustrated* (June 9, 1975), 79; Michlovic to the editor, *Pittsburgh Post Gazette* (April 7, 1971), 10; Garfolo to Richard Hammer, *Interviews with My Lai Veterans* (25-minute film, 1971). Cf. Polner, *No Victory Parades* 24, 49, 58; Jonathan Schell, *The Village of Ben Suc* (New York, 1967), 104-5; *Winter Soldier Investigation*, 24-25; *U.S.* v. *Sgt. V____ B____*, CM 415080, 38 CMR 199; *U.S.* v. *Sp4 C____ M____*, CM 424384; Starr, *Jennison's Jayhawkers*, 20, 28; account of Pfc. L____ M____, in *Esquire* (October 1970) 198-99.

Data gathered by Gordon Zahn from British military chaplains suggest that Evangelicals, whose theology is more "egalitarian," are more willing to challenge violations of the laws of war than Roman Catholics or Church of Englanders (Episcopalians in the United States), who belong to more authoritarian, hierarchical religious groups. See Zahn, *The Military Chaplaincy* (Toronto, 1969), 143-45. But Catholics and Church of Englanders, probably responding to St. Thomas's "Principle of Proportionality," were quick to criticize the World War II bombing of Dresden (*loc. cit.*, 162; Father John Ford, "The Morality of Obliteration Bombing," *Theological Studies* [September 1944], 261-309). One's religious affiliation, per se, is a poor indicator of one's capacity to observe the laws of war.

34. E. F. M. Durbin and John Bowlby, *Personal Aggressiveness and War* (London, 1939), 108; Douglas Leach, *Flintlock and Tomahawk* (New York, 1958); Pierce G. Fredricks, *The Sepoy and the Cossack* (New York, 1971); Stuart Miller, "Our Mylai of 1900," *Transaction 7* (September 1970): 20-28; Jonathan Schell, *The Village of Ben Suc* (New York, 1967), 104; David Parks, *GI Diary* (New York, 1968), 81; R. J. Lifton, *Home from the War* (New York, 1973), 192n; and various interviews with veterans. Compare *The Holy War*, ed. Thomas P. Murphy (Columbus, Ohio, 1975).

Thus in 1900 General S. B. Young told a Pittsburgh audience: "The keynote of the insurrection . . . is race. This, then, gentlemen, is the whole thing in a nutshell. If you ask me the quickest and easiest way to bring peace and good order to the Filipino, I can only say that, like the chameleon, we must put him on such a background that he can change his color" (cited in Miller, *op. cit.*, 26). Compare Georges Tamarin, *The Israeli Dilemma* (Rotterdam, 1973), 138.

35. J. W. Thompson, *Wars of Religion in France*, 148, 154, 274; Toland, *Last 100 Days*, 120 (on the Croatian *Ustachi*); Samuel Stouffer et al., *The American Soldier* (Princeton, 1949), II, 34, 159, 161 (cited by John Helmer, *Bringing the War Home* [New York, 1973], 30-31, as Helmer compared the racism of World War II GIs with that of those in Vietnam); various interviews with U.S. veterans of the war with Japan, for some of which I am indebted to Captain William Goodman, USAR; *Once a Marine: The Memoirs of General A. A. Vandegrift, USMC*, as told to Robert B. Asprey (New York, 1964), 142. Compare Oldenbourg, *op. cit.,* 120; Hitti, *op. cit.*

36. See, for example, Hitchcock, *Marching with Sherman*, 242-43, passim. Compare *Letters of Private Wheeler*, 25.

37. Reitz, *Commando*, 225, passim; Jock Haswell, *Citizen Armies* (London, 1973),. 141; S. Hoig, *Sand Creek Massacre*, 161; John Toland, *The Rising Sun* (New York, 1970), I, 365 (for a notable exception to these generalizations in the Boer War, see Ken Griffith, *Thank God We Kept*

the *Flag Flying* [New York, 1974], 52-55); Milgram, *Obedience to Authority* (New York, 1974), 40. Compare Milgram's views with those of Yolande Diallo, a legal expert working for the ICRC in West Africa:

Traditionally war between people belonging to the same ethnic group was less cruel than a war declared against a neighbouring country or against people of a different ethnic section of the population. Every African is profoundly conscious of his adherence to an ethnic unit. There is a proverb which says: "You may chew your brother, but do not swallow him." In such conflicts, the rules are identical for both groups of belligerents and are therefore respected most strictly. A man belonging to a different ethnic group may be kept in bondage, but not a fellow-countryman. Similarly, a sacred place belonging to an enemy of the same ethnic group will not be desecrated, because it is venerated by both parties. (ICRC Bulletin, May 5, 1976, p. 5).

38. Westington, *op. cit.*, passim; Thucydides, *Peloponnesian War, III, 82, 84: "Indeed, men do not hesitate, when engaged in acts of vengeance, to abridge common principles upon which all must rely in the event of misfortune, thus reducing the chance that these principles be observed by others when in peril oneself."

39. Ramsay, *History of the Revolution in South Carolina,* II, 270; cited in Don Higgenbotham, *The War of American Independence* (New York, 1971), 384.

40. Lynn Montross, *Rag, Tag and Bobtail* (New York, 1952), 386, 369-70; John Shy, "The Military Conflict Viewed as a Revolutionary War," in Stephen Kurtz and Joseph Hutson, eds., *Essays on the American Revolution* (Chapel Hill, N.C., 1973), 134-5, 135n; U.S. Cong., *House Committee . . . to enquire into . . . the manner in which the war has been waged by the Enemy* (Troy, N.Y., 1813), 76.

41. Starr, *Jennison's Jayhawkers,* 100; Haswell, *Citizen Armies,* 205. Compare Bryant Wedge, "The Anticommunist Complex," *American Journal of Psychiatry* (November 1970): 548 ff.; and Charles Foley, ed., *The Memoirs of General Grivas* (New York, 1965), 38, where Grivas tells us that his orders to his men during the civil war on Cyprus were to engage in "murderous attacks" on Cypriot policemen who "get in our way."

42. See, for example, 57th Cong., 1st Sess., Senate Document 20 (5), pt. 1, *Charges of Cruelty to Natives of the Philippine Islands* (Washington, D.C., 1901), passim; and George Palmer Diary, USMC Box, Spanish-American War Survey, Military History Research Collection, Army War College.

43. Leslie Guile folder, USMC Box, *op. cit.*

44. Stuart to his father, September 1778, cited in Shy, *op. cit.,* 146; Toland, *Last 100 Days,* 491; David Burwell, "Civilian Protection in Modern

Warfare," *Virginia Journal of International Law* 14 (1973): 136*n*. Compare Toland, *Last 100 Days*, 186.

45. Captain B. H. Liddell Hart, ed., *The Letters of Private Wheeler* (Boston, 1952), 9. It will be recalled that Wellington was distressed at the amount of pillage and rapine his men engaged in.

46. Richard Tregaskis, *Guadalcanal Diary* (New York, 1962), 22; personal interview with F___ R___, August 13, 1973; Grinker and Spiegel, *Men Under Stress* (New York, 1945), 132; J. Glenn Gray, *The Warriors: Reflections on Men in Battle* (New York, 1966), 9.

Former Pfc. Robert Bonner's remarks may be worth quoting as a possible example of this phenomenon, despite the real questions raised about the reliability of other accounts appearing in the same volume as this one:

I don't see how anybody who really could go through a month in a line company in Vietnam and at least not hear somebody's story about something. Because that's the whole thing in Vietnam. When a new guy comes into the company, a replacement for about the first three or four days, everybody's telling them about their great adventures or how our outfit did this. And just lays down the whole history of, you know, of your outfit and our platoon and your squad, and then you go on your own ego trip and rap out about how you killed so and so. . . . Anybody who has any kind of relations with a combat unit, I don't see how they could not hear about some type of atrocity. (Mark Lane, *Conversations with Americans* [New York, 1970], 238.)

47. See, for example, S. L. A. Marshall, *Men Against Fire* (New York, 1961), 78-79, for a discussion of controlled observations in World War II of combat units that revealed that only 15 to 25 percent of the men would fire at the enemy, even when attacked themselves. The Judaeo-Christian inhibition against killing was deemed to be one of the reasons for this reluctance to fire. "Train-Fire" (a process of controlled, collective fire) and the counseling of men found to be unwilling to shoot ("You've got to support your buddies"), coupled with a better ammunition replenishment system, resulted in a much higher rate of fire among men in Korea (55-60 percent) and Vietnam (over 80 percent) (*ibid.*, 9; remarks of Marshall in Pittsburgh, 1971).

48. Charles Levy, *Spoils of War* (Boston, 1974), 80-81.

49. *Ibid.*, 129-30, 134.

50. The inability to distinguish enemy guerrilla from truly innocent civilians is as old as guerrilla warfare, of course. It troubled the British in the American Revolution, and it troubled the Americans in the Philippine Insurrection. (Corporal John LaWall, for example, found it difficult to distinguish friendly Filipinos from unfriendly or truly dangerous ones.) Charles Moskos reported that the GI in Vietnam regarded "virtually all

indigenous people" as "actual or potential threats to his physical safety." Hence Smith's reaction, and hence the behavior of the sergeant who threw a phosphorous grenade into a hut, wounding women and children, and left the wounded untreated: "Fuck 'em. They're VC too. Around here everybody's VC." See LaWall, "16 months in the Philippines" (1901), 88, 27th U.S. Volunteer Infantry Box, Spanish-American War Survey, U.S. Military History Research Collection, Carlisle Barracks; Charles Moskos, "Why Men Fight," *Transaction* (November 1969): 13 ff.; Paul Avery, in the *San Francisco Chronicle* (December 5, 1969), cited in Edward Herman, *Atrocities in Vietnam* (Philadelphia, 1970), 45.

51. Duncan and Martinsen testimony in John Duffett, ed., *Against the Crime of Silence* (New York, 1968), 499, 434.

52. Westington, *op. cit.*, 95, 101, passim; Ian Roy, ed., *The Hapsburg-Valois Wars . . . by Blaise de Monluc* (Hamden, Conn., 1972 [orig. pub. 1591]), 54: Howell Lloyd, *The Rouen Campaign* (Oxford, 1972), 166; Montross, *op. cit.*, 424, 452, 387, 172.

53. U.S. Cong., *House Committee appointed to enquire into the . . . Manner in which the War has been Waged . . .* (Troy, N.Y., 1813), 101-3; "The Papers of Major D. McFarland," *Western Pennsylvania Historical Magazine* 51 (1968): 104-05. Compare George Smith and Charles Judah, eds., *Chronicles of the Gringos* (Albuquerque, N. Mex., 1974), 268-71.

54. Margaret B. Roth, ed., *"Well, Mary": Civil War Letters of a Wisconsin Volunteer* (Madison, Wis., 1960), 57. Compare Carl Mydans, *More Than Meets the Eye* (New York, 1959), 173.

55. Starr, *Jennison's Jayhawkers*, 357.

56. Joseph Schott, *Ordeal of Samar* (Indianapolis, Ind., 1964), 55; Dominique Eudes, *Kapetanios* (trans., London, 1972), 141-42, 154; Toland, *Last 100 Days*, 155-5; interview with G____, ex-Russian tank commander, 1973. (I am grateful to Captain William Goodman for the last reference.) Rybalko's men spoke very imperfect German, but one of them was still able to explain his behavior in concise terms. Friendly to Viennese at first, he and his comrades shot a wounded prisoner in anger after suffering a casualty to sniper fire. When an Austrian woman protested, the Russian soldier replied in German: "You good—we good. You bad—we bad" (Toland, *Last 100 Days*, 352).

57. *Memoirs of Grivas*, 96-97. Later, in 1958, in response to further guerrilla attacks, a group of British soldiers organized a secret vengeance squad that called itself "Cromwell" (ibid., 153).

58. *U.S. v. Lance Corporal F____ S____*, NCM 66-2846; 39 C.M.R. 133; *U.S. v. Staff Sergeant R____ B____*, CM 421583: His recon team took three men into custody, and Sgt. B____ ordered them shot. He had lost some comrades the week before. David Halberstam, *The Making of a Quag-*

mire (New York, 1965): After a "particularly bitter" battle near Bac Lieu, U.S. Marines "lined up" and shot seventeen captives "in cold blood" when they began shouting anti-American slogans. Other evidence of this phenomenon is derived from personal interviews with veterans.

59. "Rich" to his father, in Bill Adler, ed., *Letters from Vietnam* (New York, 1967), 22. Compare the remarks of Vietnam veteran Peter Martinsen: "The men told me they weren't taking any prisoners. They said, 'We aren't taking prisoners, because one of our platoon leaders was killed three days before.' One fellow, 18 years old, I think he was, said to me with a grin, 'You should have seen the girl I shot yesterday' " (Duffett, ed., *Against the Crime of Silence,* 440).

60. If they *are* able to vent their anger on the enemy, of course they may not commit any violations of the laws of war. Seaman H___ was on the U.S.S. *Quincy* when that vessel was sunk off Guadalcanal in 1942. He and his shipmates were fired on in the water by Japanese destroyers. His means of retaliating was to be as good a fire controller as he could when assigned to another warship directing fire on Japanese-held islands (interview with Captain William Goodman, 1973).

61. See, for example, Gray, *The Warriors,* 40; Willard Waller, *The Veteran Comes Home* (New York, 1944), 39, 54; Grinker and Spiegel, *op. cit.,* 278. Compare Lieutenant Ned_____, to his parents, from Vietnam, 1966: "I hope you both realize that over half of the men I knew at West Point have been or are here. I could never again face my buddies unless I came here." Bill Adler, ed., *Letters from Vietnam* [New York, 1967], 70-71).

62. R. J. Lifton found that some veterans feel profound guilt at having survived while close friends perished *(Home from the War,* passim). My own interviewing appeared to bear this out.

63. Major W. H. Parks, "Crimes in Hostilities," *Marine Corps Gazette* (August 1976), 10.

64. Wellington, *Selections,* 267; U.S. Cong., *House Committee appointed to enquire into the Spirit and Manner in Which the War has been Waged by the Enemy* (Troy, N.Y., 1813), 10; Joint Committee on Conduct of War, 38th Cong., 2nd sess., *Massacre of Cheyenne Indians* (G.P.O., 1865), 27, 144; Lloyd Lewis, *Captain Sam Grant,* 192; Hoig, *Sand Creek Massacre,* 182, 186.

65. LaWall, "Sixteen Months in the Philippines,"-27th U.S. Volunteers Box, Spanish-American War Survey, U.S. Military History Research Collection, Carlisle Barracks; General James Woolnough Oral History Transcript, I, February 25, 1971, p. 3, Oral History Program, U.S. Military History Collection, Carlisle Barracks; Charles McDonald, *The Last Offensive* (Department of the Army, Washington, D.C., 1973), 333;

Sergeant D____, 1973, interviewed by Captain William Goodman, USAR. Compare Andrew Wilson's opening remarks in "The Rules of War," *The Observer* (November 30, 1969).

66. Parks, *GI Diary* (New York, 1968), 95, 109; *Winning Hearts and Minds*, 1; Compare *U.S.* v. *1st Lt. L____ M____*, 23rd (Americal) Division, 41 *C.M.R.* 650 (who led two men into a nearby village one night and raped Vietnamese girls at gunpoint).

67. *U.S.* v. *Pvt. M____ S____*, NCM 71-0028, 45 *C.M.R.* 852; *U.S.* v. *Captain L____ G____*, CM 420332; *U.S.* v. *Pfc. U____ W____*, CM 419872. Compare *U.S.* v. *Sgt. W____ G____*, CM 416805, 39 *C.M.R.* 586.

68. Hodt, cited in Frank McNitt, *Navajo Wars* (Albuquerque, N.M., 1972), 426; *New Yorker* (September 4, 1970), 39; Vietnam Veterans Against the War, *Winter Soldier Investigation* (Boston, 1972), 78.

69. Anderson to his wife, December 8, 1901, and undated, ca. 1901 (in undated file), Edwin Anderson Papers, Southern Historical Collection, University of North Carolina Library; Leo Alexander, "War Crimes and Their Motivation," *Journal of Criminal Law and Criminology* 38 (1948): 314.

70. Hackworth, quoted in Pyle and Merron, "Angry Colonel About to Quit," *Washington Post* (June 24, 1971), sec. F, pp. 1, 6; Lang, *Casualties of War*, 60-62; E. Herman, *Atrocities in Vietnam* (Philadelphia, 1969), 67. Compare the remarks of Lieutenant Colonel Edward L. King: "The primary motivation [at the Joint Chiefs of Staff and the Army General Staff] appeared to be a desire for career promotion no matter what the cost. . . . many foreign officers comment unfavorably on the fawning servility displayed by Army junior and middle grade officers toward their colonel or general officer superiors. (They had not heard about the efficiency report!)" King, "Death of the Army," *Navy Times* (February 17, 1971); and 92nd Cong., 1st sess., *Hearings Before House Ad Hoc Committee on Command Responsibility for U.S. War Atrocities in Southeast Asia*, Pt. 1, April 26, 1971, 18-95.

71. See, for example, the account of the attempted cover-up of the mutilation of enemy dead in *U.S.* v. *Sgt. C____ H____*, CM 420341. See also Seymour Hersh, *Cover-up* (New York, 1971), on the My Lai aftermath.

72. Woolnough Oral History transcript, I, February 18, 1971, p. 30, Oral History Program, U.S. Military History Collection, Carlisle Barracks.

73. Douglas Leach, *Flintlock and Tomahawk* (New York, 1958), 149; M. De W. Howe, ed., *Marching with Sherman* (Boston, 1927), 114-15; F. Wiener, *Civilians Under Military Justice* (Chicago, 1967), 120; M. Roth, ed., *"Well Mary,"* 57, 59-60; Paul Wellman, *Death on the Prairie* (New York, 1934), 21n; *Politics* (January, 1946), 5; (October 1946), 319; German

Foreign Office, *Polish Acts of Atrocity*, 218; *Tragedy of Silesia*, 396, 406, 407, 428; Elbridge Colby, "War Crimes," *Michigan Law Review* 23 (1925): 501 ff.; Farquharson, *op. cit.*, passim; *Memoirs of Grivas*, 167; personal interviews; Anthony Herbert, *Soldier* (New York, 1972), 62, 147, 268, 320, 521-30 (on which pages appear the affidavits of several officers in Herbert's battalion, whose words are the ones I have quoted).

74. "Bill" to "the menfolk of the family," in G. Munson, ed., *Letters from Viet Nam*, 60.

75. *Winter Soldier Investigation*, 63. Compare Schell, *The Village of Ben Suc*, 25; Lang, *Casualties of War*, 18-19: "A corporal who was still enraged over the ambush tried to strangle another of the prisoners; he had knotted a poncho, nooselike, around the captive's neck and was tightening it when a merciful lieutenant commanded him to desist."

76. Peter Petersen, *Against the Tide* (New Rochelle, 1974), 162.

77. Edward Waterhouse, *A Declaration of the State of the Colony and Affaires in Virginia* (London, 1622), 22, 24. (Waterhouse, the Secretary of the Virginia Company, was the nephew of Sir Edward Waterhouse, Chancellor of the Exchequer in Ireland [See *Dictionary of National Biography*])

78. La Corne St. Luc and Tryon are both cited in Montross, *op. cit.*, 210. Compare Colonel Banastre Tarleton's Proclamation to the Inhabitants of the Carolinas, November 1780; "It is not the wish of Britain to be cruel or to destroy, but it is now obvious to all Carolina that Treachery, Perfidy, and Perjury will be punished with instant Fire and Sword" (Robert Bass, *The Green Dragoon* [London, 1957], 112).

Obviously, Tarleton regarded the rebels as being on the illegal, far side of the fine line between legitimate, protected guerrilla warfare and illegitimate, treasonable brigandage, while Francis Marion and other southern militia leaders saw themselves as being on the legal, near side. We shall subsequently consider the issue of the legitimacy and legality of various types of guerrilla warfare.

79. Lewis, *Captain Sam Grant*, 159-60; Starr, *Jennison's Jayhawkers*, 48-49, 254. Compare Hoig, *Sand Creek Massacre*, 161.

80. Howe, ed., *Marching with Sherman*, 53, 69, 75, 86; W. T. Sherman, *Memoirs* (New York, 1875), 146, 152; John Walters, *Merchant of Terror: General Sherman and Total War* (Indianapolis, Ind., 1973), 81, passim.

General Phil Sheridan's raids in the Shenandoah Valley are notorious, and, by his own admission, Sheridan did use Confederate prisoners to clear the roads of mines during the campaign, but inasmuch as this region sustained Jubal Early's rebel raiders, other "delicate but necessary" orders of Sheridan may well have been lawful "military necessity." (*Personal Memoirs of P.H. Sheridan* [New York, 1888], 1, 380, 485).

81. See p. 16 for my argument and evidence on this score.

82. Arthur Bryant, *Unfinished Victory* (London, 1940), 3, 9-10; Fuller, *Conduct of War,* 178.

83. S. Hsü, *War Crimes of the Japanese* (Shanghai, 1938), 169-70; Toland, *Rising Sun,* I, 63; Sheldon Glueck, "War Criminals . . . ," *op. cit.,* 65-125; Stein, *Waffen SS,* 42, 76, 92, 126, 133, 136; Fuller, *Conduct of War,* 280; Churchill, quoted in Angus Calder, *"The People's War": Britain 1939-1945* (New York, London, 1969), 491. Compare Kingdom of Belgium War Crimes Commission, *War Crimes . . . The Destruction of the Library of the University of Louvain* (Liege, 1946); Toland, *Last 100 Days,* 155, 156 (on the provocative language of some Soviet war leaders and propagandists); and C. W. Sydnor, Jr., *Soldiers of Destruction* (Princeton, 1977).

84. E. Andrade, "Submarine Policy in the U.S. Navy, 1919-1941," *Military Affairs* (April 1971), 55; William Bosch, *Judgement on Nuremberg* (Chapel Hill, N.C., 1970), 174; Address to the Nation of President Truman, August 9, 1945, quoted in Robert Tucker, *The Just War: A Study in Contemporary American Doctrine* (Baltimore, 1960), 21-22.

85. Gabriel Kolko, in *Crimes of War,* Kolko et al., eds. (New York, 1971), 404; Raphael Littauer and Norman Uphoff, eds., *The Air War in Indochina,* rev. ed., (Boston, 1972), vii, 9, 82n, 91 ff.; Michael Krepon, "Weapons Potentially Inhumane: The Case of Cluster Bombs," *Foreign Affairs* 53 (April 1974): 595.

86. Chester Cooper, *The Lost Crusade* (New York, 1970), 262; Lifton, *Home from the War,* 359.

87. Predictably, military personnel (N = 128) were less willing to fight without air support (80 percent said they would call in the air strike) than the random sample of Pennsylvania males (62 percent), the *civilian* Pentagon officials (63.5 percent), or the Council on Foreign Relations members (56 percent). As with the "Cobra Strike" and "electronic battlefield" situations discussed in this chapter, this difference in responses would suggest that civilians (especially *elite* civilians) may well expect more of military men regarding observance of the laws of war than military men are inclined to deliver.

88. Littauer and Uphoff, *op. cit.,* 163n; *Air University Review* (January-February 1968), 2-9; Herman, *Atrocities in Vietnam,* 82; Tucker, *The Just War,* 59; Lifton, *op. cit.,* 349.

Branfman claims that the American Ambassador to Laos told him: "You gotta understand, Fred—We had all those planes coming in to Laos [because of the November 1968 pause in the bombing of North Vietnam]. What could we do? We had to bomb villages" (Lifton, *loc. cit.,* 350). Incredible! (If credible.)

89. Jonathan Schell, *The Military Half* (New York, 1968), 181; personal interviews; David Binder, Special to the *New York Times*, "Equipment Flaw Hinted in 2nd Raid" (August 7, 1973); Littauer and Uphoff *op. cit.*, 158*n*, 159*n*.

90. Wulff, in Duffett, ed., *Against the Crime of Silence*, 531; Hoopes, *The Limits of Intervention* (1969), 116, passim.

91. Command and General Staff College "Symposium on Officer Responsibility," April 21, 1975, p. 5.
A better illustration of this behavioral distance between distant, relatively safe policy makers and commanders on the one hand, and insecure field unit "grunts" on the other, may be that of John Sack's account of the burning of a village in his journalistic novel of an infantry company in Vietnam (*M* [1966], 141). In this excerpt, the battalion commander ('Smoke") is circling above the battlefield in a helicopter:

Not far away, Morton was burning down Vietnamese houses, having been asked to. *"Stop burning all those houses!"* Smoke yelled into his radio, hitting the ceiling (the plexiglass, rather) half a mile above Demirgian's helmet. "Stop burning down those houses!" Smoke told his captains by radio. "There's no VC in those houses!" The captains told their lieutenants don't burn the houses if there's no VC in them — the sergeants told their men go and burn those houses, there may be VC in them — and Morton kept striking his C-ration matches. Or something or other — anyhow, soon there wasn't a Vietnamese farmhouse that wasn't just a layer of smoldering black dust.

92. Hart, in *Naval War College Review* (September-October 1972), 31-32; Paust, *loc. cit.* (January-February 1973), 104 (quoting Hart).

93. Grinker and Spiegel, *Men Under Stress*, 35; Harry Maule, ed., *A Book of War Letters* (New York, 1943), 321; personal interviews.
Compare Sergeant H____'s World War II fascination with the B-24's capabilities to Sergeant K____'s Vietnam-era satisfaction with the Starlight sniper scope: "It was like watching a TV" (personal interview).

94. Howard Zinn, *The Politics of History* (Boston, 1970), 259, 264-65, 273.

95. Stanley Milgram, *Obedience to Authority* (New York, 1974).

96. Lifton, *Home from the War,* 349; Stone, *Legal Controls of International Conflict* (New York, 1954), 339, quoted in Guenter Lewy, "Superior Orders, Nuclear Warfare, and the Dictates of Conscience," in Richard Wasserstrom, ed., *War and Morality* (Belmont, Calif., 1970), 130.

97. Personal interviews; Stanley Gold and Lawrence Smith, "Interrogation Under the 1949 POW Conventions," *Military Law Review* 21 (July 1963): 153 (an article that is basically admirable and sound but that may have led some to believe that the law regarding POWs was not going

to be applied strictly); *Naval War College Review* (September-October 1972), 36 (following the thoughtful, if not entirely persuasive article by Lt. Col. Franklin Hart, USA, "Yamashita, Nuremberg and Vietnam; Command Responsibility Reappraised," *loc. cit.,* 19-36). Captain Jordan Paust complained to the editors of their choice of quotation in a brilliantly drawn letter, but the editors defended their choice of Smith's words with the claim that they were "stimulating thought." I take it that they do not view the *ius belli* as settled policy.

98. Verb (colloquial), meaning to cause attrition.

99. Frances Fitzgerald, *Fire in the Lake* (New York, 1972), 344; *New York Times Magazine* (September 19, 1965), 136. In any event Komer *definitely* called the laws of war "largely irrelevant" (*American Society of International Law 66th Proceedings* [1972], 195).

100. Major General George Prugh, *Law at War: Vietnam, 1964-1973* (Department of the Army, 1975), 74-77; Hart, *op. cit.,* 43; O'Brien, *Georgetown Law Review* 60 (February 1972): 606; *U.S. News & World Report* (June 30, 1975), 41.

101. Parks, *GI Diary,* 107; Bill Adler, ed., *Letters from Vietnam* (New York, 1967), 37.

102. *Winter Soldier Investigation,* 75; Lane, *Conversations,* 159; Broughton, *Thud Ridge* (Philadelphia, 1969), 76; personal interview with former N.S.A. official "X."

103. Duffett, ed., *Against the Crime of Silence,* 419, 452-53, 434; Polner, *No More Victory Parades,* 113. See also Red Cross Society of China, *Out of Their Own Mouths* (Peking, 1952), a similar effort during the Korean War to brand American policy makers as war criminals that failed for the same reason: All of the printed admissions of wrongdoing were descriptions of unmistakably personal volition. Compare E. Herman, *Atrocities in Vietnam,* 67.

Jean Paul Sartre has charged that the United States deliberately committed genocide in Vietnam (Duffett, *op. cit.*); this charge is analyzed most effectively by Hugo Adam Bedau in Virginia Held, ed., *Philosophy, Morality and International Affairs* (New York, 1974).

104. Thompson to the editor of *Newsweek* (July 17, 1972).

105. Helmer, *Home from the War,* 197, 199, 202.

106. Keen, *Law of War in the Late Middle Ages,* 190; *The Chronicles of an Old Campaigner: M. de la Colonie, 1692-1717,* trans. W. C. Horsley (London, 1904), 174.

107. *Journals of Major Robert Rogers* (New York, 1961 [originally published 1765]), 93, 105, 126; Montross, *op. cit.,* 354. Compare Lewis, *Captain Sam Grant,* 180; R. Asprey, *War in the Shadows* (New York, 1975), I, 106.

108. Gordon, *Reminiscences of the Civil War,* 308.

109. Robert F. Kennedy, *Thirteen Days* (New York, 1969), 14-15, 127.

110. J. K. Miriithi, *War in the Forest* (Nairobi, 1971), 50. Despite the orders, Miriithi used his own judgment. At one point he "drew a bead" on one foe and "was already squeezing the trigger" when he "sud-denly . . . realized what I was about to do and a cold sweat broke out on me. The baby [that the man was carrying], I knew, whatever the crime of the Home Guard [that is, native collaborator] father, was innocent; I turned and fired without aiming into the camp . . ." (*ibid., 73*).

111. John Bagot Glubb, *A Soldier with the Arabs* (London, 1957), 81, 211, 286-87, 309, 318-20; Erskine Childers, "The Other Exodus," *The Spectator* (May 12, 1961), 672-75; Charles Foles, ed., *The Memoirs of General Grivas (New York, 1965), 43*.

112. Leon Trotsky, *Their Morality and Ours* (1969 Merit ed.), passim; Hans Werner Bracht, "Kriegsrecht and Ideologie," *Revue de Droit penal Militaire et de Droit de la Guerre* 6, no. 2 (1967): 359-406. Compare Lenin, "Partisan Warfare," *Proletarier* (December 13, 1906): "Marxism is pre-pared to adopt any form of strife providing the means achieve the end. . . . Marxism . . . does not pretend to lay down for [partisans] rules of combat." See also G. Ginsburgs, " 'Wars of National Liberation' and the Modern Law of Nations—The Soviet Thesis," *Law and Contemporary Problems* 29 (1964), 910-942, esp. 935.

But see the Soviet Union's proposed new article that would extend "without any discrimination to all victims of the conflict without regard to the causes espoused by the party to which they belong" (*Report of the U.S. Delegate to the Diplomatic Conference . . .* [July, 1975], 98).

113. Mao Tse-tung, *Yu Chi Chan* [*On Guerrilla Warfare*] (1937); Mao, "The Military Problem," in William J. Pomeroy, ed., *Guerrilla Warfare & Marxism* (New York, 1968), 173; Winston, "Unity and Militancy for Free-dom and Equality," *Political Affairs* (February 1968): 7. Compare John Armstrong, ed., *Soviet Partisans in WW II* (Madison, Wis., 1964), 188-89; and Pomeroy, "Philippines: The Mass Base," in Pomeroy, *loc. cit.,* for other examples of orders to socialist revolutionary forces to respect local persons and property.

114. Ramon Bonachea and Marta San Martín, *The Cuban Insurrec-tion, 1952-1959* (New Brunswick, N.J., 1974), 37, 90, 193, 197; Hugh Thomas, *Cuba* (New York, 1971), 840-43, 940, 998, 999, 1202.

115. MacArthur, commenting on General Yamashita, cited by Jordan Paust, *Naval War College Review* (January-February 1973), 106.

116. Walker, *History of Laws of Nations,* I, 41; Stanley Layne-Poole, *Saladin and the Fall of the Kingdom of Jerusalem* (Beirut, 1964), 224-34; Montross, *op. cit.,* 369; F. P. Crozier, *The Men I Killed* (London, 1937), 121; Toland, *Last 100 Days,* 156, 355; Toland, *Rising Sun,* I, 398; Alexander

Dallin, *German Rule in Russia, 1941-1945* (London, 1957), 73n. Compare Cyril Falls, *The Art of War* (London, 1961), 148.

117. Marcus Cunliffe, *Soldiers and Civilians* (Boston, 1970), 270-71.

118. Robert Ege, *"Strike Them Hard"* (1970), 68-69, 139-45; Max Heyman, *Prudent Soldier* [Canby] (Glendale, Calif., 1959), 123, 131; Robert Utley, *The Last Days of the Sioux Nation* (New Haven, Conn., 1963), 224-25n; Utley, *Frontiersmen in Blue* (New York, 1970), 101n, 173, 236, 256, 295, 330-31. Compare Thomas Leonard, "Red, White, and Army Blue," *American Quarterly* 25 (1974): 176-90; Paul Wellman, *Death on the Prairie* (New York, 1934), 21n.

James Combs told the Court of Inquiry that Colonel Chivington had told him: "I long to be wading in gore" (Representative of the Secretary of War, 39th Cong., 2nd sess., Senate Document 26, *Sand Creek Massacre Inquiry* [1867], 117).

119. Batson folder, diary entry for September 24, 1899, Spanish-American War Survey, Military History Research Collection, Carlisle Barracks.

120. Grinker and Spiegel, *Men Under Stress*, 307; Herbert, *Soldier*. Compare Lifton, *Home from the War*, 58.

Ex-navy hospital corpsman Gary Giaminoto's complete veracity has been questioned by Neil Sheehan (*New York Times Book Review*, December 27, 1970, p. 5), but he was with the marines in Vietnam, and the volunteered remarks that follow (from Lane, *Conversations*, 212) could not be said to have strengthened any "case against the military" that might have inspired the rest of his account. Hence these barely literate remarks, relevant to what we have said of professional officers and irregular soldiers, may be quite credible: ". . . it was really, you know, the officers, the captain, the CO, whoever it was that yelled back, you know. 'Stop burning the villages down,' but you know it didn't really do too much good because these men, that's the way they felt, you know. They didn't know."

121. Robin Higham, ed., *Bayonets in the Streets*, (Lawrence, Kans., 1969).

122. Burgoyne, in Peter Force, ed., *American Archives* (Washington, D.C., 1837), I, 1620; *Obedience*, a film produced by Stanley Milgram and released by New York University Film Library, 1965; Milgram, *Obedience to Authority* (New York, 1974), 47, 185, passim; von Blomberg, quoted in Hans Gisevius, *To the Bitter End* (Boston, 1947), 355 (the remarks were made before the war began); Dwight McDonald, *The Root Is Man* (1953), 10.

123. Compare Kelman and Lawrence, "Assignment of Responsibility . . . ," *op. cit.*, passim.

124. Arthur Bryant, *Unfinished Victory* (London, 1940), 18; H. Deutsch, *Conspiracy Against Hitler*, 179n; Alexander Dallin, *German Rule in Russia*

(London, 1957), 515; Gene Sharp, *The Politics of Nonviolent Action* (Boston, 1973), 320-25. Compare Milgram, *Obedience to Authority,* 159, for evidence that Milgram's obedient subjects were prompting the victim in order to avoid the dilemma of giving him shocks.

Sometimes the protest is made to a political figure far from the scene. Obviously, this is not likely to solve the immediate problem confronting the soldier, but it is sometimes effective in the last resort as a means of alerting responsible civilians to wrongdoing, initiating prosecutions, and reducing the likelihood of future crimes. Ronald Ridenhour's letters to congressmen are known to have precipitated the My Lai investigation. Letters from soldiers in the Philippines led to a similar investigation in 1900. (See, for example, Leon Wolff, *Little Brown Brother,* 274-75; "To Bomb or Not to Bomb," *Newsweek* [May 14, 1973]; Seymour Hersh, "Senators Are Told U.S. Bombed Cambodia Secretly . . . ," *New York Times* [August 8, 1973]; *Against the Crime of Silence,* 517.)

125. *United States* v. *Captain L____ G____,* USA, CM 420332.

126. Bullard, "Cardinal Vices . . . ," *Journal of the Military Service Institution* 36 (1905); Wilfried Strik-Strikfeldt, *Against Stalin and Hitler* (New York, 1973), 30, 170; Toland, *Rising Sun,* I 368; personal interviews; *New York Times* (November 21, 1970), letters to editor; Heinl, "The Collapse of the Armed Forces," *Armed Forces Journal* 118 (June 7, 1971): 30-38.

127. And if one's superior was well regarded, reporting him for ordering violations of the laws of war could be dangerous too: Captain Si Soule testified against his commanding officer Colonel J. M. Chivington at the investigation of the Sand Creek massacre. Shortly thereafter he was murdered, as was the officer who captured his murderer (Stan Hoig, *The Sand Creek Massacre* [Norman, Okla., 1961], 164-65).

128. Robert O. Paxton, *Parades and Politics at Vichy* (Princeton, 1966), 177.

129. Dallin, *German Rule in Russia,* 76n; Gray, *The Warriors,* 185-86; Fredborg, *Behind the Steel Wall* (New York, 1944), 234; Les Evans, ed., *Disaster in Chile* (New York, 1974), 239-49. Compare the Yugoslav film *Joseph Schultz,* which celebrates the courage of one such *Wehrmacht* soldier.

130. Jacques van Doorn, *Soldiers and Social Change,* 137.

131. James Finn, ed., *Conscience and Command* (1970), 246; Jeff Needles, quoted in Lifton, *Home from the War,* 313. The most famous courts-martial of this kind were probably those of Captain Howard Levy (concerning the training of Green Beret medics) and Captain Dale Noyd (concerning the air war). Professor Gary Wamsley speaks of an earlier case of an air force graduate of officer-training school (OTS), a nuclear

weapons control officer, who had refused to arm nuclear weapons whose most likely destinations were to be Soviet cities. See also the refusal of Captains Dwight Evans and Michael Heck to participate in the December 1972 carpet bombing of Hanoi and Haiphong. Heck believed that the "goals do not justify mass destruction and killing" and that "a man has to answer to himself first." Three junior officers on the *Coral Sea* submitted public resignations in November 1971 noting their moral obligations, and numerous air force and navy enlisted personnel indicated similar reservations. See David Cortright, *Soldiers in Revolt* (New York, 1975), 110, 112, 134 ; *New York Times* (January 12, 1973), 1.

132. Cartwright to Howe, February 6, 1776, Frances D. Cartwright, *The Life and Correspondence of Major Cartwright* (London, 1826), 1, 76.

133. John Mahon, *The Second Seminole War* (Gainesville, 1968), passim; Lewis, *Captain Sam Grant,* 137, 159; W. A. Croffut, ed., *Fifty Years in Camp and Field: The Diary of Major General Ethan Allen Hitchcock* (New York, 1909), 111, 123, 198, 203, 214, 218, 225-29, 395, passim; *Chronicles of the Gringos,* 27.

134. M. DeW. Howe, ed., *Marching with Sherman,* 53, 62, 87, 93, 125.

135. Levinson, in Marshall Cohen et al., eds., *War and Moral Responsibility* (Princeton, 1974), 144.

136. Crozier, *Ireland Forever* (London, 1932), 90-91.

137. Harold Deutsch, *The Conspiracy Against Hitler in the Twilight War* (Minnesota, 1968), 29-31; Margaret Boveri, *Treason in the 20th Century* (London, 1956), 242-43; Mother Mary Alice Gallin, *German Resistance to Hitler,* 45; Hans Gisevius, *To the Bitter End* (Boston, 1947), 280-83.

138. Deutsch, *Conspiracy,* 185; Alexander, "War Crimes . . . ," *Journal of Criminal Law and Criminology* 38 (1948): 321-22.

139. Personal interviews with retired Colonel Harry Latimer and "X"; Peter Petersen, *Against the Tide* (New Rochelle, 1974), 193, 194.

140. See, for example, "Guardsman at Kent State Wins Ruling for Discharge," *New York Times* (October 3, 1971).

141. Raymond Schmandt, "The Fourth Crusade and the Just-War Theory," *Catholic Historical Review* 61 (1975): 191-221; personal interview with Czeslaw Raczkowski; Daniel Lang, *Patriotism Without Flags* (New York, 1974), passim; Edward R. Sowdens, "Surrender," *The Progressive* (July 1973), 37.

142. Carleton McCarthy, *Detailed Minutiae of Soldier Life in the Army of Northern Virginia* (Richmond, 1888).

143. Hans Bernd Gisevius, *To the Bitter End* (Boston, 1947), 335, 463; Joachim Kramarz, *Stauffenberg* (trans. N.Y., 1967), 71-72, 148; Royce et al., eds., *Germans Against Hitler: 20 July 1944,* 248.

144. Kramarz, *Stauffenberg,* 148, 153, 185; Mary A. Gallin, *Resistance to Hitler,* 20, 30-31; Gordon Zahn, *The Military Chaplaincy (1969),* 206.

145. H. Deutsch, *Hitler and his Generals* (Minneapolis, 1974), 42, 45-49; Deutsch, *Conspiracy Against Hitler* (Minneapolis, 1968), 35-36, 49; Hans Gisevius, *To the Bitter End,* 468-69, 473; Royce et al., eds., *Germans Against Hitler,* 176-78; Erich Raeder, *Mein Leben* (Tubingen, 1956-57), II, 294; Walter Baum, "Marine Nationalsosialismus und Widerstand," *Vjh für Zeitgeist* 11 (1963): 16-48; "Steiff," *op. cit.,* passim; Fabian von Schlabrendorff, *Offizierne gegen Hitler* (Zurich, 1946), passim. Compare Colonel A. A. Afrifa, *The Ghana Coup* (London and New York, 1966), 52, 72, 95, 99, 104.

146. Deutsch, *Conspiracy Against Hitler,* 75, 95, 320. Compare the account of anti-Nazi *Wehrmacht* officers in Soviet POW camps who organized a League of German Officers and sought to persuade their colleagues still fighting in the *Wehrmacht* to overthrow the Nazis: Bodo Scheurig, *Freies Deutschland, das Nationalkomitee und der Bund Deutscher Offiziere, 1943-1945* (Muenchen, 1961).

147. Gray, *The Warriors,* 185.

148. E. S. Wallace, "The Battalion of Saint Patrick in the Mexican War," *Military Affairs* 14 (1950): 84-91; Diary of Charles Harris, pp. 66-68, Harris Folder, 42nd U.S. Volunteers Box, Spanish-American War Survey, U.S. Military History Research Collection, Carlisle Barracks; Willard Gatewood, *"Smoked Yankees"* . . . (Urbana, Ill., 1971), 15.

149. A. P. Ryan, *Mutiny at the Curragh* (New York, 1956), 211; R. Meinertzhagen, *Middle East Diary* (New York, 1960), 3-4, 19, 48, 66, 84, 222; Christopher Sykes, *Orde Wingate* (London, 1959), 35, 39, 48, 112, 163, 170, 194, 197; Robert Paxton, *Parades and Politics at Vichy* (Princeton, 1966), passim; Winfried Strik-Strikfeldt, *Against Stalin and Hitler* (trans. New York, 1973), 89, 165. Compare the *Penkovskiy* Papers, Introduction by Frank Gibney (Garden City, N.Y., 1965), 56-57, 205, 309, 358.

CHAPTER 3

Some Conclusions and Recommendations

Where are we at this point in our analysis? We have explored the evolution of the laws of warfare and have noted the concern of its proponents with practical, damage-limiting principles. We have considered a number of violations and observances of these laws in order to learn why such violations occur and have organized them into two groups—the "internal" (personality traits, character deficiencies, ethnocentric and ideological value systems) and the "external" (the combat environment, the quality of leadership, the nature of certain weapons). I have commented on the significance of socioeconomic status, child-rearing practices, insecurity, military socialization, frustration-aggression, fear, revenge, misperception, cognitive dissonance, professionalism, technology, racism, and ideology, and have examined the options open to the conscience-stricken soldier who is confronted with illegal superior orders. It remains for me to advance a series of policy recommendations designed to reduce the likelihood that violations of the laws of war will occur in the future and to increase the clarity and effectiveness of such laws. I conclude with additional observations that an analysis of my data leads me to believe are valid.

SOME RECOMMENDATIONS

Screen recruits, in order to identify persons predisposed to commit war crimes, and remove from combat zones persons whose behavior indicates that they may be on the verge of committing war crimes.   One would have thought that this was being done, at least in the military systems of the more advanced countries where psychological testing skills are readily available to military elites. In the United States, for example, the Human Resources Research Office (HumRRO) has for decades provided psychological services for the army, and similar groups serve the navy and the air force. HumRRO has developed techniques for identifying "fighters" and "leaders" among recruits and trainees.[1] But they have not, as yet, been directed to help identify potential Calleys. Brig. C. N. Barclay assumes that "our modern psychiatric techniques for prejuding behavior under stress" has enabled modern military systems to keep from the front lines all but "a few" who "lose all ability to judge clearly" in combat "and act only on impulse." Unfortunately, he is mistaken. Stephen Herbits, a former Department of Defense official (Manpower and Reserve Affairs), referred recently to a "moral standards" requirement of all enlistees but immediately confessed that "this means checking into a candidate's police record. If he has more than six moving-traffic violations in a year, he can't get in unless he has a special waiver."[2] The degree to which hard-pressed recruiters are "checking into a candidate's police record" has recently been questioned. In any event, the "moral standards" test appears to be somewhat crude.

Every military system ought to be using as sophisticated a screening device as possible (preferably in "boot camp," where recruits can be carefully observed) to reduce the likelihood that sadists and men prone to lose self-control be allowed to exercise life-or-death control over prisoners and noncombatants. Obviously, such a measure would not eliminate all war crimes. But if turning away the 1 or 2 percent who do not measure up resulted in only a modest reduction in such crimes, it would be well worth the effort.

Some might argue that the identification and removal from

combat billets of atrocity-prone soldiers may coincidentally result in the removal of "good leaders" or "good fighters." We very much doubt it. In the first place, what kind of a leader wantonly and unnecessarily injures helpless or innocent persons? In the second place, the background and personality characteristics that HumRRO found "fighters" to possess differ greatly from those that we have herein found to characterize our "violators." In any event, the loss of a few "fighters" or "leaders" would be a small price to pay, and one that *should* be paid, to eliminate a more substantial number of atrocity-prone individuals from the front lines.

Admittedly, it is no easy task to identify potential "violators" from a series of questions or tests put to every recruit.[3] But one would have thought that combat veterans sent to psychiatric units for attention and care would be more easy to screen. After all, they have already demonstrated some inability to cope with the stress of combat. Yet many were returned to combat in Vietnam, and one army psychiatrist maintains that "there is no medical or psychiatric follow-up on the boys after they've returned to duty. No one knows if they are the ones who . . . gun down unarmed civilians. . . . The army doesn't seem to want to find out." If this is true, it is hard to understand. Army Medical Corps personnel could still be able to correlate evidence of psychiatric care and combat behavior in Vietnam. It is not too late to interview squad and platoon leaders, to check disciplinary records, to reinterview ex-patients. We ought to know more of the behavior of ex-psychiatric patients released to return to combat.

Provide more elaborate and sophisticated training in the laws of warfare. Surely this is something that could be done in every nation in the world today.[5] Given my own proclivities and sources of information, I shall focus the discussion somewhat arbitrarily on the U.S. military, though I do not mean to imply that additional training is not needed in the military of other nations.

In fact, the training on the laws of warfare offered within the modern U.S. military is more substantial than that offered in a number of other nations. But that isn't to say that it is unexceptionable. General James Woolnough, the man responsible for the army's school system in the late 1960s, maintains that "we had as adequate instruction [in the laws of warfare] before [My Lai] as we could have."[6] However, prior to My Lai, U.S. ground forces received only one hour of training in the laws of warfare before being sent into combat, and the air force offered no instruction whatsoever! General Woolnough feels that such time as was devoted to such training "has to be taken from something else," and is "not profitably spent" inasmuch as "you cannot teach judgement. There is no black and white rule you can lay down." The ill-fated American Division had *scheduled* an hour of instruction on the Geneva Conventions as part of a day of training in Vietnam several months before the My Lai massacre, but an Army Inspector General's report of July 31, 1968, scored the American as deficient in such instruction; it would appear that someone had decided that the hour to be devoted to the laws of warfare would not be "profitably spent," inasmuch as it would have to be "taken from something else." Kurt Baier has put it well: "A society prepared to turn men like Calley into officers incurs an additional responsibility to make clear to them the distinctions they are supposed to draw particularly if society seriously intends later to charge them with failure to do so."[7]

As a result of the disclosure of the My Lai massacre, the ensuing Peers Commission Inquiry, the resultant courts-martial, and the VVAW's "Winter Soldier" hearings, the U.S. military has begun to give more serious attention to instruction in the laws of warfare. The army has made six fine training films, and it has increased to two hours the instruction on the laws of warfare* offered in basic career officer schools. More significantly, this instruction is now to be offered *both* by an army legal officer from the Judge Advocate General's staff *and* by an officer having combat experience.[8] The presence of the former is, of course, an important assurance that the instruction and responses to questions are accurate and complete, but the addition of a combat veteran should add authority and credence to the classroom setting—that is, unless one of the instructors construes his mission to be that of a debater. If the two offer mutual *support* for the laws of warfare as they describe, define, and illustrate them, the instruction should be more effective than if one acts as if these laws are insufficiently clear, or as if these are unnecessary hindrances.

Woolnough feels that the Pentagon has "over-reacted"to My Lai and that this added attention to the Geneva Convention is unwarranted.[9] Another view is that although the Army is on the right track, it has not yet moved far enough. The films, although admirable, are inadequate as vehicles for the instruction of enlisted recruits, noncommissioned officers, and officer candidates. It is certainly desirable that career officers receive ample instruction, but it is just as important that all lower-ranking personnel receive similar, expert legal instruction. After all, it has often been the private, the sergeant, or the lieutenant who has made on-the-spot decisions to harm persons who should have been protected by the laws of warfare. Col. Jared Schopper has argued that an instruction manual be prepared to complement the films.[10] The Army's Training and Doctrine Command has been using a twenty-eight-page pamphlet, *Your Conduct in Combat Under the Law of War* (TRADOC Pam 27-1), for over two years. Written by the International Law Division of the Army's Judge Advocate General School, this is a clear and superb statement of the laws and could be rewritten slightly to incorporate questions relating to the films. It could then be made a part of a four-hour unit led by judge advocate general (JAG) officer-combat veteran teams assigned the mission of instructing *all* personnel, and especially all combat arms personnel.

If the Army is on the "right track," the Air Force may be said—at last!—to have left the "switching yards." Defense Department Directive 5100.,77 of November 5, 1974, which requires that servicemen learn the rules of warfare ("the extent of such knowledge to be commensurate with their duties and responsibilities"), evoked two memos from the office of the Air Force Judge Advocate General to all air force judge advocates. By March 1977, the Air Force had available three new films dealing specifically with the laws of warfare. It has finally ordered the creation of teaching materials on these laws. Judge advocates were referred to an air force compilation of relevant U.S. treaties (AFP 110-20) and a collection of essays on "the law applicable to air operations," and were directed to "familiarize themselves" thoroughly with their contents in order that they might fulfill their obligations "as legal advisors to [their immediate] commander in areas of the law of particular importance to him." They were also told of a draft version of a new pamphlet dealing with the laws of warfare.[11]

There have been one or more draft versions of the Laws of Air Warfare in circulation within the air force since at least the late 1950s. Will Carroll, the Deputy Chief of the Air Force Judge Advocate General's International Law office, was one of those who wrote one of the early draft versions. I'm sure he was pleased when the pamphlet appeared, but in conversation he defended the record: The Air Force did not really *need* such a manual. "What good would it do for someone in an F4 [air force jet] at Mach 2? Moreover, there are many professionals who function without manuals." A senior air force officer had a very different reason for feeling that his service could do without such a manual. "I'll put it to you frankly. If they come out with a book on the laws of air warfare, and then *go* by it, we're all going to be out of jobs." Such a manual would have to point out that the "political," "strategic," or "terror" bombing of targets essentially without intrinsic military value was illegal. It would also have to explain that long-range weapons fired at tremendous speeds could only be employed in a lawful fashion if there were adequate means of verifying (1) that the targets designated for such strikes were lawful targets and (2) that the air controllers were able to guide the strikes to the targets with enough accuracy to ensure that the Principle of Proportionality was not likely to be violated. Such restrictions would *not* put the air force out of business. This particular officer was simply exaggerating. But it might well lead air commanders to define their business somewhat more carefully—to the advantage of those who are pleased to see that the laws of warfare are being adhered to, and to the advantage of those noncombatants who suffer when they are not.

The Air Force intends to delay no more. The pamphlet has been published. It is in many ways admirable, but it has deficiencies. In the first place, it is not an manual, but a "pamphlet" (Air

Force Pamphlet 110-31). It is described on the first page as suggestive but "not directive in nature." In the second place, it is already dated, inasmuch as it appeared before the signing of the new Geneval Protocols. The authors were clearly conscious of the changes in the law being agreed to at Geneva, and they generally reflect these changes faithfully, but their discussion (in chapter 5) of the law regarding aerial bombardment of "dangerous forces," such as dams and dikes, does not strike *this* reader as being consistent with the final language of Geneva (Articles 52-57). In the third place, the pamphlet is designed for an unnecessarily narrow band of air force personnel "particularly concerned" with the laws of war. This pamphlet, or another like it, ought to be used in the training of *all* air force personnel, and especially combat pilots, air controllers, air operations staff officers, and air commanders. (I am told one will be.) Those responsible for these initiatives deserve our thanks and our support. But the process is still fluid and uncertain. It does not as yet include plans for team-teaching by JAG and combat officers. We shall have to wait and see what comes from these beginnings.

Help create a less atrocity-prone combat environment by providing (1) a better weapons development legal review process and (2) better command-and-control procedures. New weapons are constantly being developed and used on the battlefield, but few such weapons have ever been subjected to systematic review by any reasonably objective agency or organization to ascertain whether they conform to existing international law. In the United States, for example, such systematic legal review of weapons was first prescribed in 1975, with the appearance of regulations implementing DOD Instruction 5500.15 of October 16, 1974, an instruction that was itself a direct result of the anticipated adoption of Protocol I of the Diplomatic Conference on the Reaffirmation and Development of International Humanitarian Law Applicable in Armed Conflicts. (Article 36 of that Protocol I spells out the "obligation" of signatories to determine whether any new weapons "would, in some or all circumstances, be prohibited" by any of the laws of warfare.) As is the case with recent developments in the training of military personnel, this move toward the effective legal review of weapons in the development stage is clearly a step in the right direction. But, as with the training developments, it does not go far enough.

Consider, for example, the new air force weapons review process. The air force regulation that implements the review process defines weapons as "mechanisms or devices designed for, or which have the necessary effect of, causing injury or disablement to an adversary, or physical destruction of enemy property." Unfortunately, it thereupon explicitly exempts from legal review items such as "electronic warfare devices not physically destructive or injury producing."[12] If my analysis has been sound, it would appear that some electronic warfare devices used in Vietnam may well have led to the "blind" use of force. They would appear to be proper subjects of such a legal review system. To be sure, it was individuals who, while using such "sensors," may at times have ordered fire inappropriately on noncombatants. Their lack of judgment was the direct or proximate cause of the injuries. But underlying such acts was the nature of the weapons control system itself and the absence of clear and careful commands to and supervision of such operators. The legal review of weapons control devices and their operator manuals may help to reduce injury to protected persons and places; it should not be omitted from any review process.

There is another problem with the legal review of weapons envisioned by Air Force Regulation 110-29 of May 30, 1975. The review process in entirely "in-house," conducted exclusively by air force officers themselves. This is not to say that such in-house review is invariably wrong headed, or that review by an external agency is inevitably more objective. Regulatory and review agencies do have a tendency to treat those whom they regulate or review as their "clients."[13] But a well-designed review agency is still preferable to the in-house review process. The air force regulation in question calls for review by an air force legal officer from the office of the Air Force Judge Advocate General in conjunction with a representative of the Air Deputy Chief of Staff for Research and Development, and specifies that the review must contain "a statement as to the weapon's consistency with applicable international law. . . ." But one must ask how objective such a review can be, given the potential biases and interests of its authors. One must also ask whether such a review is likely to be regarded as credible. One of the first such reviews declared that the proposed use of residual uranium in a particular weapon would be lawful. It probably would be, but how many will believe it? And does not such use of residual uranium merit a formal review by an interested party such as the Arms Control and Disarmament Agency? To be sure, residual uranium is not fissionable, and thus is hardly on a par with an H-bomb, but will other nations accept the distinction? It *is* uranium, and it is highly poisonous, even if it is not being designed to be employed as poison. I hope the use of residual uranium was considered by national security officials other than those within the air force, but my inquiries did not establish that it was. In any event, this case may illustrate the danger of such an in-house review process. And the process becomes more problematic when one considers that the same officer who found the use of residual uranium to be lawful also recently spoke out in defense of the legality of the December 1972 "carpet" bombing of Hanoi.[14] To be fair, he is also an air force JAG officer most active in and enthusiastic about the publication of the new pamphlet on the laws of war. But that is but further cause for alarm, for if one of the air force JAG's more sympathetic officers did not question the legality of the carpet bombings of Hanoi, how careful and objective can we expect the air force JAG's legal review of weapons to be?

The adoption of Protocol I is imminent. Consequently nations will soon be expected to adopt formal review processes with both legal and technical expertise and with the necessary objectivity. In the United States, for example, the Arms Control and Disarmament Agency would appear to be the appropriate reviewing authority *and should be so designated by the next Congress.* Given the rate of modern technological change, one can regrettably expect that a steady stream of new and awesome weapons will be developed. We ought to be ready for them with a review process that will ensure that they conform to the rules of warfare.[15]

On another plane, commanders would reduce the likelihood

of war crimes by becoming more familiar with the laws of war, by drafting their policies and strategies with greater sensitivity to the laws, and by developing more effective command-and-control mechanisms for the supervising and monitoring of those policies and strategies. The commander who avails himself of sound legal advice (behavior expected of combatants under Articles 82 and 87 of Protocol I), who issues clear, lawful orders, and who oversees the execution of those orders by fielding strong criminal-investigating divisions, inspector general units, and other judicial apparat is only doing what is expected of him. Gen. W. T. Sherman was of the opinion that "the presence of one of our regular civilian judge—advocates in an army in the field would be a first-rate nuisance." It is probably true that such persons would indeed have been annoying to a commander like Sherman. Major Hitchcock certainly annoyed him at times, as we have seen. But we need not be guided by counsel from such a sou e. Lawyers and investigators may well be an annoyance on the battlefield, but chiefly to those commanders who are indifferent or hostile to enforcement of the *ius belli*.[16]

How effective were American command-and-control measures during the Vietnam War? Did policy makers and field commanders take those steps that would enable them to gauge the degree to which their orders regarding prisoners and civilians were followed? Did they receive the kind of feedback that would have alerted them to the atrocity-prone character of search-and-clear operations and free-fire zones? Surely some did and others did not. But the questions cannot be answered easily, for the simple reason that no one in a responsible position appears to have posed them. For example, one might have expected that General George Eckhardt's massive study of army command-and-control in Vietnam would have included some discussion of the effectiveness of command-and-control measures with regard to war crimes. After all, General Westmoreland had issued two general orders on the subject. But the Eckhardt volume is silent on the matter.[17] We know that criminal investigators, inspector generals, and judge advocates were hard at work, but we cannot say how well they were supported. More than a few veterans of Vietnam had no idea that criminal-investigating divisions existed and that one might go to them in a last resort to report a crime that one was afraid to discuss with one's superiors or that one's superiors were ignoring.[18] General Prugh's account of courts-martial in the fields suggests that trial and defense counsels suffered from low-priority travel designations in gathering evidence, from high turnover rates, and from a frequent lack of cooperation from those controlling the availability of key witnesses.[19]

Moreover, a reading of those court-martial cases in which military personnel had been charged with mistreating prisoners or noncombatants suggests that some of the law officers (attorneys who judge matters of law as opposed to members of the court who judge matters of fact) were offering the court members dubious or downright bad law in some of their instructions. For example, in *U.S.* v. *Bumgarner* the law officer instructed the court that the accused had a right to kill his prisoners "if he honestly believed that he [or his men] were in imminent danger. . . ." And in *U.S.* v. *Medina* the law officer told the court that a necessary element of the offense charged was "actual knowledge" of the unlawful shootings in My Lai 4: "While it is not necessary that a commander actually see an atrocity being committed, it is essential that he know that his subordinates are in the process of committing atrocities or are about to commit atrocities."

As Leonard Boudin has observed, this instruction to the court constituted a "retreat from the *Yamashita* standard" and was bad law, ignoring as it did that Nuremberg and *Yamashita* principle of command responsibility that specifies that one who "ought to have known" of the crimes of subordinates is just as guilty of dereliction as one who "actually knew" of such crimes if neither takes corrective action.[20] Daniel Ellsberg has said that some policy makers and commanders appeared to have felt a "need *not* to know" what their subordinates were doing—that they behaved as if they did not want to be morally and legally burdened with such knowledge. If so, they were just as guilty as those who did nothing about war crimes of which they *were* fully aware. Every nation can expect its policy makers and military commanders adequately to supervise and monitor the behavior of its armed forces in the field. For some this will mean that criminal-investigating units may have to be made stronger, more credible and more independent of local commanders. For others it may mean that policy makers and commanders will themselves have to take more seriously their responsibilities to observe and enforce the laws of warfare. The commander who issues clear, lawful orders, and then takes steps to see to it that they are obeyed, reduces sharply the likelihood that his forces will commit war crimes, and thus serves mankind as well as his own country.

Help military personnel cope with unlawful orders by taking those steps that will reduce the pressures on subordinates to obey such orders. Telling commanders that they should not issue illegal orders and telling junior officers and enlisted men that they should refuse to obey such orders are not enough. Hanson Baldwin felt that the "loyalty down" which policy makers and commanders owe their subordinates would suffice to preclude these subordinates from being placed in compromising situations,[21] and it is surely true that "loyalty down" does just that—if one's commander has it. Unfortunately, some commanders will probably persist in issuing highly dubious and unconscionable (at times explicitly illegal) orders; some career-minded combatants subordinate to them will continue to "duck the issue" (or "fudge" or "cover-their-ass" or "compromise"); and, consequently, some war crimes will occur and go unreported. As Lieutenant Roger Woodbury, USAF, put it: "Until something is done, the average soldier will continue to be more concerned about his commander's influence over his future rather than about regulations such as the Geneva Conventions."[22]

Something must be done, then, but what? Socialization programs like the Command and General Staff College's annual symposium on officer responsibility certainly will help.[23] A strengthening of in-the-field legal apparat would also help. Independent ombudsmen, free to come and go, hear complaints, and cut through military channels to obtain relief might terrify and infuriate some commanders, but they might also help to solve the problem confronting a combatant in an atrocity-producing situation torn by a crisis of conscience. (The recently-created

Defense Investigative Service, under the control of the Secretary of Defense, is a step in this direction.) Another measure that should increase the career officer's willingness to challenge atrocity-producing orders would consist of changes in the promotion process. At present the career officer's chance at promotion rests on efficiency reports (OERs) made out by his superiors. Some officials, aware of the debilitating and mendacious "cover-your-ass" attitude of many officers and enlisted persons, are now speaking of OERs that would be filled out by peers as well as superiors. To these one might add OERs made out by subordinates (in the fashion of "professor evaluation" forms now used in many universities) in order to gauge one's "loyalty down," among other things.[24] And one might also add elaborate, and impersonal, examinations. All such reforms should serve to reduce both the junior officer's fear of career reprisal and the senior officer's congruent sense of omnipotence. And one desirable result of such alterations in the system of deference to commanders would be an officer corps with more of the courage of its convictions. We are prepared to believe that we have more to gain by helping officers gain such courage than we have to lose, especially with regard to the enforcement of the laws of warfare.[25]

Despite all such measures as those described in the preceding paragraphs, there will surely be some combatants in the future who will feel that their orders are unlawful and who will not be able to persuade their commanders to alter them. Should not there exist some mechanism, some standing panel of ombudsmen independent of the plantiff's own command, before which such persons may speedily present their case? The sheer existence of such a panel should serve to reduce the need for its services, and when its members *were* called upon to advise, or to arbitrate, one can imagine a procedural format that might, in one fashion or another quickly sustain the complainant, support fully the commander, or, while offering some support to both the plaintiff and his commander, facilitate the plantiff's reassignment to another command, or even allow for his resignation from the service altogether. As we have noted earlier, resignation is not as available an alternative as it might be to some, particularly to men of the lower rankings and ratings. One former naval officer and Annapolis graduate has suggested that citizens should "insist that the concept of Duty involve the practice of public resignation by military officers (and civilians) who conclude that their orders involve . . . a violation" of their consciences and higher responsibilities. "It would help mightily," he continued, "if we honored them . . . grandly. . . ."[26] We wholeheartedly agree with these sentiments, but we also agree with Donald Peppers that draftees and lower-level personnel as well.[27] may have need of a similar means of relief from atrocity-producing situations.

We are anxious to see that officers who resign in conscientious protest be honored (and even, in the eighteenth-century British fashion, allowed to return to service at a later time without loss of status), but we can see disadvantages to any arrangement that encourages senior officers to resign, for they, far more than lower-ranking personnel, are able to influence policies and combat behavior by virtue of their positions and authority. The dilemma such an officer may face can, indeed, lead him to believe that the only just, honorable, and wise measure left open to him is resignation. But in thus preserving his own conscience, he may well be consigning numerous subordinates to the very fate from which he is escaping. Hans Gisevius, one of those who conspired against Hitler and survived, put it well:

Once we had discovered somewhere a trustworthy and courageous man and had cautiously established relations with him, it was discouraging to see him step out of the picture, no matter how admirable were the reasons for his resignation. Every key position that was left open was immediately occupied by an adherent of the Nazi system. How could we ever hope to bring about a change in regime if every important position was voluntarily abandoned to the Nazis?

General Beck resigned, but he later attached himself to those, like Admiral Canaris and Colonel Stauffenberg, who chose to fight the Nazis from within. Sometimes a Canaris displays greater judgment, and no less courage, than a Beck.

Encouraging resistance to orders deemed unconscionable is a tricky business; of that we are well aware. Gen. Raoul Salan defended his behavior as a leader of the 1961 coup against the De Gaulle government with the claim that officers like him had learned the propriety of rejecting superior orders that conflicted with one's conscience from the way in which Gaullists had purged the French army in September 1944 of thousands of officers unable to prove that they had taken a pro-Allied position prior to the Normandy invasion.[29] The argument may have been sophistic—may have been invented after the fact in the hope that it would embarrass the Gaullists—but it is telling, none the less. It is one thing to disobey the orders of a tyrant; quite another to disobey those of an elected or duly appointed official in an open society. Whereas "boring from within" might be proper in the former case, resignation would generally seem the more appropriate form of resistance in the latter.

Clarify and further develop the international laws of warfare in ways that will reduce unnecessary suffering for all concerned. Were we to compare the international laws of warfare as they might have been stated in 25 B.C. or A.D. 975 with those in existence and operation in A.D. 1975, and were we to consider the actual improvement in the status of prisoners of war and wounded combatants in the past century or more, we would have to agree that mankind has managed to agree upon, and impose on itself, some substantial wartime restraints. None the less, we need additional restraints and a clarification of some of those already existing.

Fortunately, the Diplomatic Conference on the Reaffirmation and Development of International Humanitarian Law Applicable to Armed Conflicts, which held its final session in Geneva in 1977, has just presented the nations of this world with some of these badly needed clarifications and addenda for formal ratification. One article in Protocol I of the conference prohibits "ecocide, or long-term, widespread and severe damage," to the natural environment. Other articles deal with the "Protecting Power," a neutral nation agreeable to both parties to an armed conflict whose mission it will be to see that the laws of war are observed. Still other articles deal with the definition of a guerrilla (what is and is not expected of such an irregular under the laws of war); the creation by mutual consent of the combatants of demilitarized undefended zones well behind the front lines (a measure designed to protect noncombatants from aerial attack); the immunization from attack of certain "installations containing dangerous forces" such as nuclear power plants, extensive dikes, or dams;[30] and the outlawing of attacks on medical supplies and foodstuffs vital to the survival of a civilian population.[31]

These are admirable rules, to be sure, but others that might have been adopted by the conferees have, to date, either not been given their consideration or have not received their imprimatur. One such measure (the original draft of Protocol II) would "lower the threshold" of civil wars in order to enable the insurgent forces to claim the protection of the various international conventions. This effort to extend protection to insurgents was supported by the United States, Canada, and most of Western Europe, and was opposed by the Soviet Union, Romania, and the Third World (e.g., Brazil, Mexico, Argentina, India, Pakistan, Indonesia, and Nigeria), many of whose governments have recent memories of insurgencies in their own countries. The latter insisted on a "high threshold," weaker Protocol II—one that would require of insurgents a number of substantial acts and measures in order for them to qualify. One would certainly want insurgents to conduct themselves *in fides* and in accordance with the laws of warfare, as we have already said, but the effect of the amendments to Protocol II is to weaken the measure and render it harmless to regimes reluctant to see insurgents granted any international status or immunities.[32]

Another measure would have limited the military objectives considered legitimate targets for aerial bombardment as specifically as possible by listing those targets "of generally recognized military importance" and excluding all others. The list—which included armed forces and their installations, airfields, missile sites, transportation and communication systems "of fundamental military importance," industrial structures engaged in the production, servicing, or storage of weapons, military vehicles, "supplies and material of a military character," and metallurgical, engineering, chemical, and energy plants "whose nature or purpose [or basic function] is essentially military"—was to be "reviewed at intervals of not more than ten years by a group of Experts composed of persons with a sound grasp of military strategy and of others concerned with the protection of the civilian population."[33]

This effort to clarify with regard to aerial bombardment the meaning of the oft-employed term "legitimate military objective" was entirely appropriate, highly desirable, and reasonably well conceived. Its omission from the present protocols is distressing. It appears that the air power nations did not want their airborne "edge" to be sheathed or blunted by a listing such as this.

The present protocols also say nothing new about submarine warfare, and this, too, is unfortunate. World Wars I and II saw numerous instances of submarine attacks upon shipping in which nothing was done to aid the lifeboat survivors. One simple step, harmless to the protection-conscious submariner, would be of great value to the defenseless survivors. After each sinking, all sub commanders should be obliged to release from their torpedo tubes universally accepted devices that, on rising to the surface near the lifeboats, would begin to beam a powerful, standard-frequency electronic distress signal within an hour or two (thus giving the submarine ample opportunity to depart).[34]

Each nation must now prohibit the recruitment on its soil of mercenaries, inasmuch as article 47 of Protocol I outlaws all such combatants. *All recruiting must be made illegal and must be prosecuted.* Eventually, the world community may consider seriously the suggestion that an international criminal court be created with the authority to extradite and try persons accused of grave breaches of the laws of warfare,[35] but that kind of legal institution is unlikely to be found acceptable to nations as fond of their sovereignty as today's; we will probably have to continue to rely upon the nation-states themselves to enforce the *ius belli*. With the continued efforts of the ICRC, the community of international lawyers, and responsible statesmen, these laws can be expected to become clearer, more adequate, and more enforceable.

SOME ADDITIONAL OBSERVATIONS

War crimes are not functional. Quite independent of any consideration of morality or legality, violations of the laws of war do not serve any practical state interests. From a strictly military

Goya's reaction to the French suppression of the Spanish Rising of 1808 was a number of etchings depicting French brutality. This one reads "Yo no hay tiempo!" ["No more time!"]

standpoint, they are simply counterproductive. Mars Westington and Robert Asprey have demonstrated that the generosity and *fides* of commanders like Quintus Sertonius were more effective than brutality in securing the foreign policy objectives of the Roman Republic, and the same may be said of the armies of Mithridates of Pontus, of the ancient Incas, and the early Islamic powers.[36] The mutual recriminations of Spanish and Dutch forces in the sixteenth and seventeenth centuries may have gratified the passions of the respective soldiery, but they served no useful military purposes. Sir James Turner, an English student of warfare, maintained in 1671 that "the fear of bad quarter, of hard and cruel usage, of the breach of Treaties and Articles, hath made many resolve to take no quarter and to chuse to dye fighting." Speaking specifically of "the Turks," who "were accustomed to keep no treaties, but to kill all or most who yielded on [promises]," he noted that these same Turkish soldiers were "finding the breach of [these promises] to be prejudicial to themselves, because it forc'd the Defendants to stand out to the last drop of their blood." The brutalities of Generals Turreau, Boucret, and Westermann did not subdue the rebels of La Vendée in 1792; the even-tempered "good faith" of those who relieved them (Generals Hoche, Kleber, Dutruy, and Vimeux) was clearly more effective. The military characteristics of General Sherman's March were of some significance in the war effort; but there is simply no evidence that the illegal features of the march served any purpose other than that of enraging the enemy. Napoleonic armies in Spain and Portugal stirred similar emotions in Iberian breasts; these emotions clearly accelerated the French departure, whereas the accommodating and scrupulous behavior of General Championnet's command in southern Italy helped to pacify that region. The terrorism of King Tewadros, a nineteenth-century Ethiopian monarch, may have helped him temporarily to cowe his subjects, but its ultimate consequence was the formation of an opposition movement that led to his downfall. The Spanish forces in Cuba in the 1890s and the German troops in Belgium in 1914 may or may not have actually *behaved* brutally, but the charges in America that they did so certainly injured their cause. The excesses of the Royal Irish Constabulary after the 1916 Easter

Rising did not succeed in extirpating the sputtering Sinn Fein movement; but it did accomplish the opposite: An outraged public came to the aid of the Sinn Fein. Similarly, Japanese atrocities drove some potentially receptive Filipinos and Indonesians to bloody guerrilla warfare. The successful counterinsurgencies in Malaya and the Philippines did not rely on terrorism, savage air raids, or open-ended search-and-destroy missions; the unsuccessful counterinsurgent campaigns of the French in Indochina and Algeria (with their air strikes, *zones interdities,* torture, and *regroupment* camps) and the Americans in Vietnam (with much the same sort of atrocity-producing strategies) did. The terrorism employed by the Saigon forces in Long An, like the terrorism of the *Bastistanos* in Cuba, simply served to strengthen the hand of their opponents. The American unit in Vietnam famed for pinning its patch on the foreheads of dead enemy soldiers soon found itself singled out for reprisals of a nature just as offensive to the American soldiers as its own acts were to the Vietnamese.[37] Terrorism and brutality served more often to weaken than to provide an advantage for the military force that used them. And this appears to have been true despite the politics, ideology, and relative strengths of the contending forces.

Signatory nations allying themselves with, or employing the soldiers of, a people who do not accept the laws of warfare bear a heavy measure of responsibility for the behavior of such allies or mercenaries, and are ill advised to enter into such relationships. This sense of responsibility for "savage" allies was clearly in the mind of General Lord Jeffrey Amherst in 1759, for he instructed the officer in charge of Britain's Indian allies during the French and Indian wars to "prevent the Indians from exercising their cruelty" upon French prisoners in the hope that "prisoners may be treated with humanity." Amherst may have been reasonably successful in curbing *his* allies, but his counterparts in 1782 and 1813 were not. In 1782 Arent De Peyster was saddened by the return of Britain's Western allies, the Delaware Indians, to "the old savage custom of putting their prisoners to death, which [custom] with much pains and expense we [thought we] had weaned the Indians from in this neighborhood." He protested to their chiefs that this kind of behavior "will throw an odium upon their friends the English, as well as prevent [us] from receiving the necessary intelligence of the enemy's motions, so essential to carry on the service for [our] mutual interests." A generation later the problem was the same: A captain of British dragoons wrote home in 1813 of Tecumseh and his men: "These savages have no mercy." He added: "We are completely in the savage's power. . . . We have spread a net which may catch us. . . . They are more plague than profit."[38]

The same might have been said of the South Korean and Saigon allies of the United States in Vietnam. Many of these troops openly abused prisoners and engaged in flagrant violations of the rights of noncombatants. Yet it was often American soldiers who had captured the prisoners and had been told by their superiors to turn these prisoners over to the Saigon forces. Article 12 of one of the Geneva Conventions of 1949 says that those who actually capture the prisoner retain the responsibility for his well-being even after he has been released to the forces of an ally.[39] U.S. commanders sometimes ignored this responsibility.

Terrorism is never a proper weapon, and its perpetrators are never above the law.   One of the chief objects of the laws of warfare is to protect innocent noncombatants. Any guerrilla chief who fields a force that cannot be distinguished from the protected civilian population *imperils that population*, and any chief who authorizes or tolerates attacks by his men upon protected persons is both violating the laws and injuring his cause. The Palestinian cause gained recognition chiefly because of the oil boycott, not Munich or Malaat. In this regard, it is worth adding that a guerrilla commander who does not or cannot control his men is also undercutting any claim his own force may have to protected status. Sensible and humane leaders will not allow their troops to attack protected persons. To be sure, the fanatic may insist that the righteousness of his cause justifies the deliberate terrorizing of the innocent and the helpless, that his end justifies his means. But such as have chosen to regard themselves as lawgivers for themselves and the rest of society properly merit the tag "outlaw." Note that we do not have in mind the guererrilla leaders of an oppressed people who seek their freedom from a colonial power or a dictatorial regime and who fight in accordance with the *ius belli*. It is sometimes not easy to ascertain whether a group of rebels represents a just cause, has the support of the populace, and merits protected status, as those debating Protocol II in Geneva in 1974 and 1975 can testify. But it is easier to say whether or not such a group is violating the laws of warfare. An attack upon a military outpost or a secret-police station is one thing; a bomb thrown into a crowded cafe is quite another. We must insist that the distinction be observed.[40]

We must also insist that the military forces of the "developed" world observe the same distinction. The "strategic" bombing of civilian communities void of military persons or defense industries, be it styled "terroristic" or "political," is illegal. It cannot be justified merely because it may help to bring the enemy to the conference table. That is precisely the argument of the urban terrorist, and it is just as reprehensible when employed by superpowers. The language of Protocol I and especially of Article 51 of that protocol now makes it clearer than ever that acts "which have the primary object of spreading terror among the civilian population" will not be allowed. Explicitly prohibited are indiscriminate attacks such as those bombardments "which treat as a single military objective a number of clearly separated and distinct military objectives located in a city, town, village, or other area containing a concentration of civilians or civilian objects" and those that "may be expected to cause incidental . . . injury to civilians . . . , which [injury] would be excessive in relation to the concrete and direct military advantage anticipated" (the Principle of Proportionality). The article also prohibits reprisals directed "against the civilian population." When Protocol I is adopted, the policy maker who chooses to force others to the conference table by means of a "carpet-bombing" raid will be seen to be just as criminal as the person who heaves a bomb into a crowded store.

All nations should observe the laws of warfare, but if some decide to behave less scrupulously than others, those more scrupulous in observance should not decide that they are released from their responsibilities.   The laws of warfare allow for acts of reprisals against *military forces* that persistently violate those laws. But reprisals directed against civilians are prohibited, and (in the language of Article 51 (8) Protocol I) "any violations" of the laws by one side "shall not release the parties to the conflict from their legal obligations. . . ." That some may violate the laws is no reason for others to violate them. After all, the more scrupulous one's forces, the more likely one is to gain the support of uncommitted parties, and the less likely one is to alienate those whose support one has already obtained. Nothing of lasting import is gained by unscrupulous warfare, and much may be lost.

Though one may be distressed by the fact that prisoners are sometimes mistreated, one may find some solace in the fact that the lot of the typical vanquished soldier is considerably better than it was in the days of Aemilius Regillus. Most can reasonably expect to get home eventually in one piece. The laws of warfare may be imprecise and ill enforced, but they are a great deal better than no laws at all. And they are frequently observed, to the relief of helpless and innocent persons everywhere. Moreover, they serve to remind us in our darkest hours that humanity is more than an anthropological term. Their self-enforcing nature may be among the better examples of the Kantian Imperative, and of the Golden Rule, in practice. Until we can manage to abolish war altogether, we shall do well to consider all reasonable ways to limit its damage, and in this regard, we hope this book has presented some useful and feasible ideas to those who must do the more difficult work of translating general recommendations into concrete and workable public policy.

NOTES

1. See Human Relations Resource Office, *Bibliography of Publications . . .* (Washington, D.C., 1969); and Robert Egbert, "Profile of a Fighter," *Infantry School Quarterly* (October 1954).

2. Brigadier Barclay, "The Devil and the Deep Blue Sea: Some Thoughts on the Actions of Regular Troops When Fighting Against Armed Civilians," *Army Quarterly* (October 1970): 71. Herbits, quoted in Bruce Bliven, Jr., "All-Volunteer I," *New Yorker* (November 24, 1975), 85.

Compare LCOL Peter Petersen, *Against the Tide* (New Rochelle, N.Y., 1973), 237; There should be "more emphasis" on the applicant's "psychological qualities."

3. It would be especially difficult to do so were the military to resort to the screening practices employed during World War II. Eli Ginsberg notes that "in many stations the psychiatric evaluation was made by physicians who had had no special training in psychiatry but who were corralled for the job. Many were sensible men who did quite well. Others did not. At one large station, it was several weeks before the authorities caught up with an examiner whose method of psychiatric evaluation consisted of suddenly approaching the nude man standing before him and slapping him very hard on the abdomen; he then purported to assess the man's emotional state on the basis of how high he jumped. Many selectees reported that the sole question they were asked by the examining psychiatrist was, 'Do you like girls?' " (Ginsberg, *The Ineffective Soldier: Vol. I, The Lost Divisions* [New York, 1959], 38).

4. Ron Glasser, *365 Days* (New York, 1971), 178.

5. Moreover, such training ought not be restricted to those within military service. Civilians could one day become soldiers, and as civilians they may find themselves some day in a battlefield or occupation environment. They ought to know their rights *and* their responsibilities. This appears to be the purpose of Article 83 of Protocol I, which calls on signatories "to encourage the study [of the laws of war] by the civilian population."

6. Woolnough oral interview transcripts, I, 6 (February 25, 1971), Oral History Project, U.S. Military Historical Collection, Carlisle Barracks.

7. Colonel Jared Schopper, *Lesson from My Lai* (U.S. Army War College, April 1973); Hamilton De Saussure and Robert Glasser in Peter Trooboff, ed., *Law and Responsibility in Warfare* (Chapel Hill, N.C., 1975), 136; Woolnough, *loc. cit.;* Baier, "Guilt and Responsibility" in Peter French, ed., *Individual and Collective Responsibility* (Cambridge, Mass., 1972), 43.

8. Schopper, *op. cit.;* "What the Army is Doing to Prevent Another My Lai," *U.S. News & World Report* (April 12, 1971), 25; SP5 Tom Bailey, "Judgement on the Firing Line," *Soldiers* 26 (August 1971): 4-7. Compare Colonel Robert Rigg, "Killing or Murder?" *Military Review* (March 1971): 5; Captain Robert Jenkins and First Lieutenant Martin McWilliams, "The Soldier and the Law of War," *Infantry* 61 (November 1971): 22-25.

9. Woolnough oral history, *op. cit.,* I, 6.

10. Schopper, *op. cit.*

11. MGEN Harold Vague, Judge Advocate General, USAF, to All Staff

Judge Advocates, November 21, 1974, and Colonel James Taylor, Director of Civil Law, Office of the Judge Advocate General, USAF, to All Judge Advocates, July 8, 1975.

12. AF Regulation 110-29 of May 30, 1975, p. 1.

13. See, for example, Samuel Huntington, "Clientism . . . ," unpublished Ph.D. dissertation, Harvard University, 1949.

14. LCOL James Miles and LCOL Norman Thorpe in Trooboff, ed., *Law and Responsibility in Warfare,* 145-152. Compare Colonel Jay Terry, *Air University Review* (November-December 1975): 36: ". . . it is useless for the law to wave anachronistic limitations in the face of inexorable technological developments. . . ."

15. This paragraph is primarily concerned with future developments, but any review process should also consider existing weapons. Air Force Regulation 110-29 addresses itself to such weapons, but, once again, one must insist that air force officers do not make the best ex *post facto* judges of the legality of napalm or cluster bombs. The ICRC's Conference of Government Experts on the Use of Certain Conventional Weapons met in 1974 and 1976 to consider the legality of incendiary, small-caliber, blast, fragmentation, and delayed-action weapons in addition to possible weapons of the future, but the Diplomatic conference on the Reaffirmation and Development of Humanitarian Law Applicable in Armed Conflicts did not resolve its disputes regarding the report of these experts. It is still possible that the use of certain existing weapons such as glass or plastic "frag" (which cannot be detected by x-rays), or "blind" mines and "booby traps" will be restricted by an agreement that might emerge at a Conference the U.N. is to call for in 1979. See ICRC, *Conference of Government Experts on the Use of Certain Conventional Weapons* (Lugano, 1976).

16. Sherman, *Memoirs,* II (1875), 397. General George Marshall also maintained that "lawyers and legal complications are inappropriate on a battlefield," but his judgment is also to be doubted on this score. Marshall was a wise administrator, but he acquired none of the experience necessary to lend credibility to such a judgment; he never commanded in combat! Compare Captain Gordon Baldwin, "A New Look at the Law of War . . . ," *Military Law Review* (March 1959): 1; General Woolnough oral history, I, March 4, 1971, p. 39, Military History Research Collection Carlisle Barracks.

17. MGEN George Eckhardt, *Vietnam Studies, Command and Control, 1960-1969* (Department of the Army, 1974). But see the unsolicited recommendations of Colonel Robert Rigg, USA (Ret.), "Killing or Murder," *Military Review* (March 1971): 5.

18. See, for example, Daniel Lang, *Casualties of War* (New York, 1969), 77.

19. General George Prugh, *Law at War: Vietnam* (Department of the Army, 1975), 100-02.

20. *U.S.* v. *Platoon Sgt. Roy Bumgarner, USA,* CM 421583, p. 385; Leonard Boudin, in Trooboff, *op. cit.,* 213.

21. H. Baldwin in *New York Times Magazine* (March 21, 1954).

22. Letter to the editor, *New York Times* (April 4, 1971).

23. See Captain Wesley K. Clark's memo to Major Robert G. Totten. May 4, 1975, concerning the symposium (a memo circulated to all participants), for one officer's opinion.

24. Conversation with MGEN Robert Gard, USA, November 1975; Josiah Bunting, "Conscience of a Soldier," *Worldview* (December 1973). See Petersen, *Against Tide,* 65-66 for information about two successful peer-group evaluations by army and air force officers.

25. But it is also likely that such changes would result in a more responsive and effective officer corps. See Morris Janowitz, "Changing Patterns of Organizational Authority: The Military Establishment," *Administrative Science Quarterly* 3 (1959): 473-93.

26. W. A. Williams, in The *New York Review of Books* (May 6, 1971), 7.

27. D. Peppers, "War Crimes and Induction: A Case for Selective Nonconscientious Objection," *Philosophy and Public Affairs* (Winter 1974): 129-66. Compare the remarks of Judge Wyzanski in *U.S.* v. *Sission,* 297 F. Supp. at 908 (1969).

28. Hans Gisevius, *To the Bitter End* (Boston, 1947), 281-82. Compare Eberhard Zeller, *Der Geist der Freiheit* (München, 1965), 39; and Gordon Zahn, *The Military Chaplaincy* (Toronto, 1969), 143, on the views of one Royal Air Force chaplain: "To resign would be the easy way out."

29. Robert O. Paxton, *Parades and Politics at Vichy,* 424, 440.

30. The immunization of such installations appears necessary, for even though the U.S. government abstained from attacks on North Vietnamese dikes, there were many who called for such attacks. (See, for example, Bem Price, "They Fought in Vietnam with One Hand Tied Behind Their Backs," *U.S. News & World Report* [June 30, 1975], 41).

31. *Report to Secretary of State of the U.S. Delegate to the Diplomatic Conference* . . . (July 1975), passim; Michel Veuthey, "Some Problems of Humanitarian Law . . . ," in M. Bassiouni and V. Nanda, eds., *A Treatise on International Law,* I: *Punishment* (Springfield, Ill., 1973), 425.

32. This version of the fate of Draft Protocol II is essentially based upon conversations with conference participants. Compare Veuthey, "Some Problems of Humanitarian Law in Noninternational Conflicts and

Guerrilla Warfare," in Bassiouni and Nanda, *op. cit.,* 425.

33. Appendix III — ICRC Draft Rules for the Limitation of the Dangers Incurred by the Civilian Population in Time of War, September 1956 (Geneva, 2nd ed., April 1958), art. 6, art. 7, Draft Annex.

34. I don't think the idea is my own; *I think* it was advanced several years ago by another author, but I am embarrassed to say that I have been unable to recall or discover that person's name.

35. R. Bierzanek, "War Crimes: History and Definiton," in Bassiouni and Nanda, *op. cit.,* 585.

Joseph Goldstein, Burke Marshall, and Jack Schwartz have recently argued that the Congress should authorize the U.S. District Court for the District of Columbia to try U.S. soldiers for violations of the laws of war. They maintain that this would overcome the military's inherent institutional reluctance to conduct war crimes trails. (*The My Lai Massacre and Its Cover-up* [New York, Free Press, 1976], 11-15). They are persuasive, and the measure might also solve the problem of how one prosecutes a soldier who has been separated from the service. My only reservations concerning such an innovation concerns the effect it would have upon the military's training and self-policing practices. If the introduction of such an external adversary figure as the U.S. District Court for the District of Columbia were to cause a weakening in the military's self-enforcement of the laws of warfare, then any increase this change produced in the likelihood that violators be punished would not be worth the cost. (It could, of course, have the opposite effect.)

36. Mars Westington, "Roman Atrocities . . . ," 121; Joseph Bram, *An Analysis of Inca Militarism* (New York, 1941), 47; Majid Khadduri, *War and Peace in the Law of Islam* (Baltimore, 1955), 102-05; Walker, *History of Law of Nations,* I, 193-94.

When Mithridates killed some 80,000 Romans in Asia Minor in 88 B.C., he made himself a permanent enemy of Rome. As late as 66 B.C., Cicero was still able to inspire cries for vengeance at the mention of this deed (James Barthelmess, "The Sullan Senate and the Army," unpublished Ph.D. dissertation, University of Washington, 1970, pp. 48, 88).

37. Turner, *Pallas Armata* (London, 1671), 345-46; Peter Paret, *The Vendee, 1789-1796* (Research Monograph no. 12, Princeton Internal War Project, 1961), passim; Donald Crummey, "The Violence of Tewardos," in Bethwell Ogot, ed., *War and Society in Africa* (London, 1972), 65 ff.; *Papers of the Military Historical Society of Massachusetts,* (1895), 148-51; F. P. Crozier, *Ireland Forever* (London, 1932); Cornell Air War Study Group, *Air War in Indochina* (rev. ed. Boston, 1972), 211-16; J. Race, *War Comes to Long An* (Berkeley, Calif., 1972), 196-97; R. Asprey, *op. cit.,* I,

22, 25, 29, 135, 140, 168, 566-88; E. Holt, *Protest in Arms* (New York, 1961), 219, 226. Cf. P. W. Fay, *The Opium War* (Chapel Hill, N.C., 1975), 278-79, 300.

38. *Journal of Major Robert Rogers* (New York, 1961 [originally published 1765]), 93, 126; Cathrine Crary, ed., *The Price of Loyalty* (New York, 1973), 257-58; U.S. Cong. House *Committee appointed to inquire into the Spirit and Manner in which the War has been Waged by the Enemy* (Troy, N.Y., 1813), 164-65. Compare Walker, *op. cit.*, I, 73.

39. See the argument to this effect in O'Brien, *op. cit.*, *Georgetown Law Review* 60 (1972): 650. Compare Jesse Frosch, "Anatomy of a Massacre," *Playboy Magazine* (July 1970): 139, 188.

40. See, for example, L. F. E. Goldie in Peter Trooboff ed., *Law and Responsibility in Warfare* (Chapel Hill, N.C., 1975), 88; Edward Hyanes, *Terrorists and Terrorism* (New York, 1974); Albert Parry, *Terrorism from Robespierre to Arafat* (forthcoming); Michael Waltzer, "The New Terrorists," *The New Republic* (August 30, 1975): 12-14; Denise Bindschedler-Robert, *Report of the Conference on Contemporary Problems of the Law of Armed Conflicts* (New York, 1971), 78 ff. Paust, *op. cit.*, *Military Law Review* (1972): 133; Institute of Law, Academy of Sciences of the USSR, *Soviet International Law Textbook* (1960), 407, 423: ". . . the laws and customs of war apply not only to armies in the strict sense of the world, but also to . . . partisans."

Cobra Strike

You are the flight commander of a Cobra fire team providing support to the armed forces of a developing country. You are in communication with the US advisor to the unit you are supporting. He directs you to attack a target which he identifies as an enemy concentration at specific coordinates. You approach the target and determine that it is in a village occupied by men, women, and children. You observe no weapons and receive no fire. Based on your understanding of the rules of engagement and the rules of land warfare, you determine that you should not attack the target.

You inform the advisor of your decision. He, in turn, passes your message to the ground unit commander (you are OP CON [Operating Control] to the unit). In about two minutes the advisor, senior in rank to you, returns to the radio. He says, "The unit commander has the final authority to clear fire missions in this area and he wants the targets hit. It's his responsibility. You are ordered to hit it."

Since you have no doubt that it is not an appropriate target you refuse to change your decision not to attack the target. However, in order to avoid a confrontation with the advisor, you simply declare a malfunction and low-fuel state, inform the advisor, and return to your base.

The next day, reading the INSUM [Intelligence Summary], you discover that the target you had been given was attacked by artillery ten minutes after you left the area. Forty-five enemy was reported KIA [Killed In Action]. Since the coordinates describe exactly the area you reconnoitered, you suspect that a war crime may have been committed.

1. What is your action now with regard to the report carried in the INSUM?

2. Have you contributed to a possible war crime?

3. Can you analyze the pressures on the advisor who said, "You are ordered to hit it"?

APPENDIX 2

The Enemy in Your Hands

1. *HANDLE HIM FIRMLY, PROMPTLY, BUT HUMANELY.*

The captive in your hands must be *disarmed, searched,* secured and watched. But he must also be treated at all times as a human being. He must not be tortured, killed, mutilated, or degraded, even if he refuses to talk. If the captive is a woman, treat her with all respect due her sex.

2. *TAKE THE CAPTIVE QUICKLY TO SECURITY*

As soon as possible evacuate the captive to a place of safety and interrogation designated by your commander. Military documents taken from the captive are also sent to the interrogators, but the captive will keep his personal equipment except weapons.

3. *MISTREATMENT OF ANY CAPTIVE IS A CRIMINAL OF-FENSE. EVERY SOLDIER IS PERSONALLY RESPONSIBLE FOR THE ENEMY IN HIS HANDS.*

It is both dishonorable and foolish to mistreat a captive. It is also a punishable offense. Not even a beaten enemy will surrender if he knows his captors will tortue or kill him. He will resist and make his capture more costly. Fair treatment of captives encourages the enemy to surrender.

4. *TREAT THE SICK AND WOUNDED CAPTIVE AS BEST YOU CAN.*

The captive saved may be an intelligence source. In any case he is a human being and must be treated like one. The soldier who ignores the sick and wounded degrades his uniform.

5. *ALL PERSONS IN YOUR HANDS, WHETHER SUSPECTS, CIVILIANS, OR COMBAT CAPTIVES, MUST BE PROTECTED AGAINST VIOLENCE, INSULTS, CURIOSITY, AND REPRISALS OF ANY KIND.*

Leave punishment to the courts and judges. The soldier shows his strength by his fairness, firmness, and humanity to the persons in his hands.

Key Portions of the Geneva Protocols of 1977

Protocol Additional to the Geneva Conventions of 12 August 1949, and Relating to the Protection of Victims of International Armed Conflicts (Protocol I)

Geneva, July 1977

PREAMBLE

The High Contracting Parties,

Proclaiming their earnest wish to see peace prevail among peoples,

Recalling that every State has the duty, in conformity with the Charter of the United Nations, to refrain in its international relations from the threat or use of force against the sovereignty, territorial integrity or political independence of any State, or in any other manner inconsistent with the purposes of the United Nations,

Believing it necessary nevertheless to reaffirm and develop the provisions protecting the victims of armed conflicts and to supplement measures intended to reinforce their application,

Expressing their conviction that nothing in this Protocol or in the Geneva Conventions of 12 August 1949 can be construed as legitimizing or authorizing any act of aggression or any other use of force inconsistent with the Charter of the United Nations,

Reaffirming further that the provisions of the Geneva Conventions of 12 August 1949 and of this Protocol must be fully applied in all circumstances to all persons who are protected by those instruments, without any adverse distinction based on the nature or origin of the armed conflict or on the causes espoused by or attributed to the Parties to the conflict,

Have agreed on the following:

Article 1 — General principles and scope of application

1. The High Contracting Parties undertake to respect and to ensure respect for this Protocol in all circumstances.

2. In cases not covered by this Protocol or by other international agreements, civilians and combatants remain under the protection and authority of the principles of international law derived from established custom, from the principles of humanity and from the dictates of public conscience.

3. This Protocol, which supplements the Geneva Conventions of 12 August 1949 for the protection of war victims, shall apply in the situations referred to in Article 2 common to those Conventions.

4. The situations referred to in the preceding paragraph include armed conflicts in which peoples are fighting against colonial domination and alien occupation and against racist régimes in the exercise of their right of self-determination, as enshrined in the Charter of the United Nations and the Declaration on Principles of International Law concerning Friendly Relations and Co-operation among States in accordance with the Charter of the United Nations.

Article 2 — Definitions

For the purposes of this Protocol:

(a) "First Convention," "Second Convention," "Third Convention" and "Fourth Convention" mean, respectively, the Geneva Convention for the Amelioration of the Condition of the Wounded and Sick in Armed Forces in the Field of 12 August 1949; the Geneva Convention for the Amelioration of the Condition of Wounded, Sick and Shipwrecked Members of Armed Forces at Sea of 12 August 1949; the Geneva Convention relative to the Treatment of Prisoners of War of 12 August 1949; the Geneva Convention relative to the Protection of Civilian Persons in Time of War of 12 August 1949; "the Conventions" means the four Geneva Conventions of 12 August 1949 for the protection of war victims;

(b) "rules of international law applicable in armed conflict" means the rules applicable in armed conflict set forth in international agreements to which the Parties to the conflict are Parties and the generally recognized principles and rules of international law which are applicable to armed conflict;

(c) "Protecting Power" means a neutral or other State not a Party to the conflict which has been designated by a Party to the conflict and accepted by the adverse Party and has agreed to carry out the functions assigned to a Protecting Power under the Conventions and this Protocol;

(d) "substitute" means an organization acting in place of a Protecting Power in accordance with Article 5.

Article 5 — Appointment of Protecting Powers and of their substitute

1. It is the duty of the Parties to a conflict from the beginning of that conflict to secure the supervision and implementation of the Conventions and of this Protocol by the application of the system of Protecting Powers, including *inter alia* the designation and acceptance of those Powers, in accordance with the following paragraphs. Protecting Powers shall have the duty of safeguarding the interests of the Parties to the conflict.

2. From the beginning of a situation referred to in Article 1, each Party to the conflict shall without delay designate a Protecting Power for the purpose of applying the Conventions and this Protocol and shall, likewise without delay and for the same purpose, permit the activities of a Protecting Power which has been accepted by it as such after designation by the adverse Party.

3. If a Protecting Power has not been designated or accepted from the beginning of a situation referred to in Article 1, the International Committee of the Red Cross, without prejudice to the right of any other impartial humanitarian organization to do likewise, shall offer its good offices to the Parties to the conflict with a view to the designation without delay of a Protecting Power to which the Parties to the conflict consent. For that purpose it may *inter alia* ask each Party to provide it with a list of at least five States which that Party considers acceptable to act as Protecting

Power on its behalf in relation to an adverse Party and ask each adverse Party to provide a list of at least five States which it would accept as the Protecting Power of the first Party; these lists shall be communicated to the Committee within two weeks after the receipt of the request; it shall compare them and seek the agreement of any proposed State named on both lists.

4. If, despite the foregoing, there is no Protecting Power, the Parties to the conflict shall accept without delay an offer which may be made by the International Committee of the Red Cross or by any other organization which offers all guarantees of impartiality and efficacy after due consultations with the said Parties and taking into account the result of these consultations, to act as a substitute. The functioning of such a substitute is subject to the consent of the Parties to the conflict; every effort shall be made by the Parties to the conflict to facilitate the operations of the substitute in the performance of its tasks under the Conventions and this Protocol.

5. In accordance with Article 4, the designation and acceptance of Protecting Powers for the purpose of applying the Conventions and this Protocol shall not affect the legal status of the Parties to the conflict or of any territory, including occupied territory.

6. The maintenance of diplomatic relations between Parties to the conflict or the entrusting of the protection of a Party's interests and those of its nationals to a third State in accordance with the rules of international law relating to diplomatic relations is no obstacle to the designation of Protecting Powers for the purpose of applying the Conventions and this Protocol.

7. Any subsequent mention in this Protocol of a Protecting Power includes also a substitute.

. . .

Article 32 — General principle

In the implementation of this Section, the activities of the High Contracting Parties, of the Parties to the conflict and of the international humanitarian organizations mentioned in the Conventions and in this Protocol shall be prompted mainly by the right of families to know the fate of their relatives.

. . .

Article 35 — Basic rules

1. In any armed conflict, the right of the Parties to the conflict to choose methods or means of warfare is not unlimited.

2. It is prohibited to employ weapons, projectiles and material and methods of warfare of a nature to cause superfluous injury or unnecessary suffering.

3. It is prohibited to employ methods or means of warfare which are intended, or may be expected, to cause widespread, long-term and severe damage to the natural environment.

Article 36 — New weapons

In the study, development, acquisition or adoption of a new weapon, means or method of warfare, a High Contracting Party is under an obligation to determine whether its employment would, in some or all circumstances, be prohibited by this Protocol or by any other rule of international law applicable to the High Contracting Party.

. . .

Article 40 — Quarter

It is prohibited to order that there shall be no survivors, to threaten an adversary therewith or to conduct hostilities on this basis.

Article 41 — Safeguard of an enemy hors de combat

1. A person who is recognized or who, in the circumstances, should be recognized to be *hors de combat* shall not be made the object of attack.

2. A person is *hors de combat* if:
    (a) he is in the power of an adverse Party,
    (b) he clearly expresses an intention to surrender, or
    (c) he has been rendered unconscious or is otherwise incapacitated by wounds or sickness, and therefore is incapable of defending himself,

provided that in any of these cases he abstains from any hostile act and does not attempt to escape.

3. When persons entitled to protection as prisoners of war have fallen into the power of an adverse Party under unusual conditions of combat which prevent their evacuation as provided for in Part III, Section I, of the Third Convention, they shall be released and all feasible precautions shall be taken to ensure their safety.

. . .

Article 44 — Combatants and prisoners of war

1. Any combatant, as defined in Article 43, who falls into the power of an adverse Party shall be a prisoner of war.

2. While all combatants are obliged to comply with the rules of international law applicable in armed conflict, violations of these rules shall not deprive a combatant of his right to be a combatant or, if he falls into the power of an adverse Party, of his right to be a prisoner of war, except as provided in paragraphs 3 and 4.

3. In order to promote the protection of the civilian population from the effects of hostilities, combatants are obliged to distinguish themselves from the civilian population while they are engaged in an attack or in a military operation preparatory to an attack. Recognizing, however, that there are situations in armed conflicts where, owing to the nature of the hostilities an armed combatant cannot so distinguish himself, he shall retain his status as a combatant, provided that, in such situations, he carries his arms openly:

(a) during each military engagement, and

(b) during such time as he is visible to the adversary while he is engaged in a military deployment preceding the launching of an attack in which he is to participate.

Acts which comply with the requirements of this paragraph shall not be considered as perfidious within the meaning of Article 37, paragraph 1 (c).

4. A combatant who falls into the power of an adverse Party while failing to meet the requirements set forth in the second sentence of paragraph 3 shall forfeit his right to be a prisoner of

war, but he shall, nevertheless, be given protections equivalent in all respects to those accorded to prisoners of war by the Third Convention and by this Protocol. This protection includes protections equivalent to those accorded to prisoners of war by the Third Convention in the case where such a person is tried and punished for any offenses he has committed.

5. Any combatant who falls into the power of an adverse Party while not engaged in an attack or in a military operation preparatory to an attack shall not forfeit his rights to be a combatant and a prisoner of war by virtue of his prior activities.

6. This Article is without prejudice to the right of any person to be a prisoner of war pursuant to Article 4 of the Third Convention.

7. This Article is not intended to change the generally accepted practice of States with respect to the wearing of the uniform by combatants assigned to the regular, uniformed armed units of a Party to the conflict.

8. In addition to the categories of persons mentioned in Article 13 of the First and Second Conventions, all members of the armed forces of a Party to the conflict, as defined in Article 43 of this Protocol, shall be entitled to protection under those Conventions if they are wounded or sick or, in the case of the Second Convention, shipwrecked at sea or in other waters.

Article 45 — Protection of persons who have taken part in hostilities

1. A person who takes part in hostilities and falls into the power of an adverse Party shall be presumed to be a prisoner of war, and therefore shall be protected by the Third Convention, if he claims the status of prisoner of war, or if he appears to be entitled to such status, or if the Party on which he depends claims such status on his behalf by notification to the detaining Power or to the Protecting Power. Should any doubt arise as to whether any such person is entitled to the status of prisoner of war, he shall continue to have such status and, therefore, to be protected by the Third Convention and this Protocol until such time as his status has been determined by a competent tribunal.

2. If a person who has fallen into the power of an adverse Party

is not held as a prisoner of war and is to be tried by that Party for an offence arising out of the hostilities, he shall have the right to assert his entitlement to prisoner-of-war status before a judicial tribunal and to have that question adjudicated. Whenever possible under the applicable procedure, this adjudication shall occur before the trial for the offence. The representatives of the Protecting Power shall be entitled to attend the proceedings in which that question is adjudicated, unless, exceptionally, the proceedings are held *in camera* in the interest of State security. In such a case the detaining Power shall advise the Protecting Power accordingly.

3. Any person who has taken part in hostilities, who is not entitled to prisoner-of-war status and who does not benefit from more favourable treatment in accordance with the Fourth Convention shall have the right at all times to the protection of Article 75 of this Protocol. In occupied territory, any such person, unless he is held as a spy, shall also be entitled, notwithstanding Article 5 of the Fourth Convention, to his rights of communication under that Convention.

. . .

Article 47 — Mercenaries

1. A mercenary shall not have the right to be a combatant or a prisoner of war.
2. A mercenary is any person who:
    (a) is specially recruited locally or abroad in order to fight in an armed conflict;
    (b) does, in fact, take a direct part in the hostilities;
    (c) is motivated to take part in the hostilities essentially by the desire for private gain and, in fact, is promised, by or on behalf of a Party to the conflict, material compensation substantially in excess of that promised or paid to combatants of similar ranks and functions in the armed forces of that Party;
    (d) is neither a national of a Party to the conflict nor a resident of territory controlled by a Party to the conflict,

(e) is not a member of the armed forces of a Party to the conflict, and

(f) has not been sent by a State which is not a Party to the
conflict on official duty as a member of its armed forces.

. . .

Article 51 — Protection of the civilian population

1. The civilian population and individual civilians shall enjoy
general protection against dangers arising from military operations.
To give effect to this protection, the following rules, which are
additional to other applicable rules of international law, shall be
observed in all circumstances.

2. The civilian population as such, as well as individual civilians,
shall not be the object of attack. Acts or threats of violence the
primary purpose of which is to spread terror among the civilian
population are prohibited.

3. Civilians shall enjoy the protection afforded by this Section,
unless and for such time as they take a direct part in hostilities.

4. Indiscriminate attacks are prohibited. Indiscriminate attacks
are:

(a) those which are not directed at a specific military objective;

(b) those which employ a method or means of combat which
cannot be directed at a specific military objective; or

(c) those which employ a method or means of combat the effects of which cannot be limited as required by this Protocol;

and consequently, in each such case, are of a nature to strike
military objectives and civilians or civilian objects without distinction.

5. Among others, the following types of attacks are to be considered as indiscriminate:

(a) an attack by bombardment by any methods or means
which treats as a single military objective a number of
clearly separated and distinct military objectives located
in a city, town, village or other area containing a similar
concentration of civilians or civilian objects; and

(b) an attack which may be expected to cause incidental loss of civilian life, injury to civilians, damage to civilian objects, or a combination thereof, which would be excessive in relation to the concrete and direct military advantage anticipated.

6. Attacks against the civilian population or civilians by way of reprisals are prohibited.

7. The presence or movements of the civilian population or individual civilians shall not be used to render certain points or areas immune from military operations, in particular in attempts to shield military objectives from attacks or to shield, favour or impede military operations. The Parties to the conflict shall not direct the movement of the civilian population or individual civilians in order to attempt to shield military objectives from attacks or to shield military operations.

8. Any violation of these prohibitions shall not release the Parties to the conflict from their legal obligations with respect to the civilian population and civilians, including the obligation to take the precautionary measures provided for in Article 57.

Article 52 — General protection of civilian objects

1. Civilian objects shall not be the object of attack or of reprisals. Civilian objects are all objects which are not military objectives as defined in paragraph 2.

2. Attacks shall be limited strictly to military objectives. In so far as objects are concerned, military objectives are limited to those objects which by their nature, location, purpose or use make an effective contribution to military action and whose total or partial destruction, capture or neutralization, in the circumstances ruling at the time, offers a definite military advantage.

3. In case of doubt whether an object which is normally dedicated to civilian purposes, such as a place of worship, a house or other dwelling or a school, is being used to make an effective contribution to military action, it shall be presumed not to be so used.

Article 53 — Protection of cultural objects and of places of worship

Without prejudice to the provisions of the Hague Convention for the Protection of Cultural Property in the Event of Armed Conflict of 14 May 1954, and of other relevant international instruments, it is prohibited:

(a) to commit any acts of hostility directed against the historic monuments, works of art or places of worship which constitute the cultural or spiritual heritage of peoples;

(b) to use such objects in support of the military effort;

(c) to make such objects the object of reprisals.

Article 54 — Protection of objects indispensable to the survival of the civilian population

1. Starvation of civilians as a method of warfare is prohibited.

2. It is prohibited to attack, destroy, remove or render useless objects indispensable to the survival of the civilian population, such as foodstuffs, agricultural areas for the production of foodstuffs, crops, livestock, drinking water installations and supplies and irrigation works, for the specific purpose of denying them for their sustenance value to the civilian population or to the adverse Party, whatever the motive, whether in order to starve out civilians, to cause them to move away, or for any other motive.

3. The prohibitions in paragraph 2 shall not apply to such of the objects covered by it as are used by an adverse Party:

(a) as sustenance solely for the members of its armed forces; or

(b) if not as sustenance, then in direct support of military action, provided, however, that in no event shall actions against these objects be taken which may be expected to leave the civilian population with such inadequate food or water as to cause its starvation or force its movement.

4. These objects shall not be made the object of reprisals.

5. In recognition of the vital requirements of any Party to the conflict in the defence of its national territory against invasion,

derogation from the prohibitions contained in paragraph 2 may be made by a Party to the conflict within such territory under its own control where required by imperative military necessity.

Article 55 — Protection of the natural environment

1. Care shall be taken in warfare to protect the natural environment against widespread, long-term and severe damage. This protection includes a prohibition of the use of methods or means of warfare which are intended or may be expected to cause such damage to the natural environment and thereby to prejudice the health or survival of the population.

2. Attacks against the natural environment by way of reprisals are prohibited.

Article 56 — Protection of works and installations containing dangerous forces

1. Works or installations containing dangerous forces, namely dams, dykes and nuclear electrical generating stations, shall not be made the object of attack, even where these objects are military objectives, if such attack may cause the release of dangerous forces and consequent severe losses among the civilian population. Other military objectives located at or in the vicinity of these works or installations shall not be made the object of attack if such attack may cause the release of dangerous forces from the works or installations and consequent severe losses among the civilian population.

2. The special protection against attack provided by paragraph 1 shall cease:

    (a) for a dam or a dyke only if it is used for other than its normal function and in regular, significant and direct support of military operations and if such attack is the only feasible way to terminate such support;

    (b) for a nuclear electrical generating station only if it provides electric power in regular, significant and direct support of military operations and if such attack is the only feasible way to terminate such support;

    (c) for other military objectives located at or in the vicinity of these works or installations only if they are used in regular, significant and direct support of military operations and if such attack is the only feasible way to terminate such support.

3. In all cases, the civilian population and individual civilians shall remain entitled to all the protection accorded them by international law, including the protection of the precautionary measures provided for in Article 57. If the protection ceases and any of the works, installations or military objectives mentioned in paragraph 1 is attacked, all practical precautions shall be taken to avoid the release of the dangerous forces.

4. It is prohibited to make any of the works, installations or military objectives mentioned in paragraph 1 the object of reprisals.

5. The Parties to the conflict shall endeavour to avoid locating any military objectives in the vicinity of the works or installations mentioned in paragraph 1. Nevertheless, installations erected for the sole purpose of defending the protected works or installations from attack are permissible and shall not themselves be made the object of attack, provided that they are not used in hostilities except for defensive actions necessary to respond to attacks against the protected works or installations and that their armament is limited to weapons capable only of repelling hostile action against the protected works or installations.

6. The High Contracting Parties and the Parties to the conflict are urged to conclude further agreements among themselves to provide additional protection for objects containing dangerous forces.

7. In order to facilitate the identification of the objects protected by this article, the Parties to the conflict may mark them with a special sign consisting of a group of three bright orange circles placed on the same axis, as specified in Article 16 of Annex I to this Protocol. The absence of such marking in no way relieves any Party to the conflict of its obligations under this Article.

Article 57 — Precautions in attack

1. In the conduct of military operations, constant care shall be taken to spare the civilian population, civilians and civilian objects.

2. With respect to attacks, the following precautions shall be taken:

(a) those who plan or decide upon an attack shall:

(i) do everything feasible to verify that the objectives to be attacked are neither civilians nor civilian objects and are not subject to special protection but are military objectives within the meaning of paragraph 2 of Article 52 and that it is not prohibited by the provisions of this Protocol to attack them;

(ii) take all feasible precautions in the choice of means and methods of attack with a view to avoiding, and in any event to minimizing, incidental loss of civilian life, injury to civilians and damage to civilian objects;

(iii) refrain from deciding to launch any attack which may be expected to cause incidental loss of civilian life, injury to civilians, damage to civilian objects, or a combination thereof, which would be excessive in relation to the concrete and direct military advantage anticipated;

(b) an attack shall be cancelled or suspended if it becomes apparent that the objective is not a military one or is subject to special protection or that the attack may be expected to cause incidental loss of civilian life, injury to civilians, damage to civilian objects, or a combination thereof, which would be excessive in relation to the concrete and direct military advantage anticipated;

(c) effective advance warning shall be given of attacks which may affect the civilian population, unless circumstances do not permit.

3. When a choice is possible between several military objectives for obtaining a similar military advantage, the objective to be selected shall be that [target] the attack on which may be expected to cause the least danger to civilian lives and to civilian objects.

4. In the conduct of military operations at sea or in the air, each Party to the conflict shall, in conformity with its rights and duties under the rules of international law applicable in armed conflict, take all reasonable precautions to avoid losses of civilian lives and damage to civilian objects.

5. No provision of this article may be construed as authorizing any attacks against the civilian population, civilians or civilian objects.

. . .

Article 75 — Fundamental guarantees

1. In so far as they are affected by a situation referred to in Article 1 of this Protocol, persons who are in the power of a Party to the conflict and who do not benefit from more favourable treatment under the Conventions or under this Protocol shall be treated humanely in all circumstances and shall enjoy, as a minimum, the protection provided by this Article without any adverse distinction based upon race, colour, sex, language, religion or belief, political or other opinion, national or social origin, wealth, birth or other status, or on any other similar criteria. Each Party shall respect the person, honour, convictions and religious practices of all such persons.

2. The following acts are and shall remain prohibited at any time and in any place whatsoever, whether committed by civilian or by military agents:

    (a) violence to the life, health, or physical or mental well-being of persons, in particular:
        (i) murder;
        (ii) torture of all kinds, whether physical or mental;
        (iii)corporal punishment; and
        (iv) mutilation;
    (b) outrages upon personal dignity, in particular humiliating and degrading treatment, enforced prostitution and an form of indecent assault;
    (c) the taking of hostages;
        (d) collective punishments; and
        (e) threats to commit any of the foregoing acts.

3. Any person arrested, detained or interned for actions related to the armed conflict shall be informed promptly, in a language he understands, of the reasons why these measures have been taken. Except in cases of arrest or detention for penal offences, such persons shall be released with the minimum delay possible

and in any event as soon as the circumstances justifying the arrest, detention or internment have ceased to exist.

4. No sentence may be passed and no penalty may be executed on a person found guilty of a penal offence related to the armed conflict except pursuant to a conviction pronounced by an impartial and regularly constituted court respecting the generally recognized principles of regular judicial procedure, which include the following:

(a) the procedure shall provide for an accused to be informed without delay of the particulars of the offence alleged against him and shall afford the accused before and during his trial all necessary rights and means of defence;

(b) no one shall be convicted of an offence except on the basis of individual penal responsibility;

(c) no one shall be accused or convicted of a criminal offence on account of any act or omission which did not constitute a criminal offence under the national or international law to which he was subject at the time when it was committed; nor shall a heavier penalty be imposed than that which was applicable at the time when the criminal offence was committed; if, after the commission of the offence, provision is made by law for the imposition of a lighter penalty, the offender shall benefit thereby;

(d) anyone charged with an offence is presumed innocent until proved guilty according to law;

(e) anyone charged with an offence shall have the right to be tried in his presence;

(f) no one shall be compelled to testify against himself or to confess guilt;

(g) anyone charged with an offence shall have the right to examine, or have examined, the witnesses against him and to obtain the attendance and examination of witnesses on his behalf under the same conditions as witnesses against him;

(h) no one shall be prosecuted or punished by the same Party for an offence in respect of which a final judgment acquitting or convicting that person has been previously pronounced under the same law and judicial procedure;

(i) anyone prosecuted for an offence shall have the right to have the judgment pronounced publicly; and

(j) a convicted person shall be advised on conviction of his judicial and other remedies and of the time-limits within which they may be exercised.

5. Women whose liberty has been restricted for reasons related to the armed conflict shall be held in quarters separated from men's quarters. They shall be under the immediate supervision of women. Nevertheless, in cases where families are detained or interned, they shall, whenever possible, be held in the same place and accommodated as family units.

6. Persons who are arrested, detained or interned for reasons related to the armed conflict shall enjoy the protection provided by this Article until their final release, repatriation or re-establishment, even after the end of the armed conflict.

7. In order to avoid any doubt concerning the prosecution and trial of persons accused of war crimes or crimes against humanity, the following principles shall apply:

(a) persons who are accused of such crimes should be submitted for the purpose of prosecution and trial in accordance with the applicable rules of international law; and

(b) any such persons who do not benefit from more favourable treatment under the Conventions or this Protocol shall be accorded the treatment provided by this Article, whether or not the crimes of which they are accused constitute grave breaches of the Conventions or of this Protocol.

8. No provision of this Article may be construed as limiting or infringing any other more favourable provision granting greater protection, under any applicable rules of international law, to persons covered by paragraph 1.

. . .

Article 82 — Legal advisers in armed forces

The High Contracting Parties at all times, and the Parties to the conflict in time of armed conflict, shall ensure that legal advisers are available, when necessary, to advise military commanders at the appropriate level on the application of the Conventions and this Protocol and on the appropriate instruction to be given to the armed forces on this subject.

Article 83 — Dissemination

1. The High Contracting Parties undertake, in time of peace as in time of armed conflict, to disseminate the Conventions and this Protocol as widely as possible in their respective countries and, in particular, to include the study thereof in their programmes of military instruction and to encourage the study thereof by the civilian population, so that those instruments may become known to the armed forces and to the civilian population.

2. Any military or civilian authorities who, in time of armed conflict, assume responsibilities in respect of the application of the Conventions and this Protocol shall be fully acquainted with the text thereof.

. . .

Article 86 — Failure to act

1. The High Contracting Parties and the Parties to the conflict shall repress grave breaches, and take measures necessary to suppress all other breaches, of the Conventions or of this Protocol which result from a failure to act when under a duty to do so.

2. The fact that a breach of the Conventions or of this Protocol was committed by a subordinate does not absolve his superiors from penal or disciplinary responsibility, as the case may be, if they knew, or had information which should have enabled them to conclude in the circumstances at the time, that he was committing or was going to commit such a breach and if they did not take all feasible measures within their power to prevent or repress the breach.

Article 87 — Duty of commanders

1. The High Contracting Parties and the Parties to the conflict shall require military commanders, with respect to members of

the armed forces under their command and other persons under their control, to prevent and, where necessary, to suppress and to report to competent authorities breaches of the Conventions and of this Protocol.

2. In order to prevent and suppress breaches, High Contracting Parties and Parties to the conflict shall require that, commensurate with their level of responsibility, commanders ensure that members of the armed forces under their command are aware of their obligations under the Conventions and this Protocol.

. . .

Protocol Additional to the Geneva Conventions of 12 August 1949, and Relating to the Protection of Victims of Non-International Armed Conflicts (Protocol II) Geneva, July 1977

PART I SCOPE OF THIS PROTOCOL

Article 1 — Material field of application

1. This Protocol, which develops and supplements Article 3 common to the Geneva Conventions of 12 August 1949 without modifying its existing conditions of application, shall apply to all armed conflicts which are not covered by Article 1 of the Protocol Additional to the Geneva Conventions of 12 August 1949, and relating to the Protection of Victims of International Armed Conflicts (Protocol I) and which take place in the territory of a High Contracting Party between its armed forces and dissident armed forces or other organized armed groups which, under responsible command, exercise such control over a part of its territory as to enable them to carry out sustained and concerted military operations and to implement this Protocol.

2. This Protocol shall not apply to situations of internal disturbances and tensions, such as riots, isolated and sporadic acts of violence and other acts of a similar nature as not being armed conflicts.

. . .

Article 3 — Non-intervention

1. Nothing in this Protocol shall be invoked for the purpose of affecting the sovereignty of a State or the responsibility of the government, by all legitimate means, to maintain or re-establish law and order in the State or to defend the national unity and territorial integrity of the State.

2. Nothing in this Protocol shall be invoked as a justification for intervening, directly or indirectly, for any reason whatever, in the armed conflict or in the internal or external affairs of the High Contracting Party in the territory of which that conflict occurs.

. . .

Index

ABOUT THE AUTHOR

Peter Karsten is professor of history at the University of Pittsburgh. He is the author of *The Naval Aristocracy, Patriot Heroes and Political Change,* and *Soldiers and Society: The Effects of Military Service and War on American Life* (Greenwood Press, 1978), in addition to many articles in such journals as *Military Affairs, Foreign Policy, American Quarterly,* and *The Historian.*